Apartheid's Noble Revolutionaries

Apartheid's Noble Revolutionaries

Bram Fischer and other noble revolutionaries

ANTHONY PEARCE

First published 2025

Typeset by BookPOD

ISBN: 978-0-6455188-2-5 (paperback)
ISBN: 978-0-6455188-3-2 (e-book)

A catalogue record for this
book is available from the
National Library of Australia

To
Gillian
Katherine and James

Contents

Noble revolutionaries

Many noble revolutionaries were detained, imprisoned, exiled, banned, or murdered because of their activism in opposing apartheid. These noble revolutionaries are mentioned in this book – there were countless others.

Neil Aggett	Lewis Baker	Esther Barsel
Hymie Barsel	Pixie Benjamin	Mary Benson
Hilda Bernstein	Rusty Bernstein	Steve Biko
Leslie Blackwell	Allan Boesak	Franz Boshoff
Breyten Breytenbach	Alan Brooks	Frank Chikane
Moses Chikane	Laloo Chila	Jeremy Cronin
Sholto Cross	Yusuf Dadoo	Eddie Daniels
Paul David	Spike de Keller	Nkosazana Dhlamini
Michael Dingake	Florence Duncan	Raymond Eisenstein
Julius First	Matilda First	Ruth First
Bram Fischer	Ilse Fischer	Molly Fischer
Elizabeth Floyd	Maurice Franks	Costa Gazides
Denis Goldberg	Arthur Goldreich	Hazel Goldreich
Joe Gqabi	Thozi Gqweta	Archie Gumede
Michael Harmel	Ann Henderson	Miriam Hepner
Bob Hepple	Anne Heymann	Issy Heymann
Baruch Hirson	Jack Hodgson	Tony Holiday
Abdullah Jassat	Tim Jenkin	Helen Joseph
James Kantor	Ronnie Kasrils	Ahmed Kathrada
Stephanie Kemp	Sam Kikine	Dave Kitson
Wolfie Kodesh	Sizwe Kondile	Moses Kotane
Mazisi Kunene	Stephen Lee	Patrick Lekota
Norman Levy	Hugh Lewin	Winnie Madikizela
Mac Maharaj	Gcini Malindi	Nelson Mandela
Tom Manthata	John Marks	Barbara Masekela
John Matthews	Vuyani Mavuso	Govan Mbeki

Thabo Mbeki

Jean Middleton

Motso Mokgabudi

Popo Molefe

Mosie Moola

Nthato Motlana

MJ Naidoo

Sylvia Neame

Mike Ngubeni

Duma Nokwe

Percy Qobozo

Sue Rabkin

Albie Sachs

Ivan Schermbrucker

Marius Schoon

George Sewpershad

Joe Slovo

Aelred Stubbs

Eric Thembani

Tony Trew

Nyakhane Tsolo

Eli Weinberg

Issy Wolfson

Donald Woods

Ismail Meer

Walter Mkwati

Peter Mokoena

Geoffrey Moelane

Thomas More

Elias Motsoaledi

Billy Nair

Isaac Ngcobo

Sisa Njikelana

Jabulile Nyawose

Fred Pager

Mewa Ramgobin

Solly Sachs

Lesley Schermbrucker

Minnie Sepel

Albertina Sisulu

Robert Sobukwe

Raymond Suttner

Raymond Thoms

Paul Trewhela

Ben Turok

Violet Weinberg

Anne Marie Wolpe

Charles Yeats

Raymond Mhlaba

Andrew Mlangeni

Joseph Molefe

Alex Moumbaris

James Moroka

James Moroka

Beyers Naude

Lilian Ngoyi

Curtis Nkondo

Petros Nyawose

David Rabkin

Ambrose Reeves

Babla Saloojee

Jeannette Schoon

Ralph Sepel

Walter Sisulu

Harold Strachan

Oliver Tambo

Ahmed Timol

Benson Tsele

Reuben Twala

Cecil Williams

Harold Wolpe

Murdered children

Many children were murdered in the struggle against apartheid. These murdered children are mentioned in this book – there were many others.

Hector Pieterson

Katryn Schoon

Stompie Seipei

Barristers (aka Advocates)

Many eminent barristers represented the noble revolutionaries in South African courts. These barristers are mentioned in this book – there were many others.

Vernon Berrange
Maurice Franks
Sydney Kentridge
Isie Maisels
Walter Pollack
Rex Welsh

George Bizos
Harold Hanson
George Lowen
Gilbert Marcus
Norman Rosenberg

Arthur Chaskalson
Joel Joffe
Ismail Mahomed
HC Nichols
Karel Tip

Judges

The judges had to interpret and apply the government's unjust and discriminatory apartheid laws. Some judges attempted to be just and fair, others aided and abetted apartheid. These judges are mentioned in this book – there were many others.

Andries Beyer
Christoffel Eloff
John Milne
Kees van Dijkhorst

Wes Boshoff
Neville James
William Ramsbottom

Quartus De Wet
Donald Kannemeyer
Frans Rumpff

Progressive Federal Party politicians

The Progressive Federal Party (aka Progressive Party or Progressive Reform Party) opposed apartheid. These Progressive Federal Party members of parliament are mentioned in this book – there were many others.

Alex Boraine
Helen Suzman

Colin Eglin
Frederik Van Zyl Slabbert

Harry Schwartz

Notable apartheid opponents

Many notable persons opposed apartheid. These notable persons are mentioned in this book – there were countless others.

Aubrey Aggett	Louis Babrow	Eddie Barlow
Christiaan Barnard	Maimie Berman	Toni Bernstein
Tony Bloom	Nat Bregman	Pat Davidson
John Dube	John Dugard	Vivian Ezra
Ruth Fischer	Trevor Huddlestone	Denis Hurley
Willem Joubert	Anton Lembede	Elizabeth Lewin
Yvonne Lewiton	Albert Luthuli	Mbuyisa Makhubo
Zindzi Mandela	Clive Menell	Leo Marquand
Sam Nzima	Harry Oppenheimer	Alan Paton
Sol Plaatje	Walter Rubusana	Pixley Seme
Lazar Sidelsky	Desmond Tutu	Mark Weinberg
Alfred Xuma	Deane Yates	

Nationalist Party politicians

The Nationalist Party designed, implemented, and enforced apartheid. These Nationalist Party members of parliament are mentioned in this book – there were many others.

M C Botha	P W Botha	R F Botha
K Coetsee	F W De Klerk	C Heunis
L le Grange	P M K le Roux	E Louw
P Koornhof	J Kruger	D F Malan
M Malan	C Mulder	J G Strijdom
C R Swart	A Treurnicht	H Verwoerd
A Vlok	B J Vorster	

Foreword

Henry Allum is a fictitious character and not modelled on any real person. Almost every other character in the book is a real person. Henry Allum's interactions and conversations with them are imaginary. I have tried to record historical events accurately and I have listed my sources in the bibliography. I apologise if my imagination has resulted in any incorrect impressions.

CHAPTER 1

New College, Oxford

I met Bram Fischer in January 1932 as I walked through the cloisters of New College, Oxford. This small blonde man, with twinkling blue eyes, was hobbling along on crutches. The books he was carrying impeded his progress. They were tucked under his arm as he manipulated his crutches, but they kept dropping. I stopped to assist and gathered up his books. He responded in a thick guttural accent: "*Ag man,* that is so kind of you, but please don't worry I can manage just fine." He pronounced "fine" as if he had said "feign".

"Henry Allum," I said as I extended my hand in greeting. It was a little silly because Bram had to hold his crutches in one hand, balance on one leg, and extend his free arm to shake my hand.

"Bram Fischer,"

"I am very pleased to meet you. My rooms are just around the corner. Please join me for a cup of tea."

"That is very kind of you. I shall be pleased to do so," replied Bram.

Bram limped along beside me to my rooms. It was the start of our lifelong friendship, and during that first cup of tea together it took little time to appreciate that Bram was exceedingly charismatic.

I invited Bram to sit. I turned on the kettle and said, "I am surprised that we have not met before."

"I only arrived two weeks ago."

"After a term. Why the late start?"

"Yes, indeed, a little unusual. I have come to Oxford from South Africa on a Rhodes Scholarship. I had to finish my university examinations in November before coming here."

"Your crutches. How did you injure yourself?"

"I played in a rugby game in my first week here at Oxford. It was all rather silly. I was just running with the ball in open play when I twisted my knee and fell."

"Rotten luck," I commented.

"You would at least think that someone should have tackled me."

"I hope that the injury is not serious."

"I hope not. I managed to hop along all last weekend in Scotland. Some of my South African friends insisted that I go with them to Edinburgh to watch the Springboks."

"How was it?"

"The knee was a blooming nuisance, but I loved the trip. Fabulous test match."

The Springboks had only lost one match during their lengthy tour of Britain and Ireland, and had narrowly won all four test matches against Wales, Ireland, England, and Scotland. Bram was very enthused in talking about these rugby matches. He described the thrill of watching South Africa's brilliant half-back Danie Craven score the winning try against Scotland before being knocked unconscious. As Bram discussed the test match, he let slip that he knew most of the players. This was because he had played with and against many of them. Bram had been selected to play for the Orange Free State in their two matches against the 1928 touring All Blacks. Bram shook his head and said, "Those All

Blacks got a fright when we came within four points of beating them in Bloemfontein."

I would soon learn that Bram's pedigree could hardly be more distinguished and he was as close to Afrikaner royalty as you could possibly get. Bram's grandfather, Abraham Fischer, had been the president of the Orange Free State. His father, Percy, was a judge in the Bloemfontein Supreme Court, and would later be elevated to become the Judge-President.

Unfortunately, Bram's knee injury turned out to be worse than first thought and he was advised to have his cartilage removed. He was admitted to Wingfield Hospital and I visited him regularly. Bram was in severe pain but never complained. He sat up in bed with his knee encased in plaster and a wire structure to keep the weight of the blankets off the leg. His cartilage was proudly displayed in a bottle beside him. I felt queasy looking at it. Bram was rarely alone and there was a constant stream of visitors. The New College Warden, Herbert Fisher, visited frequently but there were many others, especially South Africans, that dropped in to cheer him up. Bram had to remain in hospital for almost two months. I was drawn to Bram, like many others, because he was so naturally gregarious.

Every time I visited Bram, he seemed to be propped up writing a letter. He readily admitted that many of these letters were to Molly, his girlfriend. Bram met Molly when he was just nineteen years old. Molly had come to Bloemfontein with a hockey team from Pretoria to play against Grey University College, where Bram was studying. Molly was the daughter of Petrus and Emmy Krige. Petrus was better-known by his nickname Tottie, and he practised as a land surveyor in Pretoria. Tottie had been General Jan Smuts aide-de-camp during the First World War and his sister, Isie, had married Smuts. Bram confessed to being smitten by Molly and he anxiously kept up his correspondence to ensure that she did not run off with another suitor during his absence. He went so far as to say that he had already proposed to Molly but she was keeping him on a string.

Molly dated Jan Hofmeyer while Bram was away at Oxford. Jan Hofmeyer was a good deal older than both Bram and Molly. Jan Hofmeyer was also a Rhodes Scholar, and a rising political star in South Africa. He was instrumental in negotiating the formation of the United Party, which resoundingly won the 1933 general election. Jan Hofmeyer died as a relatively young man just six months after D.F. Malan's Nationalist Party won the 1948 election. The Nationalist Party immediately starting legislating its apartheid policies. Many years later I praised Hofmeyer's admirable non-racist views in a conversation with Bram and Molly. Neither of them responded, before Molly broke the awkward silence by announcing that she had dated Jan while Bram was at Oxford. I was dreadfully embarrassed but Bram merely chuckled and conceded that Jan had indeed been a good man.

Bram's father, Percy, had read law at Cambridge and I assumed that the Fischer family were well-imbibed with an affinity for the British. I soon learnt that the reality was quite the opposite. Bram was implacably opposed to British imperialism. The Prince of Wales, Edward, who would rock British Society with his abdication in 1936, toured South Africa in 1925. He was invited to visit Bram's school, Grey College, in Bloemfontein. Unfortunately, the visit was scheduled for a long weekend when the senior boys would be away. The headmaster attempted to change the long weekend so that all the boys would be present, but Bram led a successful protest. Bram recognised that this show of defiant anti-imperialism was the beginning of his political activism.

As it turned out the Prince of Wales rather skilfully managed anti-British sentiment during his tour to South Africa. When he visited Bloemfontein he allowed mounted commandos, who had fought in the Anglo-Boer War, to escort him. The Prince of Wales addressed both houses of parliament and attracted much praise for using Afrikaans in his concluding remarks. The wounds from the Anglo-Boer War ran deep though, and many Afrikaners still harboured bitter resentments towards the British. Despite their British educations, Bram and Percy Fischer were strongly anti-British in their sentiments.

Upon the outbreak of the First World War the South African parliament decided to go to war on England's side. There were many Afrikaners that resented this because scars from the Anglo-Boer War of 1899-1902 were a fresh memory. The families of many Afrikaners perished in the concentration camps that the English had set-up to intern Afrikaner women and children. The idea of fighting for the English was an anathema to many Afrikaners and a number openly rebelled. The Afrikaners resented living in a country where the national anthem was 'God Save the King,' the Union Jack was the national flag, the currency was British pounds, and the king's image was on every postage stamp. The rebellion leaders were predominantly wealthy farmers from the Orange Free State and Transvaal. The rebellion though was poorly organised and soon put down. Many of the rebels were arrested and tried for treason. Percy Fisher offered his services as a barrister to defend the rebels in court. Percy was infuriated at the stiff sentences imposed but he too paid a heavy price. He was shunned by Bloemfontein society because of his open support of the rebels, and the legal fraternity stopped sending him briefs. This caused him severe financial hardship and he was forced to rent the family home in Bloemfontein and move to the family farm. The entire Fischer family were involved in supporting the rebels. Percy Fischer's wife, Ella, visited the rebels in prison. Her sister Maude also visited and her husband, Dr Bidwell, provided medical attention to the prisoners.

During our chat about this Bram said, "Ma took me and my elder bother Paul along on some of these prison visits. I was just seven years old but I remember giving food and other parcels to these rebellion prisoners. Ma never discussed the rebellion, all she wanted to do was help them. She told me that these men had acted in accordance with their consciences. You know, Henry, you must always be true to your conscience. You are an Englishman, Henry, and your loyalties should lie with Britain. I am implacably opposed to British imperialism, yet I hold a Rhodes Scholarship. It is indeed a paradox, because Cecil Rhodes set-up these scholarships to promote the British Empire."

Bram returned to New College after his lengthy sojourn in hospital. His rugby playing days were over. It was spring and Bram played tennis for exercise. I liked tennis but quickly discovered that I was nowhere near good enough to engage him in a decent game. Bram had been the tennis champion at both his school and university. Bram was very busy and he had numerous social engagements. He would however, frequently accept my invitation to have an afternoon cup of tea, and I so enjoyed our lengthy conversations.

I was majoring in history and Bram stated this had been his favourite school subject. He attributed this to Leo Marquand, his inspirational history teacher. Marquand had read history at Oxford as a Rhodes Scholar. On his return to South Africa, he founded the National Union of South African Students (NUSAS) before accepting a post as a teacher at Grey College in Bloemfontein. After school Bram went to the University of Cape Town for a year before returning to Bloemfontein to attend Grey University College. Despite his anti-British sentiments Bram wished to apply for a Rhodes Scholarship and figured that it would be easier doing so from Bloemfontein than Cape Town. From what I could gauge of his remarkable talents I thought it hard to imagine how Bram could be overlooked anywhere. One of the benefits of returning to Bloemfontein was that Bram was able to reacquaint himself with Leo Marquand. It was through this association that Bram would experience an epiphany that would change him for the rest of his life.

We were discussing our history studies when Bram remarked, "It was Leo Marquand that encouraged me to get involved in classes he had established for black education."

"Where was this?" I asked.

"In Bloemfontein. Leo also persuaded me to join the Bloemfontein Joint Council of Europeans and Africans. This was a forum for whites and blacks to meet and discuss matters of common concern. I am an Afrikaner and proud of being an Afrikaner, but this did not stop me from wanting to understand the needs and wants of others that live in South Africa. During my first meeting Leo introduced me to various members of this council. I had to shake hands with them."

Bram paused for a long time before continuing. "When I shook the hands of these black men I felt a revulsion. I do not think that I had ever shaken the hands of a black man until that moment." I said nothing and Bram continued, "Why did I have these feelings of revulsion? It made me think deeply. I had spent my youth on my parents' farm and my earliest friends, Loel and Golokwaan, were black. I realised that I had changed. It was not the black that had changed, it was me. I had adopted a European attitude of superiority and I was wrong."

"Racial prejudice is not unusual," I said rather unhelpfully.

"It is wrong and wholly irrational. I carry the resentment of how the British have denied Afrikaners our rights of self-determination. All people however, need to be treated equally. Our rights of self-determination should not impede on anyone else's rights, like those of South African blacks."

Bram took advantage of the 1932 summer holidays to visit the Soviet Union. The idea seemed to dawn on Bram almost overnight and he put travel plans together with unseeming haste. Bram and three university companions obtained a berth on a Soviet ship, the *Janis Rudzutak*. Bram invited me to come along but I had committed myself to working at our local pharmacy during the summer break. I did go down to Hay's Wharf to farewell Bram, Tom, Mac, and Treads on their exciting adventure. They were gone for just over a month and Bram gave me a call immediately upon his return to London. I took a tube to Piccadilly circus and met up with Bram who was in an exuberant mood. He was deeply suntanned and his blonde hair had been bleached almost white. He recounted his travels with great enthusiasm. The ship had travelled through the North Sea and around the north of Denmark. It had then navigated the Kiel Canal before going through the Baltic Sea into the Gulf of Finland and finally docking at Leningrad. Bram claimed that he had caught most of his suntan lounging on deck where it was broad daylight for almost the entire day.

We indulged in a few beers. I drank bitter but Bram only drank lager. He disliked bitter and often expressed surprise at how, we English, could enjoy warm beer. Bram enthused about the beauty of Moscow's Red Square and Lenin's impressive tomb. Our conversation soon turned from sightseeing to politics. Bram saw many positives in the Bolshevik Revolution. He acknowledged that life in the Soviet Union was austere and recognised that the collectivisation of industry and lack of a profit motive limited economic success, but he believed that communism had overcome the problem of inequality. Bram was highly critical of the peasants, the inefficiency of their small farms, their ignorance, and acceptance of atrocious living conditions. Yet in communism he saw a method of engineering society to elevate the peasants and avoid national disputes between various ethnic groups. Bram saw communism as the solution to not only rampant nationalism, but also to the imperial policies of European powers. He developed a blind faith in communism and he would soon champion communism as the antidote to inequality in his homeland of South Africa.

Ever since the end of the First World War, Europe had lived under the cloud of another war. Britain and France feared both Germany and the Soviet Union, and were particularly fearful of a German-Soviet military alliance. The political problem was that European countries were falling to totalitarianism. On the far left there were communists and on the far right there were fascists. Both fascism and communism shared common totalitarian features. It might be accurate to describe communists as red fascists and fascists as brown communists. They both used pseudo-science to give credibility to their ideologies. Communists appealed to Marxist class struggles, while fascists appealed to eugenics and race. Britain and France were fearful of being openly hostile to the fascists in Italy and Germany, or the Bolsheviks in the Soviet Union. Although many in the upper classes of Britain society saw the fascists as being wisely anti-communist. Winston Churchill, who would soon rail against Nazism, was initially seduced by fascism, as he saw it as a bulwark against communism. This is what Churchill said in a 1933 speech: "The Roman genius impersonated in Mussolini, the greatest law-giver among living men, has shown to many nations how they can resist the pressures of Socialism and has indicated the path that a nation can follow when courageously led. With the Fascist regime, Mussolini has established a centre of orientation from which countries which are engaged in a hand-to-hand struggle with Socialism must not hesitate to be guided."[1]

It was in this climate of war anxiety that Bram and I attended a famous debate at the Oxford Union in February 1933. It was well-attended and the motion presented was: "This House will under no circumstances fight for its King and country." I was too shy to speak and Bram was unusually quiet. A vote was taken and the motion was carried with 275 votes in favour and 153 against. It was really a vote about pacifism and not really about loyalty to king and country. I voted against the motion, but I am not sure how Bram voted. The motion outcome was furiously condemned in both the press and House of Commons.

Students at Oxford and Cambridge were at the forefront of examining the new ideologies of fascism and socialism. At Oxford there was the Fascist Club, which followed the maverick Oswald Mosely, there was the October Club, which supported the communist principles of Lenin, and there was the Labour Club, which supported socialism. Bram was proud of his election to the Ralegh Club. This was a club open only to a select few persons from Britain and its dominions. They met to discuss matters of importance to the British empire and world affairs in general. It is ironic that Bram so happily joined a club that was so closely associated with British imperialism, but he was interested in gaining access to people of significance. Bram rose to become president of the Ralegh Club. Many impressive people addressed their meetings, which included, the Prime Minister, the Archbishop of York, ambassadors, and high commissioners.

In December 1933 Bram invited me join him at a London restaurant to celebrate Dingaan's Day This name meant nothing to me and it prompted me to read up on the history of South Africa. In 1652 the Dutch East India Company, or Vereenigde Oost-Indische Compagnie (VOC) sent Jan van Riebeeck to establish a refreshment station at the Cape of Good Hope. The VOC had no intention of founding a colony but merely wished to supply their ships with fresh produce on their trips to and from their spice trading empire in the East. Van Riebeeck arrived with just ninety Dutch employees and he eventually released some of these employees and other new arrivals from their contracts so that they could establish themselves as free burgers. The idea was that these burgers would farm and sell their produce to the VOC. The burgers though struggled to make a living because the VOC set produce prices as low as possible. The burghers also came into conflict with the Khoikhoi, the local indigenous population. The Khoikhoi were herders and they are often confused with the San, or Bushmen, who were hunters. Many historians simply refer to these indigenous people as the Khoisan. Within a few years of establishing the refreshment station at the Cape the VOC began to import slaves. These slaves were sold to the burghers to provide them with farm labourers. The burghers, who were predominantly male, mixed with the Khoikhoi and the imported slaves. This gave rise to a sizable mixed-race population that became known as the Cape Coloureds.

In 1688 around one-hundred-and eighty French Huguenots arrived at the Cape. They were fleeing religious persecution in Europe. The new governor, Simon van der Stel was determined to retain the Dutch character of the Cape and he ordered that they should be integrated with the burghers. Many of them settled in Stellenbosch, Franschhoek, and Paarl. These places are well-known today for their wine produce. The VOC continued to focus on servicing their ships, and around two to three per week visited the Cape. The burghers began to spread more widely around the Cape region. It was around the end of the eighteenth century that an Afrikaner identity began to develop. In simple terms the offspring of burgher women were considered white and those of slave women were designated black. The isolation of the burghers, their poor schooling, and interactions with Malay slaves and the Khoisan corrupted the Dutch language. The language spoken became known as Afrikaans. The word Afrikaner became commonly used for all those burgers that spoke this Dutch dialect, and the word Boer came into usage for those burghers that lived on farms rather than in urban centres.

More than half of the burger population owned slaves. The slaves were imported from places such as Batavia (Indonesia), Malaya, Madagascar, East Africa, and Angola. They brought their own languages but over time they began to speak the Dutch dialect of Afrikaans. The large slave numbers made the burghers fearful of their security and they maintained their authority over their slaves through imposing harsh punishments for transgressions. The VOC however, came down strongly upon slave-owners that punished excessively. Under Roman Dutch laws slaves were property but they were also recognised as human beings. Slaves were entitled to complain against their masters and give evidence against them. None of this though diminished the cruelty of punishments meted out to slaves, which included branding, torture, and death.

The burghers had an insatiable appetite for land. They dispossessed the Khoikhoi of their land and they slaughtered thousands of San bushmen. The burgers then expanded eastwards, where they came into conflict with the Xhosas. The Xhosas protected their cattle herds aggressively and offered much stiffer resistance. In 1778 the Cape Governor, Joachim van Plettenberg, attempted to affect a separation through designating a border along the Bushman's River. This boundary was soon pushed east to the Fish River. These border negotiations were largely ineffectual. The Xhosa chiefs had limited authority, the Xhosas had no concept of land ownership, and many simply refused to accept borders. The result was a tangled web of burghers and Xhosas living side by side, competing for access to land and ownership of cattle. The burghers and Xhosa fought one another in hostilities that were known as the Frontier Wars.

By the late eighteenth-century Britain gained ascendancy of the seas and took control of the trade routes to the east. In the aftermath of the French Revolution the Patriots Free Corps staged a revolt in the Netherlands and forced William V, the Prince of

Orange, to seek exile in England. While in England the Prince of Orange signed letters authorising Dutch governors to hand over their territories to the British. In June 1795 a British fleet landed at the Cape with a letter from the Prince of Orange demanding the handover of the Cape. The Cape officials were in a quandary because they were loyal to the House of Orange but unaware of the developments in the Netherlands. Their resistance though did not last long and they soon surrendered. The British found that maintaining the refreshment station was enormously expensive and in 1802 they returned the Cape to the Dutch.

By the early nineteenth century England was embroiled in a conflict with Napoleon. The Dutch were compelled to aid the French. Therefore, the English inevitably moved against the Dutch. In 1806 the British sent an armed force to take possession of the Cape. The British were now permanently ensconced in southern Africa and in 1820 they encouraged four-thousand British immigrants to come to the Cape Colony. They were largely tradesmen and artisans, and many of them settled in the frontier regions. Their arrival created tensions between the English and the Afrikaners. The spectacular advancement of Britain as a world power had convinced Britain that everything British was superior. The Afrikaners had a distinctively different culture and found it difficult to accept that they were British subjects. Britain attempted to anglicise everything in the Cape Colony. They made English the only language of government and the courts, and even attempted to make English the only language of instruction in schools. The British did not immediately tamper with the institution of slavery even though it had banned trading in slaves in 1807. The burghers could see that slavery was doomed and they attempted to negotiate concessions such as freeing slave children. In the end the abolishment of slavery was swift and in 1834 a law was passed that granted the emancipation of all slaves.

The Afrikaners wanted to rid themselves of British control and trekked into the interior. The people that embarked on this emigration became known as trekboers or Voortrekkers. It was known as the Great Trek and became an important part of Afrikaner folk lore. From 1835, over fifteen-thousand Afrikaners left the Cape Colony to settle in areas outside of British control. The trekboers had strong leaders, like Louis Trichardt, Gert Maritz, Piet Retief, Hendrik Potgieter, Andries Pretorius, and Piet Uys that inspired their endeavour to seek new land and greater security. The trekboers did not travel impulsively and they sent scouting parties forward to seek desirable land.

In 1817 two powerful Nguni chiefs, Dingswayo and Zwide confronted each in what is today known as Natal. One of Dingiswayo's military commanders was Shaka, a chief of a small group called the Zulus. The clash with Zwide resulted in Dingswayo's defeat and death, but Shaka avoided this battle. Shaka grew his power base and in 1818 he resoundingly defeated Zwide. Over the next eight years he established the Zulus as a powerful nation. Shaka defeated all opponents and imposed his will on a vast area. This was known as the *mfecane,* which means the crushing or destruction. The Voortrekkers clashed with many black groups but the *mfecane* had left many areas in a state of devastation and they easily fended off hostile attacks. The Zulus however, would prove to be a more powerful opponent.

In 1824 British traders obtained Shaka's consent to establish a post at Port Natal. The Zulus were now a formidable nation of over a hundred-thousand spread over an enormous geographical area. In 1828 Dingaan, Shaka's half-brother, murdered Shaka and assumed absolute power. He allowed the British to continue trading at Port Natal, but these traders lived precariously and were anxious for Britain to annex the area. In 1835 they changed the name of Port Natal to Durban in honour of the Cape Colony Governor, Sir Benjamin D'Urban.

Dingaan's passive treatment of the British traders encouraged the Voortrekkers. In 1835 over two-thousand trekboers approached Natal from the north. They paused before the Drakensberg Mountain range, which was a significant geographical barrier against entering Natal. One of their leaders, Piet Retief, asked them not to venture too far from the mountains until he had formalised agreements with Dingaan. The trekboers however, ignored this entreaty and entered Natal. Piet Relief made his way to Dingaan's capital in the hope of making an agreement over access to land. Dingaan was aware that the trekboers had successfully beaten all black resistance. As a test of the trekboers reliability Dingaan asked Retief to recover stolen cattle. Dingaan had intended to co-opt the trekboers as allies against his enemies but once he saw the scale of their advance, he became alarmed and changed his strategy. In February 1838 Piet Retief returned to Dingaan's capital with seventy men. Dingaan allowed Retief and his men to relax before he suddenly gave the order to kill them.

Dingaan's warriors then attacked the trekboers killing over five-hundred and they swept into Durban slaughtering many white traders. Andries Pretorius assembled a force of four-hundred-and-seventy trekboers, which he called the Wen Kommando, and set out to fight. The trekboers vowed that if God enabled them to defeat the Zulus, they would build a church and commemorate their victory forever. On 16 December 1838 a battle commenced on the banks of the Ncome river. Pretorius' relatively small band of men had formed a laager, which entailed tying wagons together in a circle. A force of over ten thousand Zulus attacked the laager but they were decisively beaten. The Zulus were unable to contend with the trekboers firepower. Over three thousand Zulus were killed, but only three trekboers were wounded and none were killed. The Ncome river ran red with blood and hence the fight was called the Battle of Blood River.

Pretorius arranged a truce treaty with Dingaan and the trekboers settled in the northern Natal area. There was no certainty about their future because neither Dingaan nor the trekboers intended to observe the treaty. The trekboers plotted with Mpande, Dingaan's half-brother, and in early 1840 Mpande defeated Dingaan. Pretorius inducted Mpande as king and even had himself recognised as a Zulu chief. The trekboers formed the Republic of Natalia with power entrusted to a twenty-four member Volksraad (or parliament) that met in the newly established town of Pietermaritzburg, which was named after the two trekboer leaders, Piet Retief and Gert Maritz. The two principal issues for the trekboers were land and labour. The farming methods were primitive and inefficient and the settlers had an insatiable desire for large farms. Those with influence were able to ensure that they received extraordinarily large land grants from the Volksraad. The Boers were extremely nervous of their black neighbours but needed their labour.

The British, who governed the Cape Colony, were not prepared to ignore the Republic of Natalia. In the eyes of the British the Boers were still British subjects. The Cape Governor, General George Napier, believed it was absurd for the Boers to be British subjects but not subject to British control. He also feared that if the Boers clashed with blacks, then Britain might be drawn into hostile conflicts. Trekboers had already crossed the Vaal River, and were expelling blacks from their land in the interior. These interior regions were largely unexplored and of little interest to the British. The coastal regions however, were of far greater concern and the British were determined to exercise control. The Portuguese had already occupied areas on the east and west coasts of southern Africa and the British did not want to see them or any other European nation encroach any further south. In August 1843 the British decided to take over Natal and made it a province of the Cape Colony. Some Boers remained but many others left to join the trekboers that had settled further north.

The Afrikaners never forgot their vow to keep the day they defeated Dingaan sacred and South Africa commemorates Dingaan's Day every 16th December. It is a day of great importance to the Afrikaner but the celebrations naturally offend many blacks. Bram's cousin, Theunis Fichardt, organised a lunch in London to celebrate Dingaan's Day on 16 December 1933. Bram asked Theunis to send me an invitation, which I accepted. I was distinctly out of place because almost all the other attendees were South Africans. Most of the conversation was in English, but they would periodically break into Afrikaans. Bram too, switched from English to Afrikaans with fluent ease. I was made to feel most welcome but their politeness could not camouflage their hostility towards the British. Bram gave the major address and I had difficulty in following everything because he switched languages throughout his speech.

The lunch was about honouring the Afrikaner victory at Blood River, but Bram was ahead of his audience and gave them a quite different perspective. He said: "As for the Great Trek, one stands amazed at the courage of men and women prepared to sacrifice...to start life again in the wholly unknown against overwhelming odds and unknown dangers. Today we stand again before a parting of the ways. Time out of number we have heard Blood River referred to as bringing the boon of European civilization to Southern Africa. But one point of view I have never heard Dingaan's Day considered from is the point of view of Dingaan. In everyday life we drug our consciences and critical faculties to his successors. The time has come, if it is not already growing late, for an acute examination of this attitude...I would not attempt to minimise the tasks. Many ideas as to race and nationality have to be destroyed or modified. This will require a new attitude of mind - of all human qualities perhaps the most difficult to attain...In September 1935 it will be a hundred years since Van Rensburg and Trichardt crossed the Orange...Now another great effort is needed, but it must be integrating this time, and draw together not only the two different European races, but to see to it that these two advance together with our vast black population..."[2]

Despite his mildly provocative comments, Bram was soundly applauded at the end of his speech. As soon as Bram had finished speaking, he was asked to join an impromptu choir in singing the folksong. Sarie Marais. The folksong was adapted from an American Civil War song called "Sweet Ellie Rhee," also known as "Carry me back to Tennessee". The South African version refers to Boers who were taken prisoner during the Anglo-Boer War and transported to Europe. The singer longs to be back in Transvaal with his lover, Sarie Marais. The folksong is in Afrikaans but an English translation is as follows:

> My Sarie Marais is so far from my heart
> But I hope to see her again
> She lived in the area of Mooi-river
> Before the war began
>
> Chorus:
> Oh bring me back to the old Transvaal
> Where my Sarie lives
> There by the maize
> By the green thorn tree
> There my Sarie lives

Bram was so busy that he neglected his studies. I was a more dedicated student, probably because I was more introverted and did not enjoy the wide circle of social contacts that engulfed Bram. I saw less of Bram because towards the end of 1933 he left his rooms in New College and moved into a shared house with his friends Mac and Len. His studies were interrupted again the next year when he took off with his parents and sister Ada on a holiday to Italy. I had the brief pleasure of meeting them all after their European holiday. I correctly addressed Percy Fischer as Your Honour and inquired about his European motoring trip. He said with a twinkle in his eye, "I tried to ride over as many fascists as I could, but I fear that there are too many of them."

In September 1934 Bram made a point of coming to my rooms for a last cup of tea before he took a train to Southampton to catch his ship home to South Africa. Bram professed a marginal disappointment over his academic results, but was determined to start his legal career. He was also very keen on rekindling his relationship with Molly. He had not chased after women in Oxford, although he impressed many with his charm, good looks, athleticism, wit, and thoughtful intellect. I was sorry to say goodbye to Bram, not realising how much our friendship would grow in the future.

CHAPTER 2

St. John's College, Johannesburg

After graduating I accepted a position as a history teacher at Tonbridge School in Kent. Reverend Clarke was the school chaplain and he made a special effort to welcome new members of staff. Reverend Clarke however, resigned shortly after I started to take up the position as headmaster of St. John's College in Johannesburg. My friendship with Bram Fischer had made me very interested in South Africa, I corresponded with Bram and he confirmed that St. John's College was a very prestigious school. One day I decided to write to Reverend Clarke and expressed an interest in teaching in South Africa. In September1936 Reverend Clarke sent me a letter:

Dear Mr Allum

Further to our recent correspondence, I am pleased to invite you to teach history at St. John's College with effect from the beginning of the 1937 Lent term. The terms and conditions are detailed in the enclosed annexure.

St. John's College was founded in 1898. The school was administered under the auspices of the Community of the Resurrection, a religious body of priests and lay brothers of the Anglican Church. In early 1934 the Community of the Resurrection terminated their involvement, but the school remains an Anglican Church school under the control of the Bishop of Johannesburg. Chapel worship and religious instruction, in accordance with the faith of the Anglican Church, remains a central focus of St. John's College. There are around five hundred boys in the school and the buildings compare favourably with Tonbridge. We seek to educate young men with an unswerving loyalty to ideals, with a dogged insistence on the execution of duty, and with a sense that somehow the job must be done. It is considered a good school, but we must strive to do better. The standard of work needs improvement. There is a distinct lack of imagination in the boys' essays and this is because of their failure to read widely and well. I have little doubt that you are of the right calibre and that you will be able to contribute positively in our mission to achieve excellence. You will have a specific responsibility to ensure that no boy leaves St. Johns College without a knowledge of the ancient and modern world. It will also be incumbent upon you to ensure that our boys obtain an understanding of the Afrikaner mind and culture.

The world is facing an ugly rise in totalitarian regimes. There is a choice between Christianity and totalitarian worldliness. Our goal is to train men in the Christian way of life. The school prayer articulates our mission very well indeed: "Lord God our Father, who art Light and Life and Love, look down in love upon our College of St John: make it to be a home of religious discipline, sound learning and goodwill, which may send forth many rightly trained in body, mind, and character to serve Thee well in Church and State: supply our wants, and give us increase as shall seem Thee good, and let Thine angels drive away all evil from us; Through Thy Son, our Saviour Jesus Christ."

You will have comfortable rooms, full board (during term time), and you will find that our staff salary scales ensure that we attract and retain the right people. You will be expected to perform duties in one of the boarding houses and engage fully in other out-of-school activities. If you are happy to confirm your acceptance please sign and return the copy of the enclosed annexure.

I am sure that will make a valuable contribution to the life of St. John's College. I very much look forward to welcoming you at the start of Lent term.

Your sincerely

Rev. S. H. Clarke

I was just twenty-six years old and tremendously excited by the possibility of going to South Africa. I showed the letter to my rather bewildered parents. They had no idea that I had pursued this position. My father had served as an army doctor during the Great War, but I knew nothing of that wretched war. I had grown up in peaceful times and in relative privilege. I was born on 2 January 1913, had gone to St. Pauls' College in Hammersmith, and up to Oxford in September 1930. After their initial surprise my parents encouraged me to accept the St. John's College offer. South Africa was part of the British Empire and they saw a stint in the colonies as being a positive feather in my cap. My father expressed grave fears over the unsettled state of Europe. The Olympic Games in Berlin had just concluded and we had witnessed the unedifying spectacle of Herr Hitler parading about with military menace. We were all worried about the spectre of another war but this barely influenced my thinking. I was excited about going to South Africa. because I relished the chance to live abroad. Bram Fischer had inspired me about the wonders of Africa, and I wanted to embark on an adventure. I had little idea that I would remain there for just over half a century.

Immediately after Christmas 1936 I took a train with my parents to Southampton where I boarded the Stirling Castle for the two-week trip to South Africa. My parents had bought me a first-class passage and I was allocated a sumptuous cabin. I was able to stand on deck and wave goodbye as the Stirling Castle bellowed smoke, untied its mooring lines, and slowly slipped away from the dock.

I played various games during the day, dressed for dinner, and enjoyed watching the evening dances. The highlight of the voyage was the crossing the line ceremony. The guests that were crossing the equator for the first time assembled on deck. The captain blew the ship's horn to mark the moment we crossed the equator, and a ship's officer, dressed up as King Neptune, dutifully baptised us by spraying us with water.

I was very excited on the morning we arrived in Cape Town. I pulled aside the porthole curtain as dawn was breaking. There was a golden glow above the unsettled dark water. Small white caps blew across the thrashing waves. I dressed and rushed on deck to see the black mass of Table Mountain. As the light brightened the white cloud, the table cloth, nestled above blew away and the mountain rose majestically against a clear blue sky. We passed Robben Island as we journeyed into Table Bay, A fellow passenger explained that 'robben' was the Dutch word for seal. I gazed intently at the island hoping to spot a seal. Little did I realise that this lonely windswept island would house many of South Africa's political prisoners.

My ideas of arriving in the wilds of Africa were soon deflated as I found that Cape Town was just like any other busy town. I was met on the wharf and taken to the Mount Nelson Hotel. The hotel was elegant but also rather unusual since all the walls were painted a garish pink. I picked up a handful of tourist brochures and studied them as I enjoyed a beer on the sunny veranda. I was required to dress for dinner, but I was pleased to dine alone. I ate quickly and retreated to my room for an early night. I woke early the next morning and eagerly looked forward to exploring Cape Town. I had a lavish English breakfast before consulting the concierge. He suggested that I join a hotel bus tour that afternoon. He assured me that I had sufficient time during the morning to wander into the city and recommended a visit to the Castle of

Good Hope. He politely recommended that I jettison my jacket and tie for my morning walk as it was a very hot day.

I walked past the Botanical Gardens and soon I found myself on Adderly Street, the heart of the city. The street was crammed with trams, buses, cars, and neatly attired office workers hurrying along the sidewalks. My surroundings were strange, but I could have been in any European city. Almost everyone seemed to be white and fashionably dressed. This was certainly not the Africa of my imagination. I turned right into Strand Street and walked towards the Castle of Good Hope. This was a stone fort built by the VOC. It had never been attacked and remained a powerful symbol of white settlement.

I returned to the Mount Nelson Hotel in time for my afternoon excursion. I could tell from the accents that I was in almost exclusively British company for our guided trip around Cape Town. We stopped to view the beautiful Atlantic Ocean beaches of Clifton, Camps Bay, and Llandudno, before following the spectacular route along Chapman's Peak Drive to Cape Point. This was not the southern-most point of Africa but it felt like it. The southern tip of Africa, where the Atlantic and Indian oceans meet, is at Cape Agulhas, just fifty-five kilometres further south and about one-hundred-and-seventy kilometres east of Cape Town. I stood on barren rocks as the wind howled about me. I could not see Table Bay to our north but to the east I had a spectacular view of False Bay. This was the name given to it by seventeenth century sailors who often confused it with Table Bay. We crossed over the peninsula to the naval base of Simon's Town where we had afternoon tea. Finally, we visited the wide sandy beaches of Fish Hoek and Muizenberg before returning to the hotel.

The next day I was taken to the station to board a train for the thirty-hour trip to Johannesburg. I had a first-class saloon and there was a well-appointed dining coach. I spent a great deal of time on the observation deck at the back. The train drew away from the station and I watched intently as Table Mountain and Table Bay slowly disappeared into the distance. The train climbed through the imposing Hex River pass and I was treated to a panorama of winelands, orchards, and snaking rivers. By midday we had entered the Karoo, which was flat and dry. There were numerous sheep dotted about on the landscape like snowflakes. The evening sunset lit up the countryside with a hue of orange. I faced west as I stood on the observation deck and delighted in watching the bright red sun disappear over the horizon. This was Africa!

The train arrived in Kimberley early the next morning. We had a lengthy stop so that the train could be divided. Certain carriages would continue to the coastal port of Durban in Natal, while the remainder would continue to Johannesburg in the Transvaal. Kimberley was the famed diamond mining town. It was a short walk from the train station to the Big Hole. This is the largest manually dug hole in the word. The hole is over eight-hundred metres deep but it is now filled with water and so it is hard to appreciate its size. Over fourteen million carats of diamonds were removed in just under fifty years. It was where Cecil Rhodes made his fortune and the birthplace of the great diamond mining company of De Beers.

In 1866 a Boer's son discovered a diamond in the Hopetown area of the northern Cape near the banks of the Orange River. Schalk van Niekerk, a neighbouring Boer, bought the diamond and sold it for a modest sum. Three years later Van Niekerk bought a far larger diamond that was found in the same area and sold it for a small fortune. News of this diamond unleashed a frenzy of prospecting. In 1870 prospectors discovered diamonds on two farms. Dutoitspan and Bultfontein. Even more diamonds were soon discovered on an adjacent farm called Vooruitzigt, which was owned by Johannes de Beer and his brother. Almost ten-thousand people descended upon the area in a search for diamonds. In 1871

Cecil John Rhodes, who was just eighteen years old, joined his brother Herbert who had staked out three claims near de Beer's farmhouse at a place called Colesberg Kopje. These claims were on top of a diamond pipe that became known as Kimberley. Herbert went back to England and Cecil Rhodes was left to fend for himself until Herbert and another brother, Frank, returned a year later. Cecil Rhodes found it hard to work his claims and turned his attention to various money-making pursuits. At one stage Rhodes and his friend, Charles Rudd, purchased an ice-cream making machine and sold ice-cream to the diggers. Rhodes also secured claims throughout the Kimberley diamond fields. Rhodes was the son of a well-educated clergyman, and he felt the lack of a good education keenly. So, in 1873 he returned to England and enrolled at Oxford University. He suffered from chest complaints and only stayed at Oxford for one term before deciding to return to the hot and dry climate of Kimberley. Rhodes' entrepreneurial spirit know no bounds and he, and Rudd, purchased a pumping engine to extract water from the Kimberley diggings. They used these large profits to increase their claim holdings. Rhodes returned to Oxford but he was a poor student. He was pre-occupied with securing wealth from his diamond claims and enjoying the good life of an English gentleman. The diamond diggings led to a border dispute between the Cape Colony and the two Boer republics of the Orange Free State and Transvaal. All three claimed that the diamond diggings were within their borders. The parties engaged in negotiations until Sir Henry Barkle, the Cape Governor, simply annexed the area on behalf of Britain. The British paid a large sum to the Orange Free State as compensation, but the Transvaal, despite their weak claim to the diamond fields, harboured a deep fury and resentment over Britain's annexation.

My train pulled into Johannesburg station on the morning of a hot summer's day. Johannesburg was far busier than Cape Town and my senses were assaulted as I was caught up in the frenzy of people. A black porter assisted me with my luggage and welcomed me to Johannesburg with a toothy grin. I tipped him handsomely and took a taxi to St. Johns College. I was deposited outside an imposing entrance and, as if on cue, the tower clock gonged loudly twelve times to announce that it was midday. The beautiful stone buildings were shaded by large oak trees. It was extremely hot but black clouds were forming and by late afternoon there was a short ferocious thunderstorm. The heat dissipated and the buildings positively glowed as they shrugged off their drenching. I settled into my sparsely furnished rooms and made my acquaintances with the other staff members as they drifted back from their summer holidays. There were other Englishmen on staff, mostly Cambridge and Oxford men. They were most welcoming and one of them asked if I had corrected the time on my watch. I confirmed that I had indeed moved the time two hours ahead of Greenwich Mean Time. He looked at me quizzically and said, "But surely you should have turned it back." I looked confused and he laughed raucously as he exclaimed, "Two hours forwards and ten years backwards."

The St. John's College environment was very English and the daily rhythm was very much like that of Tonbridge School. There were South African men on staff but the majority were young English men. It was hard to reconcile my new surroundings with being in Africa. The black staff were exclusively engaged in the kitchen, acting as waiters, undertaking cleaning duties, or in maintaining the expansive gardens and sports fields. I was keen to explore and took the bus into the city. The streets were a bustle of black and white people. The whites dressed smartly and they frequented the many elegant shops on Eloff Street.

Johannesburg was a city built on the wealth of the gold discovered here. It is the commercial centre of South Africa, a brash city where people flock to make money. The Afrikaner heartland of the country is in Pretoria just sixty kilometres to the north. The uneasy truce and persistent rivalry between English and Afrikaner is personified in these two cities. The English and Afrikaner fought each other in the Anglo-Boer War at the turn of the century and the bitterness had not dissipated. In my first years in South Africa, English and Afrikaner friction was way more evident than any black demands for equality. In 1910 the English and Afrikaners attempted to reconcile their differences and formed the Union of South Africa. There was a terrible lack of foresight as blacks and other races were denied political rights. South Africa had become a self-governing dominion in the British Empire. The Afrikaner longed to reclaim power, and when they did so in 1948, they were determined to never lose power again. This obsession with maintaining white Afrikaner political power would lead to the horrors of apartheid. The policy of apartheid was thoroughly racist, but it was not racism that underscored the policy, it was an obsession with maintaining power. The word 'apartheid' (which means 'separateness') had not yet been coined in 1937. It is worth understanding how the English and Afrikaner fought, how they reconciled, and the short-sightedness of excluding other racial groups from the political dispensation that became the Union of South Africa.

CHAPTER 3

The Union of South Africa

In the late mid-nineteenth century the trekboers clashed with the Zulus in Natal and many of them decided to venture further north. Some moved into the interior across the Orange River and some went even further north across the Vaal River, which is a northern tributary of the Orange River. There they clashed with the Basuto, Griquas, Tswana, Pedi, and Ndebele. Britain found that the expenditure on intervening in the wars with various black tribes was expensive and tiresome. Britain decided to grant the Boers independence. In 1852, at the Sand River convention, Britain recognised the independence of those that had crossed the Vaal River and called their territory the Zuid-Afrikaanse Republiek ("ZAR"), which also became known as the Transvaal. Then in 1854 they recognised the independence of the Orange Free State at the Bloemfontein convention. Both the ZAR and Orange Free State were somewhat chaotically run and survived precariously. The Boers claimed large areas of land and clashed brutally with angry blacks that resented their intrusion. This may have all been unremarkable except that the discovery of gold unleashed a titanic struggle for southern Africa.

In 1874 the British Tories, under the leadership of Benjamin Disraeli, won government. Disraeli was an unashamed imperialist and appointed a like-minded imperialist, the Earl of Carnarvon, as the colonial secretary. They saw the Cape as vitally important to British interests because it was essential for protecting trade routes to India, Ceylon, Malaysia, Singapore, China, and Australia. They were gravely concerned by instability in southern Africa. Disraeli and Carnarvon felt that Britain's security interests demanded that it control all southern Africa.

The ZAR was in a parlous state. The government had virtually no funds since the Boers generally refused to pay taxes. This meant that there were few government services, high government debt, and no ability to maintain an army. Instead, volunteers offered to fight under a commando system. The ZAR found itself in dispute with the Pedi over land, the provision of labour, and taxes. In 1876 President Burgers raised a large commando of Boer volunteers to attack the Pedi. Under the leadership of their chief, Sekhukhune, the Pedi successfully repelled the Boers. This gave Carnarvon an excuse to ask Theophilus Shepstone to proceed from Natal and annex the ZAR on behalf of Britain. In January 1877. Shepstone arrived in Pretoria, the capital of the ZAR, The Boers were mildly pleased to see Shepstone because they were rattled by the Pedi and feared that Sekhukhune would attack Pretoria. In February the ZAR signed a peace treaty with the Pedi, but now Sekhukhune advised Shepstone that the treaty was a fraud and that the Pedi feared reprisals from the Boers. Shepstone reasoned that many settlers favoured annexation, the ZAR was bankrupt, blacks resented Boer rule, and the ZAR was vulnerable to attack. On 11 April 1877 Shepstone issued a proclamation whereby Britain annexed the ZAR and it became the Transvaal Colony. President Burgers objected but was powerless to oppose British rule.

The Transvaal Boers had meekly accepted British annexation but they were highly resentful. One of the main reasons for leaving the Cape Colony was to escape from British rule and yet here they were again under a British yoke. Paul Kruger became the Boer leader. He had little education but was charismatic and a dynamic commando leader. He had fought in many campaigns against black opponents. He was a staunch Calvinist and belonged to the very conservative Afrikaner church that were called the Doppers because they believed in extinguishing the Enlightenment. (Dopper in Afrikaans means extinguish). Kruger claims to have read nothing other than the Bible and accepted the literal truth of all biblical texts, including that the earth was flat. Kruger was present at the signing of the Sand River convention, and he was appalled when Burgers was made President of the ZAR. Burgers was not religious and Kruger saw this as a fatal flaw. Kruger refused to assist Burgers in the war against the Pedi and he blamed him for the British annexation. Kruger did not accept that the Transvaal had agreed to the annexation and argued that a plebiscite should be held to see if the majority (of whites) were in favour of annexation. He made two trips to London to plead his case but was rebuffed each time. There was huge Afrikaner resentment in the Transvaal to the annexation and this anger spilled over into the Orange Free State and Cape Colony. Shepstone proved to be an incompetent administrator and he was recalled at the end of 1878. This did little to abate Afrikaner anger and in January 1879 several thousand Boers came to Wonderfontein to hear Kruger describe his lack of success from his second trip to London. They demanded revolution but Kruger urged calm.

The Transvaal Boers continued to agitate for independence. Over two-thousand Boers met again at Wonderfontein and on 15 December 1879 they resolved that they no longer wished to remain as British citizens. Afrikaners throughout the country were now growing more vocal in their support of the Transvaal Boers. Kruger travelled to the Cape and pressed members of the Cape parliament to support the Transvaal's claim for independence. The

British, under the leadership of a new Prime Minister, William Gladstone, refused to countenance independence. Kruger now decided to quietly build up arms in preparation for a fight against the British.

In December 1880 some five thousand Boers assembled at a farm called Pardekraal where they resolved to declare their independence. The war of independence was exceedingly brief but it gave Afrikaner nationalism a terrific boost throughout southern Africa. The Boers killed fifty-six British soldiers and wounded almost another hundred in a skirmish near Bronkhorstspruit. General George Colley, the Governor of Natal, set out with soldiers from Natal to reinforce the British units in the Transvaal He was determined to put down the rebellious Boers and teach them a lesson in what is known as the First Boer War. He attacked the Boers at Laing's Nek on the Transvaal border but suffered heavy casualties and suffered further casualties when the Boers attacked his supply lines. Colley decided to seize the summit of a hill called Majuba that overlooked Laing's Nek. The Boers expected to be bombarded from the summit of Majuba but Colley had failed to bring any significant artillery guns. The Boers rallied and began an assault on Majuba hill. Colley was killed and the remaining British forces fled. It was a humiliating defeat. Britain was shocked and the public wanted vengeance for the defeat at Majuba. The British Prime Minister, Gladstone, though had no appetite for an expensive and protracted conflict in southern Africa and he agreed to grant the Transvaal its independence. The ZAR, or Transvaal Republic, resumed under the leadership of Paul Kruger.

Kruger was anxious to protect the Afrikaner character of the Transvaal from British influence. He visited Amsterdam and encouraged over five thousand Dutch to immigrate to the Transvaal. He promoted the Calvinist faith and was convinced that God had assisted the Boers in their determination to establish independent Afrikaner republics in the Transvaal and Orange Free State. He ensured that Dingaan's Day, commemorating the victory over the Zulus at Blood River, was celebrated each year. Kruger equated the Afrikaners with the biblical accounts of the Israelites. God had led the Israelites out of bondage in Egypt to the promised land of Canaan. The Israelites had frequently disobeyed God and had been punished through foreign conquests and periods of exile. In the same vein Kruger believed that God had led the trekboers to the interior and ensured their victory at Blood River. The Boers however, had ignored their covenant to honour God every year for this victory. This had resulted in the Boers loss of Natal and the Transvaal to the British. Kruger believed that regaining independence was a sign of God's commitment to the Afrikaner and he ensured that their vow was remembered on 16 December each year.

Various alluvial gold deposits were found in the Transvaal during the 1870s and 1880s, but in 1886 there was a momentous gold discovery on a farm called Langlaagte in the region of the Witswatersrand just south of Pretoria. The first serious prospector was Colonel Ignatius Ferreira, a Boer from the Cape Colony. Within months Ferreira's camp was crowded with prospectors. A new town called Johannesburg sprung to life beside the gold diggings. Cecil Rhodes floated a company called The Gold Fields of South Africa and attracted investors because of his reputation for having made a fortune from diamonds. There was a frenzy of speculation with over four hundred companies raising funds through the newly established Johannesburg Stock Exchange. Gold revenues caused an enormous rise in the financial strength of the Transvaal, which dramatically altered the balance of power between the Transvaal and Cape Colony. Kruger wished to use these new revenues to build a railway line to Delagoa Bay. This would allow the Transvaal to avoid having to use the Cape for the trafficking of goods. Rhodes, aided by his wealth and prestige, had obtained a seat in the parliament of the Cape Colony, and in July 1890 he was appointed prime minister. Rhodes now had power, as well as money, at his disposal. Rhodes had an insatiable appetite for territory and he expanded both British interests and his own pecuniary interests. Rhodes took up the cause of attempting to colonise everything on behalf of Britain from the Cape to Cairo.

Kruger was able to use the wealth generated from gold to transform the capital of Pretoria. He built an impressive parliament and other government buildings. Nevertheless. Pretoria remained little more than a quiet country town, while just to its south, Johannesburg was fast growing into a lively city. Kruger was far from impressed with Johannesburg. Drunkenness, prostitution, and debauchery offended his religious sensibilities. Kruger was pleased to benefit from gold revenues but he was very unhappy about the large ex-patriate, or uitlander, community that was attracted to Johannesburg. He also noted how many of the mining magnates, dubbed Randlords, had made fortunes and then fled with their profits to London. Above all Kruger feared that the increasing numbers of uitlanders would soon outnumber the Afrikaners, and so Kruger took steps to limit their political rights. In 1882 the qualification period for the franchise had been set at four years residency. In 1891 Kruger decided to lift the franchise qualification period to fourteen years and limited it to those over forty years of age. There was, of course, no consideration at all given to granting the franchise to blacks who were physically confined to compounds in Johannesburg and not allowed to mix freely with the white population. The uitlanders protested on the grounds that they were being taxed but denied political representation. Rhodes threw his support behind the uitlanders and began to conspire against Kruger.

Rhodes gathered influential people into his conspiracy. One of his main accomplices was a Scottish doctor, Leander Starr Jameson, who he had first met in Kimberley more than a decade earlier. Rhodes and Jameson devised a plan to support a 'spontaneous' uprising in Johannesburg. Rhodes did not simply want to remove Kruger and change the government in the Transvaal, he intended to make the Transvaal a British colony. Rhodes was able to secure the support of Joseph Chamberlain, the new colonial secretary, although Chamberlain subsequently denied knowing anything about the plot. Jameson was filled with enthusiasm but he was a military novice. The plan was for Jameson to invade the Transvaal from Bechuanaland (now called Botswana) with a force of fifteen hundred men. Then thousands of uitlanders would take up arms, which had been smuggled into Johannesburg, and join forces with Jameson to remove Kruger's government. It was a simple but entirely amateurish plan, especially given Jameson's lack of military experience. The other conspirators realised that it would be very difficult to secure an uitlander uprising of the scale they required. They advised Rhodes to abandon or at least postpone the planned invasion. Rhodes reluctantly agreed to the postponement and one of the conspirators sent a telegram to Jameson advising him to halt his invasion preparations. Jameson received the telegram but since it was not from Rhodes personally, he sent an impatient telegram to Rhodes declaring that he intended to invade the following day unless he heard to the contrary. In circumstances of high farce Rhodes attempted to stop Jameson but the telegraph lines had already been cut in preparation for the invasion. Jameson launched his invasion on 29 December 1895 with a force of only five hundred men. His forces were almost comically inept. They had cut the telegraph lines to Cape Town, but they had failed to cut the lines to Pretoria. News of his invasion was quickly relayed to Kruger, who despatched armed commandos to intercept Jameson. The

Boer commandos confronted Jameson's force at Krugersdorp and after a brief fight Jameson surrendered. The Transvaal Afrikaners were incensed and they agitated for the execution of Jameson and other conspirator ringleaders. Kruger however, saw an advantage in being magnanimous and handed over Jameson and his raiders to Britain. If they were not punished, then Britain would be seen to be aiding and abetting criminals. Jameson was sentenced to fifteen months in prison, but only served four months. The British parliament set up a committee of inquiry into the Jameson Raid. Rhodes was only mildly rebuked, while many others, including Joseph Chamberlain, claimed they knew nothing and stated that Jameson had acted alone.

In 1897 Sir Alfred Milner arrived in Cape Town as the new High Commissioner for Southern Africa and Governor of the Cape Colony. Milner was an ardent British imperialist. In a statement, he called his Credo, he wrote: "I am a British (indeed primarily an English) Nationalist. If I am also an Imperialist, it is because the destiny of the English race, owing to its insular position and long supremacy at sea, has been to strike fresh roots in distant parts of the world. My patriotism knows no geographical but only racial limits. I am an Imperialist and not a Little Englander, because I am a British Race Patriot."[3] Milner and Chamberlain saw the Transvaal as a threat to the British Empire. They feared that the Transvaal would have the economic muscle to absorb the Orange Free State and Cape Colony. Milner and Chamberlain wanted to prevent this and they were determined to secure a British dominion over all southern Africa. Kruger was wary of Britain and ordered a great deal of equipment from Germany and France to bolster the Transvaal's military capability. Kruger also took steps to draw closer to the Orange Free State and secured a mutual defence treaty.

In 1898 Kruger was elected President of the Transvaal for the fourth time. He appointed Francis Reitz as secretary of state and Jan Smuts as state attorney. They were both from the Cape and both were British-trained lawyers. Reitz and Smuts gave a great deal of attention to engaging in talks with the mining Randlords to address uitlander grievances. They came up with a set of proposals known as the Great Deal. One of the proposals was to reduce the franchise qualification period from fourteen to nine years. The Randlords though declined to accept the Great Deal and sent a petition, signed by over twenty-one thousand uitlanders, to the British government detailing their grievances. Milner sent despatches to the British government warning that intervention on the side of the uitlanders risked war. He argued however, that the uitlander grievances gave Britain a unique opportunity to stamp its authority over southern Africa.

In early June 1899 Kruger and Milner met in Bloemfontein. Bram's grandfather, Abraham Fischer, the Vice President of the Orange Free State, was in attendance and acted as the interpreter. Kruger wanted to talk about a range of issues but Milner was only prepared to discuss the franchise issue. Milner wanted the franchise to be given to all foreigners with over five years residency. Kruger objected because this would mean handing the Transvaal over to British control. Kruger attempted to make concessions and proposed various alternatives. Milner was obstinate and refused all compromises. As Kruger repeatedly observed it was not really about the franchise, the British wanted his country. Smuts persuaded Kruger to make additional concessions and on 18 July 1899 the Transvaal Volksraad, or parliament, reduced the franchise qualification period to seven years. Almost everyone believed that this had averted the crisis, but Milner decried the new franchise arrangements a sham, untrustworthy, and designed to fool the British. Milner claimed that Kruger could not be trusted. The British knew that the franchise was not the real issue, but rather it was about ensuring British supremacy. Lord Salisbury, the British Prime Minister made this comment: "The real point to be made to South Africa is that we, not the Dutch, are Boss."[4]

The British parliament decided that there should be a joint inquiry into the Transvaal franchise. Many influential politicians from the Cape Colony, Orange Free State, and Transvaal urged Kruger to accept this inquiry to head off war. Kruger however, believed that if he complied with the joint inquiry request it would be tantamount to surrendering the Transvaal's independence. Instead, he attempted to appease Britain through dropping the franchise qualification and reserving ten seats in the parliament for mining areas. In return he asked Britain to drop its suzerainty claims over the Transvaal. The British though merely saw the franchise issue as a pretext for gaining control over the Transvaal. It no longer mattered what concessions Kruger made as the British were determined to intervene. Britain advised that they accepted Kruger's franchise concessions but would not abandon their suzerainty claim. War was now inevitable and both the Transvaal and British mobilised. The parliament of the Orange Free State met and resolved to join forces with the Transvaal. Abraham Fischer explained the reasoning for this decision as follows: "Every reasonable concession has been granted and the British Government's requests complied with, and the only result of every concession has been trickery and increased demands. Further compliance would, I feel sure, only be an inducement for, and lead to further dishonourable and insulting treatment of [the Transvaal]... We have honestly done our best, and can do no more: if we are to lose our independence – since that is palpably what is demanded – leave us, at all events, the consolation that we did not sacrifice it dishonourably."[5]

The British struggled to find a *casus belli*. Lord Salisbury and Chamberlain were especially fearful of explaining to the British people why they were at war. In the end it was Kruger that made it easy for them. On 9 October 1899 the Transvaal presented the British with an ultimatum demanding the withdrawal of their troops from their borders within forty-eight hours and a failure to do so would be regarded as a declaration of war. Abraham Fischer was asked to draft the ultimatum. Both sides believed in swift victories and neither side foresaw that the Anglo-Boer War would drag on for almost three years. The Boers assembled commandos on the Natal border and prepared to attack. The plan was to capture Durban and thereby thwart the landing of British troops. At the same time the Boers cut off the railway line from the Cape and laid siege to the towns of Kimberley and Mafeking. The idea was to incur early victories, much like Majuba, so that the British were forced to negotiate a settlement. The Boers laid siege to Ladysmith in Natal and commandos set out for Pietermaritzburg. A train was ambushed and Winston Churchill was one of the sixty prisoners captured. A few months later Churchill managed a daring escape from Pretoria. It took until late October for Britain to assemble their expeditionary forces and place them on transport ships to Cape Town. The arrival of these forces was destined to turn the tide of the war in Britain's favour, but not before the British had suffered some disasters.

General Redvers Buller was placed in charge of the British forces. He sent half the army to relieve Ladysmith and the other half to relieve Mafeking. He led the army force in Natal and his initial attempt to relieve Ladysmith was a spectacular failure as Boers fired upon exposed British soldiers from well-fortified positions. In similar fashion, the Boers in the Cape routed the British forces on their way to relieve Kimberley. The British expected to finish the war by Christmas, but instead they were suffering defeats. The British government was incensed and ordered Field Marshal Frederick Roberts to take command. British volunteers signed up to fight and reinforcements came from Canada, Australia, and New Zealand. The overwhelming size of the British forces would slowly turn the tide in their favour. The sieges of Kimberley and Ladysmith were broken and Roberts was able to capture Bloemfontein. Soon thereafter Mafeking was relieved and Roberts was able to cross into the Transvaal. Abraham Fischer had managed to board a ship to Europe on the very day that Bloemfontein capitulated. He and his delegation travelled throughout Europe seeking support for the Boer cause. Abraham Fischer spent most of the war in Holland where he was joined by his wife Ada and son Percy, who was studying at Cambridge. They were later joined by his other son Harry, who had been captured and taken to Britain.

Kruger was forced to escape from Pretoria and went to a hide-out in the east of the Orange Free State. He contacted President Steyn, of the Orange Free State, and suggested surrender. President Steyn was furious and argued that they should fight to the bitter end. Roberts made a triumphant entry into Pretoria on 5 June 1900 and confidently expected the Boers to lay down their arms and surrender. On 1 September 1900 Roberts formally announced that Britain had annexed the Transvaal. Kruger retreated to Nelspruit in the eastern Transvaal and issued a defiant statement rejecting the annexation. Eventually Kruger was forced to flee as British troops advanced towards Nelspruit. He caught a train to Delagoa Bay and then a ship to Holland where he remained in exile until his death in 1904, a tired and defeated man. Lord Roberts handed over command to his chief of staff, Lord Kitchener, and left the Transvaal. He was widely feted upon his return to Britain as everyone imagined the war had been won. They were to discover however, that the war would drag on for almost another two years.

The Boers under the leadership of Jan Smuts, Louis Botha, Koos de la Rey, and Christiaan de Wet, engaged in guerrilla warfare. They sabotaged infrastructure, set ambushes, and carried out daring raids. The lumbering infantry columns of the British were unable to deal with this style of engagement and they became increasingly frustrated as they chased Boer commando units across the countryside. The frustrated British began to adopt brutal tactics. They burned farms, confiscated livestock, and destroyed water reservoirs. The idea was a form of collective punishment. Lord Kitchener built a network of blockhouses and barbed wire fences to restrict the free movement of Boer commandos. He reasoned that the Boer women were providing the men with supplies and intelligence, and so he ordered women and children to be rounded up and placed in concentration camps. These concentration camps would leave a shameful legacy. Hygiene and food rations in the camps were inadequate and thousands perished from disease and malnutrition. It fuelled an Afrikaner hatred for the British. Kitchener's scorched earth policy made it impossible for the Boers to continue fighting. The Boer leaders met the British at Vereeniging to discuss peace terms. The Transvaal and Orange Free State would be run by a British administration until circumstances allowed self-government. The terms included the recognition of King Edward VII as the sovereign. The Boers were divided and some, particularly the Orange Free State Boers, wished to fight on. The bitter enders, as they were called, realised that their cause was hopeless and on 31 May 1902 they signed the peace agreement at Kitchener's headquarters in Pretoria.

Lord Milner promptly moved to Johannesburg to oversee the British administration of the Transvaal, and what was now called the Orange River Colony. He recruited young Oxford graduates to assist in his administration and they were dubbed 'Milner's Kindergarten.' Milner was determined to encourage British immigration so that the Afrikaners were outnumbered. He wanted to anglicise the former Boer republics in every possible way. He saw education as one of the principal ways of achieving this and ordered that English should be the chief medium of instruction in all schools. The gold mining industry was suffering from a shortage of labour. Many blacks simply refused to work for the low wages offered and so Milner imported indentured Chinese labourers. The importation of indentured Indian sugar-cane labourers had worked successfully in Natal. The Afrikaners resented Milner's anglicisation policies and were particularly affronted by the insistence of the use of English in education. They established their own schools and began to vigorously promote the use of Afrikaans as a language. Afrikaner writers and academics began to campaign for the recognition of Afrikaans.

In 1878 Henry Bousfield, a graduate of Cambridge University, was appointed the first Anglican bishop of Pretoria. Bousfield visited Johannesburg and realised that the new town needed an able Anglican priest. He recruited John Darragh who was working as a curate in Kimberley. Darragh was a dynamic leader, tough, and highly energetic. He acquired property on behalf of the Anglican Church, on which he established churches, schools, and orphanages. On 1 August 1898 John Darragh founded St. John's College on the porch of St. Mary's Church. After just a few weeks the school was relocated to more suitable premises in Plein Street. The school was popular and there was no shortage of pupils. The outbreak of the Anglo-Boer War in 1899 caused many to flee Johannesburg, including St. John's College staff, parents, and pupils, and the school was closed for the entire duration of the war. After the 1902 peace treaty Darragh returned to Johannesburg and re-opened St. John's College with almost two hundred pupils. The school was to face great difficulty in surviving because of Milner's education policies. Milner did not support the existence of private schools as this interfered with his plan for state schools. These state schools were well funded and Milner's acolytes even contacted parents of St. John's College pupils to tell them about the advantages of enrolling at the state schools. Some of these schools performed very well indeed and many of them, such as King Edward VII College, located just a few hundred metres from St. John's College, were (and still are) excellent schools. St. John's College however, managed to survive and made the following statement in its 1903 prospectus: "St. John's College was founded six years ago to meet the demand for a school for gentleman's sons on the lines of English Public Schools... The Council have decided to continue St. John's College, not in any sense as competing with the Government, for that is impossible, but in the belief that they are meeting a demand wholly different in character."[6]

Louis Botha and Jan Smuts emerged as outspoken critics of Milner. They formed a political party called Het Volk and agitated for self-government. Het Volk was popular and won the support of most Afrikaners in the Transvaal. Barry Hertzog and Abraham Fischer formed a political party called Orangia Unie, and it won the support of most Afrikaners in the Orange River Colony. Milner's policies had paradoxically helped the Afrikaners in the Transvaal and Orange River Colony come together as one nation. In the Cape Colony the British and Afrikaners were divided. The British supported the Progressive Party while Afrikaners supported the South African Party which was an alliance of parties, of which the largest was called the Afrikaner Bond. Milner left southern Africa in 1905 after achieving next to nothing in terms of anglicising the Afrikaner. In 1906 the Liberals won government in Britain, under the leadership of Sir Henry Campbell-Bannerman, and they granted the Transvaal and Orange River Colony self-government. In February 1907 Het Volk won the election in the Transvaal with Louis Botha becoming prime minister. In November 1907 Orangie Unie won all the seats in the Orange River Colony election and Abraham Fischer became prime minister. Abraham Fischer would shortly celebrate another very important event. On 23 April 1908 his son Percy and daughter-in-law Ella had their first child. They named him Abram after his grandfather, but he would always be known as Bram.

Blacks were disillusioned over the granting of self-government to the Transvaal and Orange River Colony. The Transvaal Native Congress and Orange River Colony Native Congress sent protests to the British government. They claimed that blacks had shown loyalty to Britain but black political rights were ignored when the British handed over self-government to white only voters. The Cape Colony had a non-racial franchise. Anyone could vote, provided they met certain income or asset ownership thresholds, and many blacks and Coloureds qualified. In the Natal Colony the franchise rules were so complex that it was virtually impossible for any black to qualify for the franchise. In Natal blacks openly revolted against poll taxes and unfair land measures, but they were brutally repressed. In the Transvaal and Orange River Colony the blacks were denied all political rights.

Jan Smuts proposed a national convention to discuss the formation of a union of the Transvaal, Orange River Colony, Natal Colony, and Cape Colony. In October 1908 delegates assembled in Cape Town. All four prime ministers attended: John Merriman (Cape), Louis Botha (Transvaal), Abraham Fisher (Orange River), and Frederick Moor (Natal). There were other notable delegates, including Jan Smuts, but no black, Indian, or Coloured delegates. One of the most contentious issues concerned black political rights. The Cape were in favour of a qualified franchise, but this was strongly opposed by the Transvaal and Orange River Colony. Smuts commented as follows: "I sympathize profoundly with the native races of South Africa whose land it was long before we came here to force a policy of dispossession on them. And it ought to be the policy of all parties to do justice to the natives and to take all wise and prudent measures for their civilization and improvement. But I don't believe in politics for them."[7]

By early 1909 the delegates had agreed on a draft constitution. The four colonies were to become provinces in the Union of South Africa under a Westminster-style of government. Only whites would be allowed to sit in the parliament. Blacks, Coloureds, and Indians were appalled at the draft constitution and protested. William Schreiner, a former prime minister of the Cape Colony, objected strongly to the exclusion of blacks and unsuccessfully attempted to have the constitution amended. An official delegation went to London to present the case for Union. Schreiner argued passionately against the short-sightedness of excluding blacks and other racial groups from the franchise. The British parliament debated The South Africa Bill in July 1909. There were a few that spoke strongly against the whites only franchise, but the bill still received overwhelming support. On 31 May 1910 the Union of South Africa came into being. Louis Botha became the first prime minister. South Africa remained part of the British empire, with God Save the King as the national anthem and the Union Jack featuring prominently on the national flag. The Privy Council in London retained judicial authority, and the British government retained control over matters concerning war and peace. South Africa had self-government but British influence ran deep. Afrikaners resented this British domination and many harboured a deep-seated desire to be rid of all British influences.

The blacks had good reason to be disgruntled with the new Union of South Africa. They were to suffer from a barrage of legislation designed to relegate them to subordinate servant roles. The 1911 Mines and Works Act barred blacks from skilled positions, the 1913 Natives Land Act prohibited blacks from purchasing land in white areas and reserved only thirteen percent of the land for blacks, and the 1923 Natives Urban Areas Act only permitted blacks to reside in urban locations if their labour was required to service white needs. Pass laws were expanded to control the influx of blacks into urban areas.

Afrikaners fell between British domination on the one side and dispossessed blacks on the other. In accordance with their Calvinist faith, Afrikaners believed that their survival was ordained by God, but they feared both the British and the blacks. In time Afrikaner fear of British imperialism would decline but they would see blacks as an existential threat.

CHAPTER 4

A very strange society

I called Bram at his chambers shortly after my arrival in Johannesburg. Bram was delighted to hear from me and he invited me to a *braai*, which is the universally used South African word for a barbeque. Bram offered to pick me up because I did not yet have a car. Bram cautioned that public buses in South Africa, especially on a Sunday, would be nothing like the well-established English system of public transport. Bram ushered me into his flat and it was soon evident that we would not be alone. People began to drift in, all carrying bottles of alcohol. Bram relocated everyone down stairs to the small communal garden and he took elaborate pains in building a fire for the *braai*. His guests spoke mainly English with a smattering of Afrikaans now and again. I was warmly greeted by everyone. I explained our Oxford University connection and my recent acceptance of a position at St. John's College. Someone warned me to keep out of the sun. I was absurdly pale in comparison to the deeply tanned collection of men and women. He said jocularly, "If you get sunburn, we shall have to call you a *rooinek*." I did not understand and raised a quizzical frown. He explained, "*Rooinek* means red neck. It is because your pale necks get so easily burnt in our African sun." I promised to be careful. *Rooinek* was a common expression used to describe Englishmen. It was mildly pejorative depending on the context in which the word was used. Another even less flattering way of referring to an English-speaking South African is to call them a *sout piel*. This translates as "salt penis" and suggests that English speakers have one foot in South Africa, one foot in England, and their penis hanging in the ocean. I was living in a very strange society.

Bram and I reminisced about various Oxford friends and it was clear that Bram had been far more diligent than I in staying in touch through letter-writing. He was pleased to tell me that he was now engaged to Molly. I congratulated him on this great news and naturally asked when I was going to meet her. Bram advised that I could not do so because Molly was working as a school teacher in Windhoek. A month later Bram told me that Molly had boarded a ship in South West Africa and gone to Europe. Bram was delighted that Molly would visit so many of the places he had seen on his travels. While Bram claimed to be pleased that Molly was enjoying a great adventure, I could tell that he was anxious about her absence and was determined to get married as soon as she returned. Bram took off to Cape Town in August to meet her returning ship. I met Molly just once before they left to get married. She was strong-willed and exuded an independent spirit. Bram and Molly were a very good match.

I was pleased to receive a wedding invitation. It was to take place in Bloemfontein on 18 September 1937. When I met Molly she stated that she did not want to wear a white dress and she did not want to be married by a *dominee* (Afrikaner church minister). I do not know what brought on her change of heart but Molly looked resplendent in a white wedding dress when she and Bram took their marital vows in front of a *dominee*. They were married in the garden of Bram's parents, Ella and Percy Fischer on a Saturday morning. The black staff formed a choir and sang joyfully in Sotho at the end of the ceremony. I felt rather privileged to be in attendance since most of the guests were relatives or close family friends. I have only a blurred memory of the guests I met that day, but I can recall meeting Bram's brothers, Paul, Pieter, and Gus, and his sister, Ada. Then there was his aunt, Maude, her husband Dr Charles Bidwell, and their children (Bram's cousins) Joan and Connie. Molly's parents, Emmy and Tottie Krige, and her sister Pauline, had come from Pretoria to attend the wedding. I was rather disappointed that Molly's aunt, Isie, could not be there. She was married to General Jan Smuts who had been the Prime Minister, and was the leader of the parliamentary opposition. I was introduced to Tibbie Steyn, the widow of Theunis Steyn, a former President of the Orange Free State. It was to my great surprise that she spoke with a distinctly Scottish accent. I asked if she was Scottish but laughed and said that she was a true Afrikaner but had lived in Scotland as a child. She sensed that I was unacquainted with most of the guests and so she grabbed me by the arm and shepherded me along. I observed that many of the guests referred to her as "Ouma." I asked what this meant and she told me a broad smile, "This means that I am a very old lady." I would learn that Ouma is the Afrikaans word for grandmother and the word is used as a mark of respect when addressing elderly ladies.

I had driven to Bloemfontein in my second-hand Oldmobile. The car was reliable but tended to overheat. I had to make regular stops to let it cool down. I carried a drum of water to allow me to fill up the radiator. I did not want to spend the rest of the weekend in Bloemfontein as I had been warned that virtually everything would be closed on the Sunday. I decided to make a detour through the northern Natal Zulu wars battlefields before returning to Johannesburg. The roads were terrible and I spent hours sitting beside my cooling car hoping that I would not be stranded permanently. I drove to the town of Dundee, and then bumped along dirt roads to the battlefields of Rorke's Drift and Isandlwana.

Dingaan's half-brother, Mpande had succeeded Dingaan shortly after the trekboers had defeated him at the Battle of Blood River. Mpande fathered twenty-three sons with multiple wives. There was a great rivalry amongst his sons over the succession. Cetshwayo was the first-born son but his succession was not guaranteed as the king often chose his successor late in his reign to prevent being usurped. Cetshwayo defeated and killed his main rival, Mbuyazi, in a fierce battle, but it took another five years before Mpande recognised him as his heir. Mpande died in 1872 and Cetshwayo became the Zulu king. Cetshwayo was anxious to receive British support and quite extraordinarily it was Theophilus Shepstone, the British secretary for Native Affairs in Natal, that placed the crown upon Cetshwayo's head. Cetshwayo had no quarrel with the British, but the British were fearful of Zulu power. Cetshwayo did everything he could to avoid war but the British were determined to crush the Zulu nation. Cetshwayo supposedly said, "I have not gone over the seas to look for the white man, yet they have come into my country... What shall I do?"[8] His generals replied that they would attack the British and refuse to allow them to capture their king.

In January 1879 Lord Chelmsford led a British column into Zululand. He crossed the Buffalo River (or Mzinyathi river) at Rorke's Drift and camped a little further on in the shadow of a hill called Isandlwana. Chelmsford neglected to set up a protective camp despite warnings from Boers, experienced in fighting the Zulus, that it was essential to take precautions. Chelmsford then made another cardinal mistake and split his forces in two. He sent part of his forces ahead to find the Zulu army and left a garrison of five companies behind at Isandlwana. The main Zulu army of twenty thousand warriors was in a nearby valley and they attacked the Isandlwana camp in a classic chest and horns formation. A message was sent to Chelmsford advising that the Zulu army was descending upon the camp at Isandlwana. Chelmsford received the news with indifference and it took him most of the day to return. Chelmsford discovered that the Zulus had overrun the camp and massacred almost everyone. Over one-thousand British soldiers were killed in this humiliating defeat. The Zulu army then attacked the small British garrison at Rorke's drift. This small British detachment of eight officers and just over a hundred men fought valiantly to hold off a Zulu force of almost four-thousand warriors. Eleven Victoria crosses were awarded to the courageous defenders, which may have had something to do with compensating for the disaster at Isandlwana. The outcry was enormous when the news of the Isandlwana defeat reached Britain. Disraeli, responded by sending out General Sir Garnet Wolseley to sort out affairs in southern Africa. He was given civil and military authority over all of Natal, Zululand, and the Transvaal. Wolseley defeated Cetshwayo and broke up the Zulu kingdom. Cetshwayo died a broken man in 1884.

There was little to see at Rorke's Drift but I was thrilled with my visit to Isandlwana. The grave sights of the British soldiers were marked and I was able to pick up shell casings that were still easy to find. I had always thought that the British had brought the benefits of its advanced civilisation to its colonial outposts. This battlefield visit made me think about colonial intrusion. I knew that the British defeat at Isandlwana was only a brief humiliation. In the long-run the British had treated the Zulus most unfairly. I had begun to see that perhaps this British commonwealth country was deeply flawed. I started to think that the whites, both English and Afrikaner, had brought more misery than benefits to the indigenous people of southern Africa.

Over the next year or so I saw Bram and Molly regularly, but seldom alone, because they were almost always surrounded with friends. I had settled down at St. John's College, Bram was busy establishing his credentials as a barrister (or advocate as barristers are called in South Africa). In late 1938 they proudly announced that Molly was pregnant. Bram and Molly decided that they needed a house and Bram was painstakingly diligent in his research. They decided to buy a vacant block of land in Oaklands, which was very close to St. John's College. I could drive there in five minutes but I often preferred to jog there. It was an easy route to their house but it was a tougher run back to school up a steep and winding road called Munro Drive.

Bram gave me a book called *Coming of Age* that Jan Hofmeyer and other academics had published in 1931. Bram and Molly had recently dined with General Jan Smuts and Jan Hofmeyer. This was not altogether unsurprising given that Molly's aunt, Ilse, was married to Jan Smuts. In the book Jan Hofmeyer identified three causes of discontent in the Union of South Africa. First, there was a lack of unity between the white English and Afrikaner groups. There was a view that the English cared more for Britain than South Africa, while the counter view was that the Afrikaners did not appreciate the benefits Britain brought to South Africa. Secondly, there were major economic shortcomings. Gold and diamonds had created an illusion of unlimited wealth. Mineral resources are a wasting asset and South Africa needed to create a vibrant manufacturing and agricultural sector to accommodate its growing population. Thirdly, there was the white fear that ultimately black numbers would overwhelm their political power. Whites also feared black retribution for their treatment.[9]

After the creation of the Union of South Africa in 1910, the South Africa Party, with Louis Botha as prime minister, formed the first national government. His cabinet included Jan Smuts and Barry Hertzog. The Afrikaners feared that South Africa would become just another outpost of the British empire. Hertzog became the leader of disaffected Afrikaners that were determined to retain a separate South African identity. Hertzog left the government in 1913 and formed a new political party, called the National Party. Hertzog campaigned against entering the First World War on Britain's side and many Afrikaners broke out in open rebellion. In 1919 Afrikaner intellectuals formed a secret society called the Broederbond. They were driven by a sense of cultural despair and sought to capture an idealised past through promoting Afrikanerdom. Their vision was to establish an Afrikaner domination of South Africa.

At the conclusion of the First World War, Botha and Smuts represented South Africa at the Versailles Peace Conference. They noted the harsh terms imposed upon the Germans and contrasted this with the efforts to bring about reconciliation after the Boer War. Botha and Smuts were hoping that the post-war settlement would enable South Africa to expand its borders into Southern Rhodesia and German South West Africa. The Rhodesians resisted and demanded self-government, while South West Africa became a protectorate under a mandate from the newly formed League of Nations. Industry had grown significantly in South Africa and there were post-war labour stresses. There was an increased demand for labour and workers were demanding higher wages. Blacks became more militant in their demands for better conditions and wanted the removal of discriminatory laws. In 1921 white mine workers went on strike to protest the proposed removal of the colour bar, which protected white semi-skilled jobs. Smuts declared martial law and there were fierce confrontations which resulted in over two hundred deaths. Smuts was depicted as a tyrant and in 1924 a political alliance of the National Party, Labour Party and Communist Party won the general election. The National Party were never happy to be reminded of the inclusion of the communists in this alliance. The Communist Party of South Africa was formed in 1921 and was initially only concerned with the rights of white workers. The principal group that represented black interests was the South African National Native Congress, which the Reverend Walter Rubusana, Pixley Seme, John Dube, and Sol Plaatje established in 1912. It was later re-named the African National Congress (ANC).

Barry Hertzog became the prime minister from 1924 to 1939. Hertzog's primary mission was to promote the interests of Afrikaners. Black discontent soon became one of the main issues that concerned the government. In 1929 the National Party won another general election. Smuts, as leader of the opposition South African Party, was incorrectly accused of wanting to hand over political power to the blacks. South Africa suffered during the 1930s Great Depression. Mineral and agricultural exports plummeted and there was mass unemployment. While the Afrikaners dominated the farming industry, many Afrikaners were rapidly becoming urbanised. The urban Afrikaner however, found himself in a subordinate role to the English who controlled virtually every economic sector. The Great Depression heaped pressure on Hertzog's government. He feared that the National Party would lose the next general election. Hertzog brokered a deal with Smuts to fuse their respective political parties. They joined to form the United Party and resoundingly won the 1933 general election. There were however, members of parliament, led by Dr Daniel Malan, who were unhappy with the fusion arrangement. They saw Jan Smuts, and his protege Jan Hofmeyer, as being far too accommodating towards Britain and the blacks. Jan Hofmeyer was often criticised for his belief in political rights for blacks. Jan Hofmeyer was the Minister of Education during my first years at St John's College. I never met him but Reverend Clarke enjoyed many meetings with this Minister and he spoke highly of him. Malan left the United Party and went into opposition as the leader of the Nationalist Party.

A topic that garnered much discussion was that of a qualified franchise. A group of parliamentary liberals argued that blacks should be given the franchise provided they met certain qualification standards. A larger group of parliamentary conservatives feared that whites could not survive in South Africa if blacks were granted the franchise. Hertzog and Smuts accepted that blacks were permanent citizens of South Africa and proposed extending the franchise to them through a separate voters' roll. Daniel Malan and his henchmen were adamantly opposed to extending any political rights to blacks, and were also determined to remove Coloureds from the voters' roll. One of Malan's most ardent supporters was Hendrik Verwoerd who was the editor of *Die Transvaaler,* a Johannesburg Afrikaans newspaper. Verwoerd was strongly antisemitic in his views. He was opposed to South Africa admitting Jews, who were fleeing Nazism, because he believed they would interfere with the economic advancement of Afrikaners. In time Verwoerd would become prime minister and the grand architect of aparthed. The Jews would become some of the most active critics of his policies.

Afrikaner nationalists planned to celebrate the Great Trek centenary through a re-enactment. In August 1938 nine ox wagons left Cape Town and wound their way through the country until they reached Pretoria. Afrikaners enthusiastically greeted the trekkers along the way. Bram was rather proud to learn that his mother, Ella Fischer, had been asked to address the trekker memorialists as they passed through Bloemfontein. Her speech was broadcast on the radio but Bram missed it because he was visiting a friend. Nevertheless, Bram was not overly impressed with this expression of Afrikaner nationalism. The event culminated in Pretoria where a massive crowd assembled on 16 December 1938, to lay the cornerstone of a monument to commemorate the Voortrekkers. These celebrations did a great deal to galvanise Afrikaner nationalism and the profile of Daniel Malan and his Nationalist Party.

In April 1939 Bram and Molly, now visibly pregnant, moved into their new home at 12 Beaumont Street, Oaklands. Their home was on the doorstep of St. John's College and it was easy for me to pop in to see them. I was always welcomed but this warm welcome extended to everyone. There was a constant stream of visitors. I soon became part of the large community of friends that dropped in whenever it took our fancy. During my first visit Bram and Molly gave me a detailed tour of the home they had so carefully planned. The builders had only recently completed their work, building rubble was scattered everywhere, and the garden was non-existent. Bram explained his plans for the garden and he had even laid out the exact site of a swimming pool. He admitted to unreasonably stretching their budget, but confessed to receiving a small loan from his father to tide him over his excesses. I joined them for a drink on their new porch. We discussed the recently drawn cricket test in Durban. The test had lasted for twelve days, but there was only ten days of actual play because two Sundays were designated rest days. England led the five-test series 1-0, and it was agreed that the fifth and final test would continue with no time limit until there was a result. The batting was desperately pedestrian and thoroughly boring. Yet spectators crowded into the ground, especially on the last day. The English were only 41 runs shy of victory when the heavens opened and rain washed out play. The match was abandoned so that the English could board their ship that was due to depart the next day. It was to be the last timeless test ever played. Bram was convinced that South Africa could have claimed those last five wickets. I scoffed at this suggestion. I was pleased to point out though that the South African batsman and occasional slow bowler, Bruce Mitchel, had been schooled at St. John's College. Mitchell would later join the staff as the school bursar. He loved watching the school 1st XI and was ever so modest about his own achievements. I engaged him once over the timeless test and he simply remarked. "Yes, it was a very long match. I remember it well. I did not last too long in the first innings but I foolishly squandered a century in the second through standing on my stumps."

On 14 August 1939 I got a delighted call from Bram to advise that he had become a father. Molly had given birth to a beautiful little girl named Ruth. A fortnight later I went around to meet their new baby daughter. Bram brought out a bottle of whisky and invited me to have a celebratory drink. Our conversation soon turned to the tensions in Europe and the rising threat of war. In September 1938 Neville Chamberlain had spinelessly capitulated to Hitler's demands at Munich. Bram saw this Munich agreement as just another example of British imperialists selling out their friends, in this case the Czechs, to protect their own interests. Despite this agreement, Britain and France had hastily started re-arming. Now Hitler and Stalin had just signed a non-aggression pact. I said, "There is little doubt that Hitler and Stalin have armies that surpass all other European war machines. There must be a danger that if Hitler and Stalin collude, everyone will be powerless to stop them."

Bram retorted, "I do not think that there is much chance of Hitler and Stalin co-operating. I think it is quite the reverse. Hitler cannot stand the communists. It is far more likely that Hitler will attack Russia. Chamberlain is a ditherer that seeks to avoid a confrontation at all cost. Stalin is aware that Britain will allow Hitler to pursue his territorial policies in Europe. It is only Russia that has the fortitude to stand up to Hitler. Mark my words, Henry, Stalin knows that one day Hitler will seek to attack Russia. In many ways we need to be grateful that Stalin has more mettle than Chamberlain."

Hitler had already taken over all of Czechoslovakia and ostentatiously flaunted his success in Prague in much the same way that he appeared in Vienna to celebrate the Austrian Anschluss the year before. Hitler's fascist ally, Mussolini, was emboldened and launched an invasion of Albania. Stalin knew that Hitler's territorial ambitions would extend to attacking the Soviet Union and so he almost certainly signed the non-aggression pact to buy time to re-arm. Europe was in a very dangerous state as Hitler now turned his attention to Poland. Bram saw it as a conflict between imperial powers and of no real consequence to South Africa. I believed that there would be war if Hitler invaded Poland. Bram disagreed, and argued that Chamberlain would prevaricate and let Hitler have his way in Poland. I was right about the outbreak of war over Poland, but Bram had correctly predicted that Hitler would attack Russia in due course.

A mere fortnight later Hitler invaded Poland and Britain declared war on 3 September 1939. It threw me into a terrible quandary because I was uncertain of my obligation to sign up for the armed forces. Britain immediately conscripted all men between the ages of eighteen and forty-one. As a twenty-six-year-old I was firmly in the frame, but being abroad I was unsure of my status. Reverend Clarke asked if I would be signing up. I explained that I was uncertain as to what I should do. I suffered from asthma and figured that I would either be rejected or assigned to clerical duties. Reverend Clarke assured me that, since I was not resident in Britain, I was under no obligation to sign up and he encouraged me to remain at the school. He said to me, "It is important that we protect the school and maintain normal standards. Your valuable contribution is much appreciated and needed." I was grateful for his encouragement to stay, but he faced a staffing exodus. A good number of staff immediately resigned and returned to England to join the war effort. The school also saw staff sign up for the South African Armed Forces and within months many of the matriculation class immediately volunteered their services.

CHAPTER 5

War years

South Africa's engagement in the war was not without controversy and momentous political consequences. South Africa was once again engulfed over the vexed question of its participation. Smuts saw fascism as an evil that needed to be defeated, while Hertzog saw European quarrels as having nothing to do with South Africa. Smuts managed to persuade parliament to narrowly vote in favour of declaring war on Germany. Hertzog immediately resigned as prime minister. He attempted to form a new political party but resigned altogether from the parliament in December 1940 and died two years later.

In general, English-speaking whites saw it as their duty to support the Allies. Not all Afrikaners rejected the war effort and many signed up, although for some it may have been for pecuniary reasons. There were other Afrikaners though that adopted a more militant opposition to the war. The most significant of these movements was the Ossewabrandwag. In English it means Ox Wagon Sentinel, and the organisation was formed in early 1939 on the back of enthusiasm for the Great Trek centenary celebrations. The leadership of the Ossewabrandwag were open admirers of the Nazis. They hoped that a German victory in the war would aid them in turning South Africa into an Afrikaner republic.

The Ossewabrandwag was styled on military lines and its storm troopers carried out acts of sabotage. The government were forced to respond to their activities and interned many of its leaders. Those interned include John Vorster, who would one day become prime minister.

Daniel Malan advocated that South Africa should remain neutral, but he was opposed to violent resistance. Malan would prove to be a shrewd politician. South Africa's war participation was the main issue in the 1943 general election. Smuts argued that the government was making the world safe for democracy. Malan argued that he rejected imperialism and was in favour of promoting white democracy within South Africa. Smuts' United Party won the election with 89 seats, but Malan's National Party accumulated 43 seats. Afrikaner nationalists were now united behind Malan and he began to promote himself as a credible leader of an alternative government.

The United Party government were ambivalent about white superiority. The war economy had created a strong demand for labour. The blacks gained greater economic freedoms and government spending on black education was significantly increased. Yet the government also instituted segregationist policies, which would later find full expression under the Nationalist Party's apartheid policies. In 1941 employers were required to provide segregated work, recreation and eating areas. Nevertheless, under the United Party there was a recognition that all races were South African citizens. Various black organisations though began to challenge white supremacy. The ANC had become lacklustre but during the war years its leader, Dr Alfred Xuma, began to galvanise the organisation. He did this primarily through attracting motivated and talented young men like Anton Lembede, Nelson Mandela, Oliver Tambo, and Walter Sisulu.

The Communist Party of South Africa (CPSA), embraced all racial groups, openly supported the Soviet Union, and promoted communism as the solution to inequality and oppression in South Africa. During the 1930s the CPSA had dwindled into a small group of a few hundred, mainly white, members. The Second World War gave the CPSA a new impetus. The leaders were primarily white Jews, but many blacks also joined because the CPSA promoted equality, offered night school education, and created a sense of unity through social gatherings. Bram was introduced to the CPSA by a fellow lawyer, Miriam Hepner, who had approached Bram to donate funds to the party.

Bram argued that the war was all about maintaining imperialist domination over empires. He was opposed to exploitative capitalism and believed that the socialist policies of the Soviet Union provided a better alternative. Bram supported communism as an ideology that addressed inequities in society. He saw it as particularly appealing in the South African context because of race, language, and class conflicts. Bram would never recognise the failures of communist ideology, or concede that Stalin was an authoritarian dictator who inflicted misery on countless millions of people. Bram was upset when Germany attacked the Soviet Union as he had predicted. In his mind this changed the war from one about imperialism to a war about ideology. Bram believed it was essential for the Soviet Union to prevail so that fascism could be defeated. Once Hitler attacked the Soviets it became easier for the CPSA to campaign in support of the Soviet communists. Bram made speeches at various rallies, and I still have a CPSA pamphlet titled "Meet the Communists." It read in part:

"Communism is more than party politics. It is a way of life. It is a philosophy of life. We have to decide between Fascism and Communism...The Communist Party makes no reservation about the colour of a worker's skin...What about intermarriage. If

prejudice is an inherent force it won't disappear under Socialism. But if it does disappear, who are we to decide such things for posterity?... Isn't this the right way? ... Can Europeans go on for ever passing repressive and degrading laws? ... Isn't this the way that makes you feel comfortable inside, that leaves no bitterness in the hearts of people? Isn't this what you mean when you talk of justice, liberty and freedom...?"[10]
(*Europeans here means white South Africans*)

At the beginning of the war, Bram, presumably on the back of his anti-British imperial sentiments, had no interest in military service. After Germany attacked the Soviet Union, Bram's passion for defeating fascism was so aroused that he volunteered to join the army. Bram was still young, only thirty-three, a multi-talented sportsman, but he had already fallen into the bad habits of smoking and drinking too much. He had high blood pressure and an ulcer. An army medical officer declared that Bram was unfit for medical service. It completely bemused me, as Bram was unbeatable on a tennis court and a naturally talented golfer. I felt somewhat mollified though because I had used my asthma as an excuse to justify not volunteering.

I did not see much of Bram and Molly for months on end because they were both so busy. Bram was away a great deal, on both legal and political activities. Molly was equally energetic and worked tirelessly for the CPSA, particularly on fund raising. I attended the Fischer's house for Christmas drinks in December 1942. The party was made particularly joyful, when Bram banged on his glass to get everyone's attention and happily announced that Molly was pregnant again. Ilse Fischer was born on 16 June 1943. I could scarcely comprehend how Molly and Bram coped with their busy lives. Bram worked enormously long days and Molly was as active as ever on behalf of the CPSA. Molly's good friend Hilda Watts, who would marry Rusty Bernstein, was a member of the CPSA.

In late 1943 Hilda campaigned for a seat on the Johannesburg City Council. Despite Ilse's recent arrival, Molly was very active in working for Hilda's campaign. Hilda successfully won the seat of Hillbrow. She was to be the first and last white communist ever to win political office in South Africa.

Bram was elected to the Johannesburg Bar Council and his reputation as a barrister spread. Even so Bram was probably living beyond his means and he took up a part-time law lecturer's job at the University of the Witswatersrand to supplement his income. I went to the Fischer's house to see their new baby, Ilse. Bram was in high spirits. It was too cold to sit outside and so we retired to his study where he brought out celebratory cigars and poured me a stiff whisky. He then said, "So, back to school after the holidays. How is it going?"

"Yes," I replied, 'We have all settled down again but our first assembly was rather distressing. Clarke read out the names of three more boys who have died in action. They only left school a few years ago. Some of them are not much younger than me. It is dreadful to recall their cheerful faces as their names are read." Bram nodded with sympathy. I paused and continued, "We have Justice Ramsbottom coming to speak to the boys next week. Clarke has certainly got some very interesting speakers to come along. Jan Hofmeyer was incredibly impressive last term, and Dr Alfred Xuma was equally brilliant before that."

"Ramsbottom," said Bram, "I have appeared before him. A good and fair judge." Bram dragged deeply on his cigar, coughed, and said, "It rather helped today that Pa is Judge-President."

"How so?" I enquired.

"I have this rather interesting student in my class. Nelson Mandela. He is black. There are Indian students in the class, but he is the only black student."

"Any good?" I asked.

"Well, he is not that good a student. Marks are poor, but there is something about that man. He is a big fellow, talks softly and quietly. He does not say much but his comments are extraordinarily perceptive. He is clearly a born leader of men. The white students do not say much to him, but I notice that even they recognise that this big fellow is special. He works for those Jewish lawyers; Witkin, Sidelsky and Eidelman. I know Lazar Sidelsky and asked him what he thought of Nelson. Lazar has a lot of time for Nelson. He says Nelson is a dependable worker but fears that he does not apply himself sufficiently to his studies. Lazar figures that the only way blacks can overcome oppression is through education. I agreed with Lazar but told him that we need educated communists, not educated capitalists. Lazar laughed and said that we need black role models. Lazar got quite worked up and said that black lawyers should not be distracted with politics. I told him that I taught law at Wits, not politics. But Lazar was not satisfied and told me that he had spoken to Nelson and said: "If you want to be a lawyer, you must be a successful lawyer, if you get into politics your practice will suffer. You will get into trouble with the authorities who are often your allies in your work. You will lose all your clients, you will go bankrupt, you will break up your family and you will end up in jail. That is what will happen if you go into politics.""[11]

"Wise counsel," I said. "All those boys leave St. John's with such a privileged education. How does a black man make up that gap?" I mused.

"It will not happen under a capitalist system," retorted Bram. "Capitalism entrenches privilege. We need to promote equality through socialist policies. I can see that Nelson is destined for politics. He has already come to a few Communist Party meetings.'

"Really," I said, is he a member?"

"No, he is not, young Nat Bregman, who also works for Lazar, has brought Nelson to some of our meetings. Nat told me that he has invited Nelson to join us but he has declined. But we digress. Nelson was arrested this week."

"Why?" I asked.

"It is all rather outrageous. Nelson and a couple of Indian students in my class, Ismail Meer and J.N. Singh, were attempting to board a tram. As you may be aware, Indians are allowed to travel on the trams but not blacks. The conductor told Meer and Singh that they could board, but that their kaffir friend could not. They exploded with rage at the conductor's offensive language. The conductor however, hailed a policeman who promptly arrested them. Ismail contacted me last night and told me that they were due to appear in court today. I hastily arranged to represent them. As soon as the magistrate worked out that I was the son of the Judge-President he gushed with awe at a meeting he once had with him. I announced that I would be pleased to ask my father all about their meeting. He hastily dismissed the charges as trivial and not worthy of the court's attention."

I laughed but hastened to say, "Such treatment is appalling."

"Terrible" said Bram, "but you will get to meet them as I have invited them to come around here next weekend. I already know Ismail and Singh from Communist Party meetings, but I need to get to know this Nelson chap better."

I did meet Nelson Mandela and many others at the Fischer house on various occasions. The biggest group of visitors were usually communists: Joe Slovo, Ruth First (who once dated Ismail Meer but later married Joe Slovo), Helen Joseph, Violet Weinberg, Rusty and Hilda Bernstein, Michael Harmel, Anne Marie and Harold Wolpe. There were a lot of Jewish South Africans, but there was usually a multi racial parade of guests, which included people like Nelson Mandela, Walter Sisulu, Ahmed Kathrada, and Ismail Meer. I once rather clumsily remarked to Ruth First that it was a very mixed group that had gathered one sunny Saturday afternoon around the swimming-pool. Ruth looked defiantly at me and said with an exasperated sigh, "It is mixed because we are mixing."

In common with almost all white families in Johannesburg, the Fischer's employed domestic servants. They had built servant quarters at 12 Beaumont Street and Matthias Mlambo worked in the garden, while his wife, Mary Mlambo worked in the house. In a sad turn of events Mary's sister died and Mary undertook to look after her niece, Nora Mlambo. In a gesture that is remarkable at any time, but particularly in a racially segregated country, Bram and Molly welcomed Nora into their home and she shared a bedroom with Ilse. I often observed Ruth, Ilse, and Nora playing together, eating together, and simply living together as part of one big family. Nora would have to attend a racially segregated school but she was simply treated as another member of the family in everyday living at the Fischer home.

Bram seemed to work an eighteen-hour day but Molly was no less active. Bram and Molly placed enormous strain on their family through their hectic involvement in public life. The war had just ended when Molly announced that she was going to run as a CPSA candidate in the Braamfontein Ward for the Johannesburg City Council. In The 1943 election Hilda Watts (now Bernstein) had succeeded in winning a seat for the CPSA. Now the CPSA added four new candidates: Molly Fisher, Franz Boshoff, Issy Wolfson, and Michael Harmel. Molly campaigned vigorously. The election took place in October 1945 and Molly and the other CPSA candidates all lost rather badly. It was probably just as well that Molly lost because she was exhausted. Bram's standing in the CPSA though continued to rise. In December 1945 he travelled to Cape Town and was elected onto the CPSA central committee.

The Fischer family spoke Afrikaans to one another but they would switch to English in an instant if they were in the company of English speakers. I could not speak Afrikaans, but I noticed a change at St. John's College towards the language. When I first started Afrikaans was virtually ignored in the school curriculum. The boys were given the option of learning French or Afrikaans as a second language, but many favoured French. Reverend Clarke however, figured that all the boys needed to be proficient in Afrikaans and it was made a compulsory subject. There was a short period when the government issued a dual-medium instruction, which dictated that the boys should be taught some subjects in Afrikaans. Reverend Clarke railed against this policy, which was fortunately short-lived.

When the war ended three of my former staff colleagues returned but sadly four of them had died in the war. Almost one-hundred old boys died during the war. Their names were engraved on a panel in the chapel, and a garden of remembrance was built alongside the chapel to honour them.

After the war Johannesburg was to experience violent industrial unrest. During the war years the number of black workers employed in industrial jobs had grown significantly and many had joined trade unions. The genial political activist, J.B. Marks, who was a member of both the ANC and CPSA, was the leader of the African Mine Workers Union. In late 1946 seventy thousand black mine workers went on strike because of low wages and poor conditions. Jan Smuts ordered the police to violently suppress the strike. The strike lasted five days, twelve mine workers were killed, and others were forced back to work at gunpoint. Bram was on holiday in the Kruger National Park during the strike but hurried back to Johannesburg soon afterwards. The CPSA had vigorously supported the strike. They printed and distributed thousands of leaflets. Over fifty people were arrested, including Bram Fischer and most of the other CPSA leaders. Bram could have pleaded that he was absent from Johannesburg during the strike but he chose to stand trial with his accused comrades on charges of sedition. Bram was released on bail and the trial only began almost a year later.

The country was soon distracted by the royal visit of King George VI, his wife Queen Elizabeth, and their daughters Princess Elizabeth and Princess Margaret. Bram had little interest in the visit but I was entranced and followed their progress with avid interest. The royal family had come ostensibly to express gratitude to the people of South Africa for their assistance in the war. The prime minister, Jan Smuts, saw it as an opportunity to strengthen ties with Britain and celebrate the importance of South Africa on the world stage. Smuts took great pride in escorting the royal family around the country. Ironically it may have been one of his greatest mistakes because he failed to sense the simmering resentment of Afrikaners towards this obsequious attention. Afrikaner antagonism towards Britain ran deep.

The sedition trial of Bram and others commenced in August 1947. Bram was the only witness called by the defence. He argued that it was not the CPSA's intent to usurp the role of trade unions but it supported the trade unions in their campaigns against unfair working conditions. In standing up in court Bram risked damage to his reputation and career, but this highly principled man was loyal to the CPSA. The accused were all found guilty and received relatively minor fines.

In the middle of the trial Bram and Molly became the proud parents of a son, Paul. I managed to drop around to see the new baby and I just could not believe Bram's composure. Paul had not been sleeping well and Molly was clearly exhausted. Ruth, Ilse, and Nora were storming around the house in some bizarre game of hide-and-seek, but Bram was able to relax with a whisky and pipe. Bram was satisfied that he had acquitted himself well at his sedition trial. As he said to me, "This case has not all been bad news for me. I have had lots of letters supporting us. It is encouraging. I know that this stuff worries Ma and Pa. Let's hope that Paul captures more of their attention. Let me find it. I want to show you a letter

I received from my old mentor, Leo Marquard. Here it is. Have a look." The letter encouraged Bram to fight the charges with a stiff English upper lip. It was a serious letter of support but written with humour. It even finished with a caution that, if any unauthorised person read the letter, he hoped that their eyes would blister and their toenails fall off.[12] Bram continued, "I know you think that us Afrikaners are a dour lot, but we can laugh at ourselves. I have just finished reading *Mafeking Road* by Herman Charles Bosman. He is very witty and perceptive. I shall give you the book. You must read it."

The book was a collection of short stories about rural Afrikaners in an area of north western Transvaal called the Groot Marico. Bosman tells most of his stories through a fictional narrator called Oom (Uncle) Schalk Lourens. Bosman was a complex character and his personal life was rather dramatic. He was an Afrikaner but attended English schools. His literary skills were evident from an early age and he published work in school magazines and local newspapers. He attended the University of the Witswatersrand, married young, and was posted to the Groot Marico district as a school teacher. While visiting his family in Johannesburg he shot and killed his stepbrother during an argument. Bosman was sentenced to death and sent to Pretoria Central Prison. Bosman's friends pleaded for clemency and his sentence was commuted to ten years hard labour. He was released on parole after serving half his sentence. Bosman's subsequent writings included stories about his time in prison. Bosman married multiple times and died at just forty-six years old after suffering a heart attack during a raucous party.

Herman Charles Bosman's observations of Afrikaners in the Groot Marico provide joyful escapism. One of my favourite stories is called *In the Withaak's Shade*. The narrator, Schalk Lourens, relates how frightening it is to come upon a leopard unexpectedly. He recalls the time when he decided to look for some strayed cattle.

He came across some Withaak trees and decides that he can easily look for his cattle sitting on the soft grass under the shade of the trees. He lies down and while he is snoozing a leopard approaches. Schalk Lourens is incapable of running away because he is frozen in terror. As he relates:

"In the meantime, the leopard had got up as far as my knees. He was studying my trousers very carefully, and I started getting embarrassed. My trousers were old and rather unfashionable. Also, at the knee, there was a torn-place, from where I had climbed through a barbed-wire fence, into the thick bush, the time I saw the Government tax-collector coming over the bult before he saw me. The leopard stared at that rent in my trousers for quite a while, and my embarrassment grew. I wanted explain about the Government tax-collector and the barbed wire. I didn't want the leopard to get the impression that Schalk Lourens was the sort of man who didn't care about his appearance.

When the leopard got as far as my shirt, however, I felt better. It was a good blue flannel shirt that I had bought only a few days ago from the Indian store at Ramoutsa, and I didn't care how many strange leopards saw it. Nevertheless, I made up my mind that next time I want to lie on the grass under the withaak, looking for strayed cattle, I would first polish up my veldskoens with sheep's fat, and I would put on my black hat that I only wear to Nagmaal. I could not permit the wild animals of the neighbourhood to sneer at me.

But when the leopard reached my face I got frightened again. I knew he couldn't take exception to my shirt. But I wasn't so sure about my face. Those were terrible moments. I lay very still, afraid to open my eyes and afraid to breathe. Sniff-sniff, the huge creature went, and his breath swept over my face in hot gasps. You hear of many frightening experiences that a man has in a life-time. I have also been in quite a few perilous situations. But if you want something to make you suddenly old and to turn your

hair white in a few moments, there is nothing to beat a leopard
– especially when he is standing over you, with his jaws at your
throat, trying to find a good place to bite."[13]

The leopard lies down next to Schalk Lourens and grunts every
time Schalk Lourens attempts to move. Schalk Lourens states that
his friends thought he was telling a fabricated story. There are
however, sightings of a leopard and he heard hunters shooting.
Then one day he walked along the path to the withaak trees, he
saw the leopard curled up in the shade, very still, and he could see
the red splash of the bullet wound on his breast.

As an Englishman I did not understand all the Afrikaner
idioms but I devoured a great many of Herman Charles Bosman's
stories. There is a small passage in a story called *Dopper and Papist*
that I particularly love. As I have mentioned Paul Kruger was a
Dopper, which was a particularly orthodox form of Calvinism.
In this story Oom Schalk Lourens and his friend Gert Bekker
are driving the Dopper priest (predikant) and a church elder
(ouderling) in a cart to a church meeting. The predikant and the
ouderling are discussing the idolatrous practices of Catholics. It
was a cold night as they travelled along. Schalk and Gert want
to drink some peach brandy to warm themselves up but they
were worried about popping off the bottle's cork without the
disapproval of the predikant and ouderling. Then they hit upon
an excellent idea. They stop the cart, open the bottle in full view
of their two passengers and advise that it is necessary to revive the
horses through swigging the brandy and blowing into the horses'
nostrils. They do this several times and the predikant shows much
interest in this old-fashioned technique of reviving the horses. At
the next stop though the predikant surprises them by holding up
his hand: "Don't you and your friend trouble to get off this time,"
the predikant calls out when Gert was once more reaching for the
bottle, "the ouderling and I have decided to take turns with you in

blowing brandy into the horses' faces. We don't want to put all the hard work on to your shoulders."[14]

I had long service leave and missed all the 1948 Lent term while I visited Mom and Dad in London. It was fortuitous that I went because Dad sadly passed away while I was there. I was terribly worried about my mother who was now alone in the United Kingdom with her only son, me, living in South Africa. Fortunately, Mom had cousins that lived close by and they took a great interest in her welfare. I was enjoying a rather hedonistic lifestyle in South Africa. My teacher's salary was modest but I was able to live well. My living expenses were minimal as I lived on the school property, ate most meals in the school dining-hall, had my rooms serviced daily, and my washing and ironing looked after in the school laundry. My salary was more than adequate to travel and enjoy myself without pecuniary restrictions. I had not been in London for almost a decade and it was a shock to see the austerity of post-war London. George Marshall, the American Secretary of State, had recently initiated a recovery plan to provide financial assistance to enable European nations to recover from the war. Under what became known as the Marshall Plan aid was dispensed to countries in Europe. The Soviet Union prevented the countries it occupied from participating and this is one of the reasons why western Europe became so much more prosperous.

The British had shown great fortitude and resolve during the war. They accepted the stringent economic environment with equanimity, and I could sense that they imagined that their lives would return to much as it was before the war. President Truman though had made it clear that the United States was not going to allow European nations to reinstate their empires. The ties between colonised countries and European imperial countries had weakened during the war, and colonised countries began to clamour for independence. Paradoxically the Soviet Union was extending its control over eastern Europe. The British needed no greater reminder of how their empire would be dismantled than the example of India. On 15 August 1947 the British flag was lowered for the last time in Delhi and soon afterwards India, Pakistan, Burma, and Ceylon became independent countries. Decolonisation heralded an era of violence. There were communist insurgents in Malaya and the Mau-Mau in Kenya. In less than quarter of a century Britain's empire was dismantled, although almost all its former colonies would remain members of the British Commonwealth. My mother was shocked at how quickly these countries gained independence. She was relieved that I was in South Africa because it was a Commonwealth country, but she did not realise that South Africa was equally determined to remove itself from the British empire. An obsession with establishing permanent white Afrikaner rule would turn the country into a pariah nation.

CHAPTER 6

The watershed of 1948

Jan Smuts failed to appreciate how many Afrikaners deeply resented South Africa's participation in the war. Furthermore, Smuts' enthusiastic feting of the royal family in 1947 had irritated many Afrikaners. The government cabinet was comprised mostly of English-speaking South Africans and they frequently ignored Afrikaner culture. There had been a flood of new immigrants from Britain, who were happy to flee bleak times at home and enjoy prosperity in South Africa. Many Afrikaners feared that these new immigrants would give English-speakers an unfair electoral advantage. Daniel Malan's Nationalist Party campaigned boldly on the issues of strictly enforcing racial segregation and promoting a return to the glorious days of Paul Kruger's Afrikaner republic. A general election took place on 26 May 1948 and the outcome astounded everyone. The United Party attracted sixty percent of the vote, but the Nationalist Party won a majority of seats in the house, since country electorates had fewer voters. Jan Smuts suffered a terrible personal humiliation and lost his seat. The new government was comprised almost entirely of Afrikaners. They had obtained political power and were determined never to lose it. It would result in the formalisation of the policy of apartheid and would unleash decades of oppression upon the country.

The Nationalist Party was determined to maintain power. One of the first things they did was create six new seats for South West Africa given that they knew that all six seats would go to the Nationalist Party. The new government swiftly purged the army, the police, and the judiciary. The replacements were loyal Afrikaners. This was not only done to promote Afrikaners but it was also to ensure that bureaucrats did not undermine their new laws. The new government enacted legislation aimed at creating a totally segregated society. The cornerstone Acts were: the Mixed Marriages Act, which banned inter-racial marriages; the Immorality Act, which made inter-racial sex illegal; and the Population Registration Act, in terms of which every person was classified by race. This was followed by other apartheid reinforcing Acts such as the Group Area Act, which allowed a geographical area to be designated for the use of one racial group only. There was also the Illegal Squatters Act, which gave the government power to evict people from specified areas. The legislation that blacks hated most of all was the perversely named Natives Abolition of Passes and Co-ordination of Documents Act, which created a national pass law that made it compulsory for all blacks to carry passes. Bram objected to the fascist leanings of the Nationalist Party, and saw Smuts as too attached to the British. In Bram's opinion communism provided the best alternative for South Africa. He saw both the new Nationalist Party government and the outgoing United Party as being unsympathetic towards socialist ideals. Bram would soon be shocked by the virulence with which the Nationalists attacked the CPSA.

In January 1949 I joined Bram, Molly, her father Tottie Krige, and her brother Jimmy Krige on a trip to Natal. Tottie had been shot in both lungs at the battle of Spionkop during the Anglo-

Boer War. Tottie had been lucky to survive, and was now still in good health at seventy-five years old. We piled into Bram's new Mercedes. Tottie sat in the front and Molly was squashed between Jimmy and I in the back. Molly complained that Jimmy hogged too much of the seat as always, and I crushed myself against the door to afford Molly as much room as possible. Bram had invited me to join them since I was an "expert" history teacher and could enlighten them on the battle. I knew scarcely more than the grand picture of the Anglo-Boer War, but I read up as much as I could. I was prepared to discuss the battle during the journey, but the conversation was all about the new Nationalist party government.

Tottie's sister Isie was married to Jan Smuts. Isie had taken the electoral defeat terribly badly and she and Jan had retired to their farm at Irene, near Pretoria. They were reluctant to socialise with anyone. Jan was almost eighty and Isie was greatly concerned about his health. Tottie argued that Smuts was a great Afrikaner patriot and he thought it was particularly galling to see his defeat as being blamed on his close relationship with the British. Tottie blamed Jan Hofmeyer for the defeat saying that he had introduced too many liberal policies. Molly objected to the accusations Tottie was levelling against Jan Hofmeyer, and Bram valiantly supported Molly. They were very good about keeping the conversation in English but, when their tempers got stretched, they started speaking Afrikaans and I could not follow their arguments precisely. Bram presciently noted that the Nationalists were extremely hostile towards communism and he feared repressive measures.

We checked into a quaint hotel in Ladysmith, which was scarcely more than a glorified pub. I had to share a room with Jimmy. He had not said much during the journey but in the quiet of our room he expressed reservations about his sister's involvement in politics. He had a fervent desire to see Molly more involved with her family and less attached to politics. Jimmy did not doubt

Molly's love for her children but he felt that Bram and Molly were excessively distracted with their Communist Party activities.

We set out for Spionkop the next day. Tottie was particularly interested in finding the spot where he had been shot, almost exactly forty-nine years ago. The Boers had attacked Natal and laid siege to Ladysmith. They strategically placed commandos on Spionkop, a hill that commanded a view of the Tugela River and protected the route to Ladysmith. The British forces, under their commander General Redvers Buller, had to cross the Tugela to relieve Ladysmith. Buller split his forces to cross the Tugela in two different places. The force to the west would clear the Boers from protecting hills, like Spionkop and then join forces with the troops to the east for the march to Ladysmith. Buller put General Warren in charge of attacking Spionkop. Warren believed that he needed more heavy artillery and he advanced painfully slowly. After lengthy delays Warren eventually ordered Lieutenant-Colonel Thorneycroft to lead a surprise attack against the Boers on Spionkop. They commenced their ascent under cover of darkness and unleashed a sudden volley of Mauser fire when they neared the summit. Thorneycroft gave the order to fix bayonets and they charged. They met little resistance as the minor force of Boers fled. The British troops immediately began to dig trenches on what they thought was the crest of the hill. Signals were despatched to Warren and Buller announcing the successful capture of Spionkop. The Boer commandos that fled from the hill presented themselves to General Botha at his camp just to the north. Botha heard the news calmly and announced that they had to re-capture Spionkop. It would be very dangerous if the British hauled up artillery and entrenched themselves on this hill. Botha knew that speed was the essence of a counter attack. Botha had insufficient guns to attack the hill with artillery fire and decided to storm the hill with commandos. It took great courage to storm the hill and Botha feared that shirkers would hide behind rocks leaving exposed comrades to their fate. Commandant Henrik Prinsloo rose to the occasion and led around four hundred men up the hill. Tottie Krige was one of these men.

We studied our maps carefully and were almost certain that we had identified the route of the Boers ascent. I was amazed at how Tottie was able to follow us up the hill, scrambling over rocks as we went. Tottie paused and then shook his head up and down a few times before declaring that it was around this spot that he had been shot in both lungs. After being shot, he had lain behind a rock struggling to breathe. His fellow Boers figured that he would die and they continued their assault. Tottie said that Walter De Vos was lying nearby severely wounded from a bullet wound in the chest and had cried out repeatedly asking if he, Tottie, was alright. Tottie's eyes filled with tears as he recalled fellow Boers that were killed as they scaled the hillside: John Malherbe, shot between the eyes, Robert Reinecke, shot in the head, De Villiers, shot in numerous places. We took off our hats and stood in silence to honour these brave men. Tottie said, in Afrikaans, "Dankie, Vader, vir die dapper kerels." *(Thank you, Father, for these brave young men.")*

The Boer assault was successful and they managed to seize the northern end of the summit. The British troops however, were in trenches on the southern side and they began to exact a terrible toll on the Boers. The Boers were exposed in the hot morning sun, they had no food, and little water. Prinsloo and the other Boer leaders exhorted the Boers to stay but they began to melt away, having no further stomach for continuing the fight. There were some courageous Boers though that crept around to the east and situated themselves on a small rise called Aloe Knoll. The British made the fatal mistake of digging shallow trenches short of the actual summit of Conical Hill and the adjacent higher ground of Aloe Knoll. The Boers positioned on Aloe Knoll were able to inflict carnage upon the British who were exposed in their badly positioned and shallow trenches. It was nothing short of a massacre as the Boers relentlessly fired on the British. Brave British soldiers attempted to rally and lead an assault upon the Boers position, but they were cut down by a hail of bullets. Thorneycroft attempted to lead a charge but he only avoided dying through twisting his ankle badly and being forced to lie flat on the ground. We made our way up to Aloe Knoll. The British trenches had been marked with white stones and we could see just how easy it was for the Boers to fire into these trenches from their higher ground. The British managed to send a message to Warren calling for reinforcements. Warren knew that he needed to get his large guns on top of the hill if the British were to prevail. He decided against shelling Aloe Knoll because he thought this was a British held position. Consequently, the Boers were able to continue their barrage of fire from Aloe Knoll. Nevertheless, British reinforcements did arrive and heavy artillery was dragged into place. The overwhelming British numbers and fire power should have secured victory.

Winston Churchill, who was a correspondent with the *Morning Post*, had accompanied General Warren. Churchill decided to see for himself what was happening and climbed to the summit. Churchill was profoundly shocked by what he saw and wrote about it as follows: "Men were staggering along, or crawling on hands and knees, or carried on stretchers. Corpses lay here and there...The splinters and fragments of shells had torn and mutilated in the most ghastly manner. I passed about two hundred while I was climbing up. There was, moreover, a small but steady leakage of unwounded men of all corps. Some of these cursed and swore. Others were utterly exhausted and fell on the hillside in stupor. Others again seemed drunk though they had no liquor. Some were sleeping heavily. Fighting was still proceeding..."[15] Churchill reported his findings to Warren and agreed to take a message back to Thorneycroft that night assuring him that heavy naval guns and reinforcements were on their way to the summit. Churchill found Thorneycroft in a state of despondency and extreme shock. Thorneycroft had already decided to withdraw and met the reinforcements on the way down. He could not be persuaded to return to the summit. The next morning a small party of Boers were confronted with an amazing sight. The British had left and the Boers waved their hats to signal that they were again in control of Spionkop. It was ironic because most of the Boers had already abandoned their positions and walked away. The Boers allowed British medical staff to evacuate their dead and wounded the next day. One of the stretcher bearers working for the British was Mohandas Ghandi. The Boer victory at Spionkop was a British humiliation but it was pyrrhic victory since they could never prevail in the long term against the superior might of the British forces. The Boers had been lucky. It was British incompetence rather than Boer brilliance that had secured their win.

During my long service leave trip to London, I persuaded my recently widowed mother to visit me in South Africa. Mom loved watching the school sport and she was happy to catch the bus to and from the city. Mom never complained much about anything but she was most certainly frustrated by the unreliable bus timetable. The new government were resolute in their determination to segregate every aspect of life. Everything was segregated from buses, park benches and post office entrances. I was sadly amused to hear my mother describe how the Johannesburg post office had two entrances: one marked Europeans and the other Non-Europeans. Mom thought that was rather odd and chose the European entrance. It only dawned on her a little later that European was a euphemism for white.

Mom and I had a wonderful visit to the Kruger National Park. I had obtained a slightly a flashy new car, a Ford Bel Air and I was very excited about taking it on a long trip. The car performed magnificently as we bumped along the park's dirt roads. September is an excellent time to see game. The grass is still short and water is scarce because there is no winter rain. The animals are easily visible as they congregate about the waterholes. We had been out one afternoon and I was conscious of hurrying back to our camp at Skukuza before the gates closed at 6.00 pm. Suddenly Mom demanded that I stop. I came to a quick halt and imagined that she had spotted a lion or something equally exotic. It was a solitary zebra and Mom had noticed that it had a badly damaged leg. Mom carefully marked our position on the map. I clasped the steering wheel with my thumb and tapped it like a drummer with my fingers. I was anxious to move on and get back to camp before curfew. We made it back in time and Mom promptly marched off to the game rangers' hut. I followed but had some doubts about the purpose of her mission. A burly Afrikaner game ranger greeted us cordially as we entered the hut. Mom placed our map on the counter and announced, "I would like to report an injured zebra." She pointed to the map and continued, "The zebra can be found at precisely this spot."

I suspect that she hoped the game ranger was going to thank her for her observation and despatch a veterinarian to the scene. Mom started to describe the zebra's injury but she was interrupted as this large man replied in a deep voice, "Madam, the lions are going to eat that zebra tonight." I could not suppress a laugh as Mom looked up with surprise. She thanked the game ranger for his attention. He smiled warmly at her and wished her a pleasant evening.

Mom and I drove to Cape Town where we spent Christmas at a seaside village called Fish Hoek. In early January Mom caught the Windsor Castle back to England. I returned to Johannesburg and caught up with Bram. He was exceedingly downcast as Paul had been diagnosed with cystic fibrosis. Paul had suffered from a chronic cough ever since birth. The initial diagnosis was that Paul had bowel problems and he was placed on a special diet. Bram's bother Paul was a doctor and Molly asked him to examine her two-year old son. The elder Paul had studied medicine in the United States and was acquainted with the newly identified genetic disease of cystic fibrosis. It arises because of a genetic malfunction in the endocrine system, which produces saliva, sweat, tears, and mucus. People suffering from cystic fibrosis develop an abnormal amount of excessively thick and sticky mucus within the lungs, airways, and digestive system. The result is that bacteria is trapped in the lungs which causes infections and leads to irreparable damage. The cystic fibrosis gene must be present in both parents but it can skip generations. Paul broke the terrible news to Molly and Bram, and suggested that his nephew's life expectancy was little more than another six years. It was a devastating diagnosis but Molly and Bram took it in their stride. They were determined to do everything possible to assist Paul and they never succumbed to self-pity.

CHAPTER 7

Suppression and defiance

T he Nationalist Party ruthlessly set about implementing its apartheid policies. I remained within my almost exclusively white urban environment of Houghton and was largely oblivious to the daily misery that these harsh policies inflicted. The African National Congress (ANC) was the main black political organisation that took up the fight against apartheid. The ANC was formed in 1912 to represent black opposition to their political exclusion from the Union of South Africa. It was initially called the South African Native Congress, but in 1923 changed its name to the African National Congress. Pixley Seme, a black lawyer, a graduate from Oxford and Colombia, convened a national conference of black leaders and chiefs in Bloemfontein. In calling for a black political movement to give voice to the disenfranchised blacks. He said: "Chiefs of royal blood and gentlemen of our race, we have gathered here to consider and discuss a scheme which my colleagues and I have decided to place before you. We have discovered that in the land of their birth Africans are treated as hewers of wood and drawers of water. The white people of this country have formed what is known as the Union of South Africa – a union in which we have no voice in the making of laws and no part in the administration. We have called you, therefore, to this conference so that together we can find ways and means of forming our national union for the purpose of creating national unity and defending our rights and privileges."[16]

This seems a relatively mild statement but it was the beginning of black political resistance. The ANC spent decades as a non-violent protest movement, but there were now young ANC members that clamoured for more dramatic action. At the ANC national conference in December 1949 the ANC's Youth League proposed a Programme of Action which called for boycotts, strikes, stay-at-homes, passive resistance, protest demonstrations, and other forms of mass action. The leaders of the Youth League were Nelson Mandela, Oliver Tambo, and Walter Sisulu. At this conference these young activists also succeeded in changing the ANC's leadership. They voted out the genial Dr Alfred Xuma as leader and replaced him with Dr James Moroka. Walter Sisulu was elected as the new Secretary-General and Oliver Tambo was elected to the National Executive.

Bram encouraged Nelson Mandela to join the CPSA, but Mandela was ideologically opposed to communism. Bram remarked, "I tried to persuade Nelson that the fight against the apartheid policies of this new government needed to be multi-racial. The CPSA represents all people and its socialist ideology is the only viable solution to addressing our society's inequalities. Nelson has been instrumental in drawing up the policies of the ANC's Youth League, but he remains highly sceptical of communism."

I was very interested and asked Bram to expand on what Mandela had said. Bram continued, "According to Nelson this Youth League document is to be a rallying cry to all patriotic African youths to overcome white domination. They reject the communist notion that Africans are oppressed primarily as an economic class rather than a race. He argues that they need to create a powerful national liberation movement under the banner of African nationalism and led by Africans themselves."

I commented, "I think he should join hands with all those fighting oppression."

Bram nodded and said, "He is ten years younger than me. A youthful firebrand. I am sure that he will moderate his stance because many of his views align with those of the Communist Party. Mandela believes land should be redistributed on an equitable basis, colour bars that prohibit Africans from doing skilled work should be abolished, and that there should be free and compulsory education for all. He recognises though that there are two competing theories of African nationalism – Africa for the Africans nationalism and the less extreme Africanism, which recognises that South Africa is a multiracial country. It seems that Mandela is more sympathetic to ultra-revolutionary nationalism and that he is angry at the white man. His parting words to me were: I am not prepared to hurl the white man into the sea, but I would be perfectly happy if he climbed aboard his steamships and left the continent of his own volition."

As a member of the CPSA executive Bram became involved in organising a "Defend Free Speech Convention." It was organised by the CPSA, ANC, Indian Congress, and African People's Organisation. It was held in March 1950 and drew thousands of people to Johannesburg's Market Square. The convention called for the abolition of pass laws and all discriminatory legislation. A resolution was passed calling for a general strike on 1 May 1950. It was to be called Freedom Day. The government reacted swiftly by banning all meetings and gatherings on 1 May. Mounted policemen violently attacked the strikers that did gather.

The government took an extreme measure to thwart protests. In June 1950 they passed the Suppression of Communism Act, which banned the CPSA and prohibited any political party from subscribing to communism. In terms of the Act the government could ban any person. Banning orders were harsh and restricted people from travelling, attending gatherings of more than one other person, and their words could not be broadcast, published, or reported. Violations of banning orders resulted in imprisonment. The CPSA met in Cape Town and decided that it had no option but to dissolve itself. Sam Kahn was the sole CPSA member of parliament as a Native Representative. On 20 June 1950 Kahn made the following announcement: "Recognising that on the day the Suppression of Communism Bill becomes law, every one of our members, merely by virtue of their membership may be liable to be imprisoned, without the option of a fine, for a maximum period of ten years, the Central Committee of the Communist Party has decided to dissolve the Party as from today."[17] The resolution to dissolve the CPSA had not been unanimous. Michael Harmel protested strongly, but Bram and other members of the Central Committee argued for dissolution. Bram was not in favour of members resigning from the CPSA because this implied a denunciation of an organisation that they had joined legally. Bram accepted though that the collapse of the CPSA was hardly inspirational because it did not demonstrate a defiant determination in the best traditions of Bolshevism.

Molly Fischer invited me to attend Paul's fourth birthday party. Paul had bright blue eyes and very blonde hair. He was surrounded by a horde of children who delighted in haring around the garden before settling down to a noisy celebration of jelly, ice cream and birthday cake. I could not but help noticing how difficult it was for Paul to blow out the candles. He coughed and struggled to draw breath. I was rather amused when four-year old Shawn Slovo lent over and blew out the candles herself. She then politely turned to Paul and said, "Now make a wish."

It was mid-winter and Bram lit a wood-fire as we took refuge in the lounge away from the excited children. Bram, Joe Slovo, his wife Ruth First, Rusty Bernstein and Hilda Bernstein had decided to celebrate with Bram's best whisky. Ruth declined a drink as she was nursing her new-born baby daughter, Gillian. The baby girl slept contentedly on Ruth's lap. I could see the front door in the hallway and, as Bram was pouring the drinks, I was hugely surprised to see the door open gently. A large man was silhouetted against the dimming winter afternoon light. Bram looked up and exclaimed, "Nelson, come in, come in."

Nelson Mandela hesitated and said, "I am so sorry Bram. I was not intending to interrupt your party,"

"Not at all," said Bram. "You are not disturbing anything. We are just having a drink in honour of Paul's birthday. Please join us." Nelson Mandela attempted to resist but Bram was persuasive and Nelson was soon seated alongside me. Bram gave Nelson a whisky, but I noted that he barely took a sip.

Nelson greeted us and said, "This is very kind of you Bram, but I shall soon be on my way. We can discuss things another time."

"Yes, indeed, said Bram, "but we are all somewhat shocked by the dissolution of the Communist Party. Something that does not seem to bother you too greatly."

Nelson replied, "That is why I have come to talk to you Bram. You seem to have been greatly offended by my comments on the Communist Party."

"No," replied Bram, "I was just surprised that you were so dismissive of our mutual opposition to the policies of the government."

"That is not quite right, Bram." Mandela scratched his chin and continued, "As you are aware some of the most important figures in the ANC are your fellow communists. Moses Kotane, J.B. Marks, and Yusuf Dadoo are communists. I am not unsympathetic to the banning of the Communist Party. I suspect that this legislation may be directed against all protest movements and not just the Communist Party. I am an Africanist who believes that we must fight against our oppression. My objection to communism is that it is a foreign ideology that misunderstands the African situation and seeks to impose another form of political control over us."

Ruth interjected with a hint of annoyance, "Nelson, communists are your allies, not your enemies."

Rusty pointed at Ruth and nodded before saying. "Quite right, Ruth, communism is not an imperialist ideology. It is a universal creed that seeks equality for all. Freedom from oppression is something that should unite all the people of South Africa irrespective of colour."

Nelson replied, "It is very hard for Africans to see our oppression as something other than whites exploiting blacks. It is important for Africans to take up the struggle. I do not want us to hold onto the coat tails of others. It is our struggle and we must prevail. The Communist Party seems to have surrendered rather meekly. Africans have been surrendering all their lives and it is now time for us to fight, not give in."

Bram toyed with his glass of whisky and said quietly, "Nelson, we had to shut down the Communist Party. We could not ask anyone to break the law, continue their membership, and go to jail."

"That is precisely the problem," said Nelson. "We have been too passive. The laws are unjust. We need to be proactive. We have no obligation to obey unjust laws."

Bram put up his hand to reply and then said slowly, "All people should resist these laws, not just Africans. The Communist Party is, or was, the only organisation in South Africa that has leaders and members from all races. The ANC would be gravely mistaken to retain a black only membership. It should recognise that all the people of South Africa, of all racial groups, have a common interest in removing this fascist government. Communism is the only alternative that advocates for the equality of all."

Nelson nodded his head and said thoughtfully, "I am not wedded to capitalism and have some sympathy with socialist ideas. There is little doubt that there is a gross inequity in wealth and measures must be taken to level the playing field. The government wants us to play by the rules but their rules are unfair and one-sided. I say we need to break the rules in the face of such injustice."

Joe made a point of saying that he and others, such as Rusty, were strongly opposed to disbanding the Communist Party. These comments irritated Bram and Joe quickly decided to change the topic. Joe asked Nelson about the progress of his legal career. Nelson said that he was still learning and was pressured to abstain from political activity. He had completed his articles with Witkin, Sidelsky and Eidelman. He had changed law firms and would soon complete his attorney's qualifying examination. He hoped to establish a black law firm with his ANC Youth League comrade, Oliver Tambo. Bram encouraged Nelson to do so and asked him to be mindful of forwarding briefs. Nelson laughed and said, "You will be too expensive for my clients, Bram."

I said little but listened to this group of passionate people with awe. I lingered and remained alone with Bram after everyone had gone home. Bram felt sure that Mandela's hostility towards communists would moderate because all opponents of the government would realise that they shared a common cause. Bram was adamant that communism was the correct political solution and said that this would become self-evident as the ANC examined alternative methods of governing more closely. Bram saw all the apartheid laws, including the Suppression of Communism Act as being motivated by the fear of losing control to British imperialists and the black masses. The move against communism was not so much to protect South Africa from a socialist system of government but rather it was psychological. The CPSA had broken ranks with the protective circle of white unity and undermined white rule. The Nationalist Party could understand black opposition but it could not understand the white communists who they saw as akin to traitors. The government was therefore determined to crush all opposition but it reserved particular disdain for white communists.

The CPSA was liquidated, but the government prepared a list of former CPSA office-bearers, members, and supporters. In October 1951 Bram received a letter from the Minister of Justice confirming that he was a listed communist. He and some of his fellow communists wrote a letter to the Minister of Justice, C. R. (Blackie) Swart, complaining that the government was attempting to not only silence communists, but all critics of their regime. Their letter concluded with these damning words: "Your tyranny will not survive the tyranny of the people."[18]

A month later Bram received another letter from Blackie Swart congratulating him on his appointment as King's Counsel. Bram had been invited to take silk years earlier but had delayed. He thought it unwise though to prevaricate further and was now delighted to be advised of his appointment. I joined other friends at Beaumont Street for a celebratory drink. Bram thought it rather ironical for the Minister of Justice, an ardent anti-monarchical nationalist, to have sent him, a listed communist, a letter of congratulation. Bram sent a letter of thanks to Blackie Swart, which read as follows: "It was friendly of you to congratulate me on my appointment as K. C. I value it highly. The disadvantage of the recognition is that if one does not succeed in the elevated status, the "appointer" – the Minister – cannot be held responsible! But whether I succeed or not, I hope nevertheless that I shall always be able to exert myself to maintain the high traditions of our profession."[19] There was a subtlety to the letter. Bram's desire to uphold the traditions of the profession was a reminder to the Minister of the importance of upholding the law. It was the government that had set course to abrogate the law to defend a wholly unjust political system.

In early 1952 the government announced plans to celebrate the tercentenary of Jan van Riebeeck's landing at the Cape. The ANC decided to counter these celebrations through launching a Defiance Campaign. This was a carefully-orchestrated programme of passive resistance. Dr James Moroka and Dr Yusuf Dadoo did most of the planning, but Nelson Mandela led the demonstrators, who contravened curfews, occupied whites only premises, and refused to carry passes. Their rallying cry was "Africa. Mayibuye," which means "Africa. May it come back to its rightful people." Mandela and around eight thousand others were arrested. The Defiance Campaign did nothing to limit the governments' draconian laws, but it did much to lift the profile and membership of the ANC. Those who were arrested were tried in magistrates' courts and fined or sentenced to a term of imprisonment. Most of those found guilty refused to pay their fines, which was in accordance with the strategy of filling the jails to capacity. This attracted media attention and magistrates were forced to release people when faced with full local jails. The government reacted swiftly. They arrested Nelson Mandela, Walter Sisulu, and other ANC leaders, and charged them under the Suppression of Communism Act. Bram, Vernon Berrange, and George Lowen appeared for the defendants. I travelled into the city and attempted to watch the trial. I got no further than the corridors as the crowds that turned up made it quite impossible to worm myself into the courtroom. I did notice that the Supreme Court walls were decorated with murals glorifying Voortrekkers. I could not help but see the irony in persecuting blacks for seeking freedom from oppression in courts decorated with pictures of the Great Trek. The accused were found guilty, but Justice Rumpff wholly suspended all the prison sentences.

In August 1952 Nelson Mandela and Oliver Tambo opened their law firm and they were besieged with clients. Bram often remarked on their success with pride. He became uncontrollably incensed though when Nelson told him that the Law Society of the Transvaal had applied to have his name struck off the role of attorneys on the grounds that his conviction under the Suppression of Communism Act amounted to unprofessional and dishonourable conduct. Bram suggested that Mandela use the services of Walter Pollack who generously appeared without charge. Judge Ramsbottom heard the Law Society's application and dismissed the case with costs. Bram was pleased because he saw it as affirmation that justice could still be upheld through the courts.

I spent the Christmas 1952 holiday on the Natal south coast with friends at their holiday homes in Margate, Uvongo, and Southbroom. Then in early January the school chaplain, Father Ted, and I took a group of boys on an eighty-kilometre hike from Port St. John's to Port Edward. It is the most easterly section of what is called the Wild Coast, which is an almost two-hundred-and-fifty-kilometre stretch of wilderness between the Eastern Cape and Natal. The coastline is undeveloped, unspoiled, rugged, and sparsely populated. Our group assembled at Port Edward. Ted went through the process of dividing the food and other minor items amongst the boys. Ted had labelled the food for each day and allocated the meals in such a way that everyone's backpack would be lightened at an equitable rate. He persuaded us to jettison most of our spare clothing as it was preferable to wear dirty clothes than carry the excess weight. Ted and I left our cars at Port Edward and our group hopped on a bus to Port St. John's. It was long two-hundred-kilometre journey that went inland via

Bizana, Flagstaff, and Lusikisiki. The road was atrocious, full of pot holes and a muddy dirt track for the last part. I marvelled at the beautiful countryside. African huts dotted the landscape, and the little boys tending cattle grinned and waved at us with carefree cheerfulness. By coincidence Molly and her children had gone to Port St. John's for the summer holidays. Bram was in Europe where he was attending the Vienna Peace Conference.

It was an extraordinarily beautiful walk as we followed the coastline. At times we walked along the beach, but we mostly followed cattle paths along the cliff tops. We drank fresh water out of the streams, which may have been risky given the prevalence of cattle. We had no tents and simply slept out in the open in our sleeping bags. River crossings were tricky. At low tide we could wade across river mouths with little difficulty. The larger rivers required us to swim across them. Ted carried a small canvas boat and pump. After pumping it up we attached a rope to the front and back and then ferried our backpacks across by having a person on each bank pull the boat back and forth. The Mboyti river though was a severe challenge. The river water gushes through the river mouth out to sea. It was too dangerous to cross near the river mouth and we had to move a little upstream. We could not go too far because the river soon became impossibly wide. Ted tied the rope around his waist and swam to the opposite bank. I was a little taken aback at how far downstream he was taken by the current but he reached the other side safely. I was a weak swimmer and was distinctly worried about the strong current. I should have been concerned about the boys but I knew that they were all competent swimmers. When it was my turn to cross, I hung onto the canvas boat and was pulled over by those on the opposite bank. There was one very frightening moment. We had just visited the magnificent site at Waterfall Bluff when one of the boys, Peter, fell off the cliff path into the ocean about fifteen metres below. I had barely time to gasp before I saw Ted jump in after him. Peter was weighed down by his backpack, but Ted grabbed him and pulled him out of the water. They were both able to scramble back up the rocks to the pathway. There was this sort of eerie calm amongst our group. Peter, a naturally cheerful boy, was non-plussed and happy to march on. Our group never discussed the incident much. We just knew that Peter had been lucky to escape serious injury and that Ted had exhibited great courage.

Bram had been in Europe for most all of the Christmas holidays. He had attended the Vienna Peace Conference as a representative of the Transvaal Peace Council. Bram and many of his fellow South African communists were not solely pre-occupied with the inequities of South Africa. They also had a world view and were strongly aligned to the global view of communism. The delegates were largely intellectuals that supported anti-colonial struggles and an end to the Cold War. Bram met Jean-Paul Sartre and Diego Riviera at the conference, and had the opportunity to speak about injustice in South Africa during one of the night sessions. I went to Beaumont Street one evening and quizzed Bram on his trip to Europe.

"I presume you were able to spend some time in England," I said.

"Yes indeed," replied Bram, "I had an entire week in London after the conference. I caught up with so many people and even managed to get up to Oxford for a day."

"How was it?" I asked.

"They are still doing it pretty tough over there. Everything seemed so bleak and austere. I guess being mid-winter does not help. It sort of adds to the depressed mood."

"I guess they are still recovering from the war."

Bram shrugged and said, "I don't think that the Second World War has really ended."

I was confused and remarked, "I do not follow"

Bram replied, "Put it this way. There can be no peace while we are arming ourselves with nuclear weapons and while there are so many conflicts. There are wars in Vietnam, Malaya, and Korea. The danger spots have spread and now there are conflicts in Indonesia, Persia, Egypt, and the entire Middle East. The Americans have threatened to extend the Korean war to the Chinese mainland. The United States wants so-called defence pacts – the Atlantic Pact, the North Atlantic Treaty Organisation, the Middle East Defence Bloc. The idea that the United States wants these pacts for defence is nonsense. They are the aggressors. It is the United States that is feverishly building up arms and sending troops to foreign soils. I fear that Europeans will be used as canon-fodder to fuel American aggression."

I was rather shocked to hear Bram's negative comments about the United States. I was firmly aligned with the West and feared Soviet aggression. I realised that Bram did not just see communism as the antidote to the injustices in South Africa. He was a strong supporter of global communism and saw the West as the Cold War aggressor.

Bram had a renewed political enthusiasm after his European trip. He got heavily involved in the establishment of the Transvaal Congress of Democrats, which soon fused with other organisations to become the South African Congress of Democrats. Bram also launched himself into forming peace councils, along the lines of those he had seen in Europe. In August 1953 Bram planned to deliver the opening address to inaugurate the South African Peace Council. Just two days before the conference however, Bram was served with notices under the Suppression of Communism Act banning him from attending gatherings and from membership of the Congress of Democrats and South African Peace Council.

Bram partially got around the notice through delivering his address via a tape recording.

Membership of the Congress of Democrats was multiracial and included ANC heavyweights such as Nelson Mandela, Oliver Tambo, and Walter Sisulu. Many communists flocked to join the Congress of Democrats. The CPSA had been disbanded but many of these communists now re-constituted themselves and established the South African Communist Party (SACP). The subtle change in name may have been made to protect those who had decided to firmly cut their ties with the CPSA. Since membership of a communist party was illegal, the SACP had to operate secretly. The SACP was organised in a cell structure and membership was a closely guarded secret. Members communicated with each other through carefully controlled channels. Bram encouraged me to join a cell. I was philosophically opposed to communism and declined. Bram worked long hours as a KC and yet he still found time to devote great energy to his anti-government activities. Molly was no less involved in many activities. She was a secret-member of the SACP and the secretary of the South African Society for Peace and Friendship with the Soviet Union. Molly's SACP cell met on park benches in the Wilds. This was a small natural bush area across the road from the St. John's College rugby fields.

In April 1953 there was another, white voters only, general election. The Nationalist Party, under Daniel Malan, won a resounding victory. This encouraged the government to enact even more repressive legislation. The most draconian of these was the Criminal Law Amendment Act of 1953, which inflicted harsh penalties on anyone found guilty of protesting against a law. They also passed the Public Safety Act, which provided for the suspension of laws if there was a declaration of a state of emergency. Bram despaired that South Africa was turning itself into a police state, but none of these laws dampened his political ardour.

One day as I walked through the David quadrangle I bumped into Father Ted. He was with Hugh Lewin, a boy in my boarding house, and another man in clerical clothing. He promptly introduced me to Reverend Trevor Huddlestone. Trevor detected my English accent and we gathered that we had both been at Oxford University. Trevor was the minister of an Anglican Church in Sophiatown, which was a multiracial township close to the centre of Johannesburg. Sophiatown was intended to be a suburb for whites, but over the years blacks had purchased houses there. Sophiatown bordered on being a slum, but it had a special character as a vibrant community. The government decided to move the blacks out of Sophiatoewn to Meadowlands, a soulless tract of land almost twenty-kilometres away. Sophiatown was then to be re-developed as a white suburb. Huddlestone mobilised opposition to the forced removal. He addressed meetings despite harassment from the police. Hugh Lewin had got to know Trevor Huddlestone through his father, who was also an Anglican minister. Hugh visited Sophiatown, and was very disturbed by the injustice of the forced removals. One Sunday evening various activists addressed a large meeting of angry Sophiatown residents. There was a significant police presence but this did not deter the speakers. Mandela spoke and he was extremely strident in his condemnation of the government. He got angry and stated that the time for passive resistance had ended. He described non-violence as a useless strategy and suggested that violence was now the weapon that should be used to overthrow apartheid. The crowd grew animated and made threatening gestures towards the police. Fortunately, Trevor Huddlestone was there to calm tensions. The police arrested many of the protesters and someone called Bram in the hope that his presence, an eminent King's Counsel, might help. Bram hurried to Sophiatown and later commented: "Can you picture the situation? 1,200 delegates at a conference – a body of police breaking in to drag a leader off the platform – outside some 300 police armed with assegais, rifles with bayonets, and sten guns. I didn't see this because by the time I got there it was all over, but I'm certain that if Father Huddlestone had not been there on the platform there would have been a bloodbath. By the time I got to the police station I saw the arms and ammunition being turned in again. God help the whites of this country within the next 10 years. Is it inevitable in history that at some stage or another a whole class commits suicide in a lunatic fashion?"[20]

I told Bram that I was concerned over newspaper reports about Mandela's call for violent action. Bram was quietly dismissive of my concerns and pointed out that the police presence posed a greater threat of violence. I countered that I was talking about a more general concern and referred to the non-violent mantra of Mohandas Ghandi. Bram simply said that I should consider the last paragraph of Karl Marx's and Frederich Engels' Communist manifesto which declared that their ends could only achieved through the forcible overthrow of all existing social conditions.

It was, of course, wrong to think that only blacks and white communists opposed the government's apartheid policies. In early 1953 a group of respected academics and intellectuals formed the Liberal Party which was strongly opposed to apartheid. It was led by the famous novelist Alan Paton and financed by the mining magnate, Harry Oppenheimer. The Liberals though were strongly opposed to communism. ANC leaders, such as Albert Luthuli, were happy to embrace the Liberals as an ally against apartheid, but Nelson Mandela was critical.

I had an opportunity to listen to Mandela's criticism of the new Liberal Party while attending a Sunday *braai* at the Fischer's home. Bram and Nelson were discussing this new political party.

Bram remarked, "The Liberal Party has some very prominent office bearers."

"It makes them feel better," said Nelson.

I chimed in, "I am sure that they have genuine intentions to improve apartheid."

Bram immediately scolded me, "You cannot improve apartheid. It is a vile and unjust and needs to be eliminated."

I stumbled for words and said, "What I mean is that they recognise that apartheid cannot work and they are advocating a fairer political system."

Nelson replied," That is precisely the problem. The Liberals concern themselves with broad generalisations without any attempt to interpret them or define their practical application in the South African context. They have announced that no person should be barred from participation in the government or other democratic processes of the country by reason only of race, colour, or creed."

"That sounds good," I said.

Nelson shook his head and said in his slow methodical way of talking, "They make these general statements but then state that they believe in a qualified franchise."

Bram interrupted, "How do you determine who is qualified? Who and how do you determine who gets the vote? One man one vote is a core democratic principle. In advocating a qualified franchise, the Liberals are creating a new political theory. It is not democracy."

"Exactly,' said Nelson, "Universal franchise rights are at the heart of democracy. I accept that the Liberal Party members are not racist, but they need to decide on whose side they are on. A qualified franchise is just another way of maintaining white privilege. I am convinced that there are there are thousands of honest democrats amongst the white population who are prepared to take up a firm and courageous stand for unconditional equality for the complete renunciation of white supremacy. In the liberation movement we extend the hand of sincere friendship and brotherly alliance. The only sure way to give all people their freedom is through the overthrow of the existing fascists and the establishment of a truly democratic government."

I conceded that Manela and Bram had correctly identified the faulty logic behind the qualified franchise platform but I still felt that the Liberal Party was making an honest attempt at seeking a better political system. I could imagine the whites accepting a qualified franchise but not a universal franchise. I could also understand though why liberation movements like the African National Congress, the South African Indian Congress, and the South African Congress of Democrats were so critical of the Liberal Party. Of course, the Liberal Party offended the Nationalist Party government who quite simply felt that it was treasonous to advocate any change to the political system.

At the end of 1953 Reverend Clarke advised that he would be retiring. I had spent seventeen years working happily at St. John's College under his leadership. A change in headmaster was a momentous event. In early 1954 it was announced that Deane Yates would be the new headmaster. Deane Yates was the first non-ordained priest to be headmaster of the school. He had been a teacher at Mill Hill School just outside London and had gone up to Oxford University where he had read the classics at Oriel College. We all felt a degree of anxiety over this change but I would come to respect Deane Yates enormously over the next sixteen years.

I managed to catch up with Bram in late July 1954. There was a roaring log fire in his living-room. Ruth, Ilse, and Paul were in their pyjamas and dressing-gowns and were jostling with one another in front of the fire. They turned the fire into a roaring blaze and Bram had to plead with them to stop adding logs. The children told me gleefully that they had all been in the swimming pool that afternoon despite it being a very cold day. I told them that I thought they were crazy but they told me earnestly that they had to use the swimming pool or else their Pa was going to turn it into a compost heap. Bram was quick to point out that he too had been swimming that day. Paul coughed repeatedly and he was clearly suffering from his lung complaint. Paul however, was cheerful and remarked in a matter-of-fact way that he now took a daily insulin injection to manage his diabetes. Molly was missing and the children told me that they had taken her to the airport for her flight to Europe. I was surprised and asked Bram what had brought about this trip. He tried to fob it off and described it as a trip to England to visit theatre shows and generally enjoy herself. It was only after her return that Molly filled me in on the details. She had indeed gone to London but from there she had gone to West Germany, East Germany, Poland, Czechoslovakia, and the Soviet Union. She then travelled to China via Mongolia. She was in Peking (now Beijing) on 1 October 1954 for the fifth anniversary celebrations of the Chinese Revolution. She stood on a podium, near to Mao Tse-tung, and watched the four-hour parade of soldiers, workers, and children. Molly attended a session of the National People's Congress and then went on to other cities such as Shanghai. Molly travelled back to London via Moscow and Stockholm before returning to South Africa. She was away for four months. It seemed as though Ruth First had been instrumental in organising her itinerary. Molly had clearly been treated everywhere as someone of importance.

The ANC came up with the idea of convening a national convention, a congress of the people, representing all the people of this country irrespective of race or colour, to draw up a Freedom Charter for the democratic South Africa of the future. In March the ANC invited some two hundred organisations to attend a planning conference in Tongaat, near Durban. Rusty Bernstein attended as a delegate on behalf of the Congress of Democrats and he was largely responsible for issuing a statement calling for people to make submissions for a Freedom Charter. His statement became known as "The Call" and it was widely circulated throughout the country. The opening lines were: "We call the people of South Africa black and white - let us speak together of freedom."[21]

There were thousands of responses, written and verbal. Rusty and his colleagues on the drafting committee attempted to sort through them all. The task was overwhelming and Rusty drafted much of the Freedom Charter by himself. On 25 and 26 June 1955 almost three thousand delegates met at Kliptown, a small town near Johannesburg, to consider the Freedom Charter. The government had banned many people from attending public gatherings, and these included Walter Sisulu, Nelson Mandela, Bram Fischer, Rusty Bernstein, and Joe Slovo. They could not attend the congress, but instead took up positions a few hundred metres away and watched proceedings from afar. Bram and Molly even brought Ruth and Ilse with them to view what they knew would be an event of historic importance. There were songs and speeches and then over the two days each section of the Freedom Charter was read aloud and the congress proclaimed its approval. As the congress was nearing its conclusion police swarmed onto the stage and announced that they suspected treason. None of the delegates were allowed to leave until they had given their name and been photographed.

The government was not able to squash the Freedom Charter and it became a document of enormous importance in the liberation struggle. It had a similar tone to that of Jefferson's American Declaration of Independence. The preamble to the Freedom Charter reads as follows:

"We, the people of South Africa, declare for all our country and the world to know: That South Africa belongs to all who live in it, black and white, and that no government can justly claim authority unless it is based on the will of the people.

That our people have been robbed of their birthright to land, liberty, and peace by a form of government founded on injustice and inequality;

That our country will never be prosperous or free until all our people live in brotherhood, enjoying equal rights and opportunities;

That only a democratic state, based on the will of the people, can secure to all their birthright without distinction of colour, race, sex or belief;

And therefore, we, the people of South Africa, black and white, together – equals, countrymen and brothers – adopt this Freedom Charter. And we pledge ourselves to strive together, sparing nothing of our strength and courage, until the democratic changes here set out have been won."

The Freedom Charter then lays out various clauses detailing how it shall ensure a democratic and free South Africa, The Freedom Charter is largely devoid of Marxist rhetoric but there is a problematic clause that states:

"The mineral wealth beneath the soil, the banks and monopoly industry shall be transferred to ownership of the people as a whole."

This clause alienated many, who saw it as promoting communism. The Liberal Party refused to endorse the Freedom Charter and many others saw the Freedom Charter as communist-inspired. I discussed it with Bram and mentioned my particular concern over the idea of nationalising banks and mining companies. Bram was dismissive and argued that the country's wealth should be shared by all. He was adamant that the country's mineral wealth belonged to all South Africans, and he believed state control was required over banks to ensure that economic resources were equitably allocated.

The government spent the next year raiding the houses and offices of individuals and organisations. The government was on a mission to gather evidence to charge those seeking a new democratic order with treason.

CHAPTER 8

Treason

In 1956 Ruth entered her final year of schooling. Ruth and Ilse attended Kingsmead College, a prestigious school for girls. Bram and Molly had given up speaking Afrikaans to the children at home and they now conversed almost exclusively in English. Paul, now nine years old, was very excited about going to St. John's Preparatory School. He would spend four years in the Preparatory School before completing his last five years of schooling in the College. It might seem odd for Bram and Molly, committed communists, to send their children to exclusive private schools. Bram and Molly though recognised that government schools, and particularly Afrikaans-speaking government schools, were indoctrinated with government ideology. In Kingsmead and St. John's College they were hoping to give their children a liberal education. Paul was aware that I was a teacher at the school but I assured him that I taught in the College and he would see very little, if anything, of me.

I did not see Paul very often but on those few occasions when we passed each other he always said hullo with an assertive "Good morning, Sir." I would call him Fischer, not Paul, as was customary at St. John's. We did meet coincidentally one day just outside the school grounds. I had no afternoon activities and had gone for a run. I was struggling up the steep hill of Munro Drive when I came across Paul walking in the opposite direction, presumably to his home. Paul was red-eyed and very upset. I stopped immediately and asked Paul what was wrong.

"Nothing, Sir", he mumbled.

"Hang on a minute," I said, "what is the matter? Have you been bullied?"

"No" he replied forcefully.

"Why are you walking home? Why didn't you catch the bus?"

Paul grimaced and said, "I went to Mark's party. He lives just back there." He nodded towards a house on the corner.

"So, what is the problem?" I enquired.

"Mark's mother told me to go home."

"Goodness me." I said, "Why? What did you do?"

"I did nothing."

"Then what on earth happened."

Paul opened his school bag and gave me a note. He shrugged and said, "Apparently, Mark forgot to give me this yesterday." I read it with astonishment:

"Dear Mrs Fischer. I am very sorry to inform you that Paul's invitation to attend Mark's birthday party has been withdrawn. Doug and I were upset to discover that Mark was in your swimming pool with Africans and Indians. We also do not want Mark socialising with communists. I regret this late notice but we do not share your values."

I stared at the note like a frozen statue and said, "Paul, your Ma and Pa are wonderful. They love you. They love all people. This is so wrong. Please don't be upset."

"Just because we let blacks swim in our pool," said Paul.

"Paul, your Ma and Pa are kind and gracious people that share."

"No-one else lets them swim in their pool."

"Paul, not many people even have a swimming pool. They are jealous."

"No, it is because my friends don't want to swim in the same pool as them."

"Does it bother you, Paul?"

"Not really, but why can't we be like other people?"

"Paul, you should be proud of your family. They treat everyone the same."

We stared at each other in silence for a few moments.

"How are you getting home?"

"I can walk, it is not far."

"Let me walk home with you."

"Thank you, Sir, but it is okay, I just want to go by myself."

I tapped Paul on the shoulder and said, "Don't worry about this Paul."

"Alright. I hope Mark will still be my friend."

He turned around and carried on down the steep hill. His head hung low and he had a dejected stoop. Then he swung his satchel off his back and tossed a small package wrapped in decorative paper into a kerbside garbage bin.

Fortunately, the incident died a natural death and Paul seemed to be a popular boy. He was clever and exceptionally good at sport. I would sometimes wander across to the Preparatory school fields and watch him play. He was in both the A-team cricket and soccer. He was smaller than most of his teammates but he was naturally co-ordinated. His talent was self-evident. I did notice that he often bent over with fits of coughing after bursts of exertion. I am not sure if anyone else took any notice, but I was all too painfully aware of Paul's lung and diabetes condition. I never once saw Bram or Molly at any of his games.

In December 1956 the government arrested one-hundred-and-fifty-six people and charged them with high treason. One morning on the front page of the *Rand Daily Mail* there was a picture of the three Slovo children: Robyn, Gillian and Shawn. Their parents Joe Slovo and Ruth First had been arrested and their grandmother had come to look after them. The newspaper quoted six-year-old Shawn Slovo as saying, "Mummy's gone to prison to look after the black people."[22] Those arrested represented numerous different organisations, although most were members of the ANC. Some of the accused did not even know one another and had to introduce themselves to each other in the dock. The number of people accused and the seriousness of the treason charge attracted national and international attention. A Treason Trial Defence Fund was established and contributions were received from varied sources. This enabled the accused to engage eminent barristers, which included Bram Fischer, Maurice Franks, Norman Rosenberg, Vernon Berrange. Isie Maisels, HC Nichols, Rex Welsh, George Bizos, and Sydney Kentridge. The preparatory examination lasted almost a year before the trial proper began. There was considerable concern in the international community and observers came from the United Kingdom and United States. South Africa's foreign minister, Eric Louw, was highly critical of these observers who openly allied themselves with the defence. The government responded by denying visas or creating lengthy visa application delays.

The preparatory examination started off on a very poor note as the accused were herded into a cage that had been specially constructed in the court. The defence barristers were outraged and threatened to walk out. An act that would have embarrassed the government given the number of international observers. The usually mild-mannered Maurice Franks could barely contain his anger and addressed the court with these words: "Your Worship confronts this unprecedented scene which we see before us today: the accused caged, as your Worship sees. Caged, one almost said

– I am most anxious not to allow my indignation to get the better of the language I use but I think I am justified in submitting to your Worship that they appear before the court caged – like wild beasts. I state on behalf of every member of the Bar and Side Bar engaged by the defence in this case, that if these are the conditions upon which it is proposed to hold the preparatory examination, then the whole body of us propose to leave this court and take no further part in the proceedings."[23] The Chief Magistrate ordered the dismantling of the cage and four days later he released all the accused on bail.

I went to the Fischer house on a February Sunday afternoon for a *braai*. Bram introduced me to George Bizos, a young barrister assisting with the treason trial. George told me modestly that his role in the treason trial was largely confined to searching documents to show that the accused had not conspired to overthrow the government by violence. George was sharing his chambers with Duma Nokwe, the first black barrister called to the Bar in the Transvaal. Duma was one of the accused and could not attend to his legal work. George told Bram that he had received an ethical clearance to attend to Duma's briefs. George related how Duma felt that in some respects their arrest and short imprisonment had been a blessing in disguise. Banning orders had severely restricted interactions between ANC colleagues, but in prison they were able to converse freely.

During the preparation examination the prosecution lodged around twelve thousand documents to support their case. The defence team spent months challenging and demolishing the accounts of the various prosecution witnesses. Closing arguments were presented in January 1958. Charges against sixty-five of the accused were dropped for want of evidence, but the court decided that there was sufficient reason to put the remaining ninety-two of the accused on trial. Charges were withdrawn against Chief

Albert Luthuli, the president of the ANC and Oliver Tambo, the secretary-general of the ANC. Bram thought that the prosecution had made a major mistake. He explained that charges against them were probably dropped because they were both Christians. The prosecution clearly felt that it would be difficult to prove that deeply committed Christians could be dedicated to the violent overthrow of the state. Bram sensed that the prosecution would have a more difficult time proving that the ANC was seeking violent revolution when charges had been withdrawn against the ANC's president and secretary-general.

The trial proper was moved to Pretoria and most of the accused had to be bused from Johannesburg each day. Fifty of the accused lived in Johannesburg but the trial caused greater hardship for those that came from afar. They lost their jobs and many were financially crippled. Helen Joseph, one of the accused, described the commencement of the trial as follows: "The spectators pack the public galleries, white along one side, non-white on the other. The press galleries are all packed. The spectators are high above the well of the court, and they stand and crane to see what is going on. The red-robed judges file in and take their seats. The public and pressmen strain to identify leading counsel in their black robes and white bibs. The clerk of the court opens the proceedings in both official languages and the prosecutor explains the absence of one of the accused; the man who is 'in custody' at Port Elizabeth – but someone blundered and failed to deliver him for the trial; the man who 'missed the bus'! The rest of the 91 accused are sitting in rows of benches closer together than ever before, Indian, European, African, men and women. All around is apartheid and the sharp division by notice and by order – black this way, white that. But here in this court, once again these 91 accused demonstrate so vividly the truth for which they stand. They worked together for justice and equal rights for all, regardless of colour. They answer the charges side by side, undivided, and so they will to the bitter end."[24]

In the gallery, the spectators were separated under apartheid prescriptions. Yet in the dock the accused, the leading opponents of apartheid, were herded together as one. The case against the accused was essentially that they subscribed to the Freedom Charter, and therefore sought the violent overthrow of the state. The prosecution had difficulty in framing an indictment and they were frequently forced to amend it. At one point all the charges were suspended while a new indictment was prepared. The defence made substantial gains because charges against sixty-one of the accused were dropped and only thirty (twenty-eight men and two women) were left to defend the charges. Of the remaining accused, twenty-four were black, one coloured, three Indian, and two white. They included Nelson Mandela, Walter Sisulu, Duma Nokwe, and Helen Joseph. The trial would drag on for years.

The prosecution called more than one-hundred-and-fifty police officers to give evidence. The defence had little difficulty in getting these witnesses to contradict themselves. One of the star witnesses for the prosecution was Andrew Murray, a Professor of Philosophy at the University of Cape Town. Isie Maisels led Professor Murray on a merry dance and trapped him into describing some of his own writings as advocating communism. Maisels got him to agree that the Freedom Charter was not a communist document and that it was in fact very similar to the Universal Declaration of Human Rights. Under cross-examination by Sydney Kentridge, Professor Murray conceded that there was nothing in communist doctrine that claimed a people's democracy could emerge only through violence, or that the objectives of the Freedom Charter could only be achieved though violence. The defence barristers thoroughly destroyed Professor Murray's credibility. Molly had no sympathy for Professor Murray and wrote in a letter to Ella Fischer: "For years he has been telling the police that perfectly innocent documents were communist doctrine. Without his advice there may never have been a trial – so he deserves everything he gets."[25]

Bram used a quiet, self-deprecating style in his cross examinations. He treated police witnesses with the utmost respect and as a result he was able to extract the replies he was seeking. While Bram appeared respectful, he was exceedingly well-prepared for his cross examinations and therein lay his success. Helen Joseph described Bram's style as follows: "Bram Fischer was Vernon's opposite: sturdily built, fresh-complexioned, with a gentle, almost boyish face, despite his now greying hair. But that gentle face was deceptive, for underneath Bram was indomitable, one of the most brilliant of advocates. He could pursue his way with a Crown witness just as relentlessly as Vernon; silver-tongued, he won the confidence of his witness with gentle skill. He didn't chase his witness into a corner and pin him down, indeed he never raised his voice, but in the end somehow, the witness turned out to have said just what Bram wanted him to say. We marvelled at his unerring technique. I think the Crown did, too, when they realised the fatal concessions, their witnesses were making so unsuspectingly."[26]

One of the oddest things about the trial was that Bram's name was mentioned frequently in court, not in his role as a defence barrister, but in his role as a comrade of the accused. Bram represented the accused, but he was one of them, even though the State had decided against charging him too. Bram and Molly regularly invited the accused to dinner. In these dinner invitations they included friends and colleagues from the bar. It was an extraordinary privilege to enjoy the company of these noble people. The guests included Nelson Mandela, Helen Joseph, Ahmed Kathrada, Duma Nokwe, Walter Sisulu. Joe Slovo, Ruth First, and Hilda and Rusty Bernstein. I always thought it strange that the white dinner guests seemed to be far more strident in their criticism of the government than the black guests, who were often more moderate in their condemnations.

The defence called Chief Albert Luthuli, the president of the ANC, as a witness, but his testimony was interrupted by the shocking events in Sharpeville on 21 March 1960. On that day the police shot and killed sixty-nine people and wounded one-hundred-and-seventy-six who were demonstrating against pass laws. The state declared a state of emergency and arrested all the treason trial accused. The accused would spend the next five months in jail until they were granted bail again. During the state of emergency, a further two thousand people were detained, including Molly Fischer.

The trial concluded in March 1961 after four long years. The trial had taken a terrible toll on the accused's livelihoods and everyone was exhausted. The State took four months to deliver its closing arguments. In March 1961 Maisels opened arguments for the defence and he was followed by Nichols and Kentridge. Bram was to follow with his arguments that were expected to last almost three weeks. As always, he had prepared with methodical care. Three days later the judges abruptly interrupted Bram's presentation and adjourned the court. The court reconvened on 29 March 1961. The prosecution again offered to amend the indictment to ensure that the court could find a guilty verdict for supposedly proven allegations. The judges however, would have none of it, and it took Judge Frans Rumpff only half an hour to read the judgment. The court found the accused not guilty and they were discharged.

The trial was a monumental folly. The Fischer's held a huge party at their home. The celebrations continued long into the night, despite the police parked outside the Fischer's home. Bram was hugged and kissed by almost everybody. It was one of the few occasions when I saw his quiet and reserved demeanour give way to unconcealed delight and joy. The judiciary had upheld the rule of law, but it was to be the last political trial where normal legal safeguards applied. The government enacted new legislation that would make it far harder for judges to acquit, and they ensured the appointment of sympathetic judges in future political trials.

CHAPTER 9

Sharpeville

The Pan African Congress (PAC) was established in April 1959. It set itself up as a rival to the ANC, it did not permit multiracial membership and only allowed black members. The PAC felt that the ANC was too passive and they preferred more militant protests. Robert Sobukwe was the PAC leader and he declared that that the government should be run by Africans for Africans. The PAC rejected the principles of the Freedom Charter and held that whites and Indians should have no role in governing the country. The PAC was able to endear itself to support from the west because it was anti-communist. Nelson Mandela respected his former ANC Youth League colleague, Robert Sobukwe, but he was critical of his efforts in establishing the PAC. He felt that many had joined the PAC because of petty grudges and disappointments over their treatment within the ANC. Nelson argued that they were thinking of their personal advancements, whereas a true freedom fighter suppressed their individual feelings and motivations.

In the early 1960s independence movements in Africa fuelled a sense of optimism that South Africa would also be liberated from white rule. This optimism was way too premature and the PAC dangerously and unrealistically promised that liberation would be achieved before the end of 1963. In Britain the Conservative Party won the October 1959 general election and Harold Macmillan became Prime Minister. In 1960 Macmillan undertook a tour of Africa. He went to Ghana, Nigeria, Northern Rhodesia, Nyasaland, Southern Rhodesia, and finally South Africa. He addressed the South African parliament in Cape Town on 3 February 1960 in what became famously known as the 'winds of change" speech. In the speech he warned that there was an awakening of national consciousness in people who have lived under a foreign power. This movement had spread through Asia and the same thing was now happening in Africa. He suggested that a wind of change was blowing through the African continent and that the growth of national consciousness was a political fact that needed to be addressed in national policies. Dr Hendrik Verwoerd, who had become prime minister of South Africa in 1958, hosted Macmillan and controlled his schedule. Macmillan wanted to meet black leaders but Verwoerd ensured that none were invited to any of the functions at which Macmillan was present. Nevertheless, Macmillan's speech had an enormous impact and organisations like the ANC and PAC were greatly encouraged.

The PAC and ANC began to vie with one another. The ANC were preparing for a massive anti-pass demonstration on 31 March 1960. The PAC decided to usurp the ANC and announced that there would be a spontaneous anti-pass campaign on 21 March 1960. Blacks were encouraged to leave their passes at home and present themselves at police stations for arrest. Robert Sobukwe and around one-hundred others walked into the Orlando police station, near Johannesburg. Sobukwe told the senior officer on duty that they had no passes and should be arrested. The police captain dismissively told them to wait outside. Sobukwe must have been disappointed because he could see people streaming off to work and the response to the anti-pass protest was small. The PAC had rushed their protest and failed to obtain a response on the national scale they envisaged. The PAC however, had succeeded in mobilising support in two areas. There was a significant response in Cape Town and in the township of Sharpeville near Vereeniging, about seventy kilometres from Johannesburg. Vereeniging is a steel-making town and Sharpeville was a township that housed black workers. The government had forcibly removed blacks that lived near Vereeniging and relocated them to Sharpeville. The method used to remove people was unfathomably cruel. The affected people were given little warning. Police arrived suddenly with trucks and bulldozers. People had to hurriedly gather up whatever they could before the bulldozers demolished their houses and possessions. Those forcibly removed to Sharpeville were given a bare patch of ground on which a crude hut and toilet had been assembled. There was no electricity or running water. Sharpeville was heavily policed to maintain order over the many disgruntled residents.

The PAC established a branch in Sharpeville, but they only recruited less than a hundred members. Despite their grievances many people were reluctant to join because they feared police informers. Those that did join were predominantly militant youths. These members were highly motivated and they spread the news about the anti-pass campaign through leaflets and word of mouth. A large crowd of around five thousand gathered in front of the Sharpeville police station in the early hours of 21 March 1960. Police lined up outside the station and the crowd began to taunt them. They demanded to be arrested for not carrying passes but the police refused because they had no room to house so many people in their cells. The police called for reinforcements who arrived in armoured carriers. Youths stoned these vehicles as they drove to the Sharpeville police station. The crowd outside the police station grew and by mid-morning it had reached almost twenty thousand. This huge crowd had not all turned up to hand in their passes, many of them were simply inquisitive and happy to provide moral support. The police attempted to persuade the crowd to move away from the station and gather in the nearby football stadium. PAC officials though acted swiftly to discourage this. The police called for reinforcements and by midday the police forces had swelled to about four-hundred. Two-hundred white policeman were carrying weapons (rifles and sten guns) and two-hundred black policeman were carrying knobkerries (clubs). There were also three armoured vehicles with machine guns.

The police claimed that the crowd were aggressive and chanting slogans such as *izwe letu* (the land is ours). Many of the crowd participants painted a very different picture. They argued that the crowd was passive and singing Christian hymns. No one was carrying weapons or clubs as there was no expectation of violence. They had come to encourage and watch the spectacle of people getting arrested for refusing to carry passes. These accounts were supported by journalists from the *Rand Daily Mail* and *Drum* who had arrived to witness events. The photographs these journalists took suggested a relaxed environment. The police reinforcements were subjected to verbal abuse and stone-throwing during their journey to the Sharpeville police station, and this almost certainly unnerved them. These new police arrivals were unfortunately unaware that crowd was largely passive.

At around 1.00 pm Nyakane Tsolo, the local PAC branch secretary, attempted to negotiate with Colonel Spengler and Lieutenant Colonel Pienaar, the police officers in charge. Spengler demanded that Tsolo order the crowd to disperse. Tsolo refused, saying that only Robert Sobukwe had the authority to give such an order. Spengler was furious and placed Tsolo under arrest. Thomas More, another local PAC branch executive, was then invited to enter the police area to negotiate, but he too refused to bring the demonstration to an end. Spengler approached the front row of the demonstrators and stumbled after seizing a man by the shoulder who thrust himself forward demanding arrest. Pienaar subsequently claimed that at this point someone in the crowd fired two pistol shots into the air. The police had formed up in firing positions and one of the rattled officers suddenly gave the order to shoot. The armed policemen proceeded to fire upon the crowd. Humphrey Tyler, a reporter from the *Drum* newspaper, stated that he saw no weapons in the crowd. He heard no warnings from the police and no warning shots. There was just a sudden avalanche of police fire. He described the massacre as follows: "We heard the clatter of a machine gun, then another, then another. There were hundreds of women, some of them laughing. They must have thought the police were firing blanks. One woman was hit about ten yards from our car. Her companion, a young man went back when she fell. He thought she had stumbled. Then he turned her over and saw that her chest had been shot away. He looked at the blood on his hand and said, 'My, God, she's gone!' There were hundreds of kids running too. One little boy had on an old blanket coat which he held up behind his head, thinking, perhaps, that it might save him from the bullets. Some of the children, hardly as tall as the grass, were leaping like rabbits. Some were shot too. Still the shooting went on. One of the policemen was standing on top of a Saracen and it looked as though he was firing his gun into the crowd. He was swinging it round in a wide arc from his hip as though he was panning a movie camera. Two other officers were with him and it looked as though they were firing pistols. Most of the bodies were strewn on the road running through the field in which we were. One man, who had been lying still, dazedly got to his feet, staggered a few yards and fell into a heap. A woman sat with her head cupped in her hands. One by one the guns stopped."[27]

The police killed sixty-nine people that day and three times that number were wounded. Most of the victims were shot in the back as they attempted to run away. The police made no effort to assist the wounded and instead witnesses accused the police of placing stones and knives in the hands of the dead in a grotesque effort to justify their action. The police immediately cordoned off the town with roadblocks and initiated a ferocious search for the protest organisers. The police even visited hospitals and arrested people with gun-shot wounds. News of the killings attracted international attention and there were riots and protests throughout the country. Robert Sobukwe and other PAC leaders were immediately arrested. Sobukwe was charged under the 1953 Criminal Law Amendment Act and sentenced to three years in prison. When he completed his sentence in May 1963, he was simply detained under the Suppression of Communism Act and taken to Robben Island where he was imprisoned alone in a small cottage for the next six years. He was released in 1969 and placed under house arrest in his Kimberley home, where he died in 1977.

The government proclaimed a state of emergency and banned both the ANC and PAC. It was now a criminal offence to belong to these political organisations. They arrested thousands of political activists, including Joe Slovo, Hilda Bernstein, and Rusty Bernstein. Nelson Mandela and all the other accused in the treason trial promptly had their bail revoked. The police came at 2.00 am one morning to arrest Molly. Ruth was away at University in Cape Town, but Ilse and Paul were at home. The children were clearly distraught and Ilse absurdly urged her mother to jump out of the window and run away. Bram figured that he had not been arrested because the government could hardly afford to arrest one of the leading defence barristers in the treason trial. Bram was furious but felt completely helpless as the police drove Molly off to prison.

Oliver Tambo, Mandela's law partner, and Yusuf Dadoo, the SACP leader, crossed the border into Bechuanaland to avoid arrest. Tambo visited many countries and would set up the ANC office in London to garner international support for the liberation struggle. Tambo proved to be a highly capable ANC spokesman and organiser.

Bram called me early that morning to tell me that he was very concerned about Paul. I promised to look out for him. In January Paul had started in Remove, the first year in the College. I sat in the back pews of the chapel, but had no difficulty in spotting Paul near the front because of his persistent coughing. I positioned myself near the door as the boys filed out after the short service. I nodded at Paul and asked him the follow me. He was reluctant to do so but could not refuse my request. I had a free period and took him to my study in Hill House. Paul was tired, clearly traumatised and suffering from fits of coughing. I told him that his father had called me to tell me about the police visit during the night. The poor fellow burst into tears. I asked if he would like some hot chocolate. Paul composed himself and I was able to busy myself with boiling the kettle and ladling a huge spoonful of chocolate powder into a mug. It was a warm day but Paul was clearly pleased to sip on the large mug of hot chocolate. He said that Ilse was fine and she had also gone to school. I assured Paul that his mother had done nothing wrong, that his father was a big deal lawyer and that the police would not dare harm his mother. Paul was upset, but very brave and clearly exhausted. I offered to take him to the sanatorium where he could have a lie down. He said he did not want to do this and said that he would rather go back to his classes. He was worried about missing the first period, a mathematics class, but I assured him that I would speak to his teacher. He looked crestfallen and said that he did not want anyone to know that his mother had been arrested. My heart bled for this poor little chap and I assured him that neither he nor I needed to discuss the arrest with anyone. The bell rang for the second period, he thanked me politely for the hot chocolate, and was anxious to head off to his next class.

I too, had to make a dash for my class but I did find a moment later in the day to bring Father Ted up to speed with what had happened. He said very little but a few days later the Headmaster, Deane Yates, walked past me and said firmly, "Henry, please keep an eye on Fischer and let me know of any problems. I have asked his Housemaster to do the same."

Father Ted was an impressive man and I thought that he was destined for high ecclesiastical office. He eventually left St. John's College to undertake a regular parish appointment, but a few years later he emigrated with his wife and four young children to the United Kingdom. Father Ted never appeared to actively engage with the anti-apartheid struggle but I perceived his departure as a quiet protest. The Anglican Church in South Africa though would have an honourable legacy of opposing apartheid. Bishop Ambrose Reeves, the Bishop of Johannesburg, was extremely vocal in the wake of the Sharpeville massacre. The government was reluctant to arrest members of the clergy and in September 1960 they simply revoked Bishop Reeves' visa and deported him back to the United Kingdom.

The government prohibited the media from publishing the names of those arrested for more than two months. These people simply disappeared and it was only family and friends that were painfully aware of who had been detained. The newspapers were simply permitted to refer to the arrest of communists and political agitators. In the staff room there was a consensus that the Sharpeville massacre was an unspeakable horror and that the police had been disgraceful in their conduct. Yet there was a surprising equanimity about the scores of people arrested and little sympathy for communists. There was this sort of contradiction, a disdain for the policies of apartheid, but an almost equal disdain for communists. I had an uncomfortable feeling that many of my colleagues saw communism as the greater of two evils. I was also quite sure that most of my colleagues were blissfully unaware that Paul Fischer's mother had been arrested.

Rusty and Hilda Bernstein were arrested and yet they had four school-age young children: Toni, Patrick, Frances, and Keith. The police allowed Hilda to telephone a friend, Yvonne Lewiton, who came and collected the Bernstein children, even though her own husband had also been arrested that day. The police arrested Joe Slovo, but for some reason they did not arrest his wife, Ruth First. Ruth did not hesitate, minutes after the police arrested Joe, she donned a red wig, packed her three children into their car, and set off for Swaziland. Ruth's parents, Julius and Matilda, who were founding members of the South African Communist Party, joined them. The three Slovo children were forced to attend a school in Swaziland for some months before their grandparents brought them back to Johannesburg. Ruth returned separately and lived underground, and in disguise, until such time as she was convinced that she was no longer likely to be arrested.

Bram could not really understand why Molly had been arrested. He had been deeply involved in SACP activities. Molly, on the other hand, had done little more in recent months than teach at the Central Indian High School. Michael Harmel had established the school after the government had attempted to remove Indians from the Johannesburg area through closing-down their schools. Teaching was hardly a subversive activity and Bram felt that arresting Molly was directed at intimidating him. Molly was detained in the Johannesburg Fort, but was moved to Pretoria in May. The women detainees were furious when they were transferred to Pretoria. They refused to enter the police vans that had come to transport them and prison warders had to physically carry them out to the vans. After they arrived in Pretoria they wrote to the Minister of Justice and threatened to go on a hunger strike if they were not moved back to Johannesburg to be closer to their families. They commenced their strike and had nothing but water with glucose. The prison authorities sent some of the women further away to Nylstroom in the Eastern Transvaal to break their morale. One woman soon became very ill and refused to stop the strike alone. The others did not want to see her suffer further and so they abandoned the hunger strike.

Bram visited Molly twice a week, and Molly was allowed to write letters to Ruth, Ilse, and Paul. Bram was proud of Molly and the other detainees, but he knew that Molly's absence was exacting a heavy toll on his family. Hilary Flegg, a family friend, moved in to assist in running the house. Ilse and Paul were both at school and needed looking after. Nora Mlambo, now a pregnant teenager, was also at Beaumont Street. Bram had to deal with the problems this teenage pregnancy presented. Nora was allowed to remain in the Fisher home, she gave birth to a little boy, and continued her schooling via correspondence. Ruth was at Cape Town University but made regular trips back to Johannesburg to visit her mother in jail. Ilse, who was in her final year of school, undertook a large share of the domestic duties. She was stoic but it was a heavy burden. Paul had to take daily insulin injections and various pills to control his cystic fibrosis. It was Molly that had attended to his medications. Bram and Ilse did their best in her absence, but Paul had to step up and take an almost unreasonable responsibility for his own health. Molly was terribly worried about how Paul was coping. Paul though never complained and simply got on with things. The insulin injections caused Paul to suffer from eye problems. Bram took time off from his schedule to ensure that Paul kept his specialist appointments. Paul suffered terribly from his cystic fibrosis affliction but he was undeterred in participating fully in school activities. His sporting talent was particularly evident. He was a prolific scorer of runs in the under 13A cricket team, despite having to squint through his glasses and lean on his bat to gather breath after a hard run single. I noticed that he was one of the outstanding performers in the annual school swimming gala and he was in the top three over all the distances in athletics. Paul would run his heart out and then collapse with fits of coughing immediately after crossing the finishing line. I once happened to see Paul taking a whole bunch of tablets in the cricket pavilion. I approached him with concern but he quickly waved me away and stated that he knew what he was doing. Bram was able to take Ruth and Ilse with him to visit Molly, but Paul was not allowed to accompany them because he was under sixteen. In May the prison authorities relented and allowed younger children to visit. Bram felt that Paul's visits though did more harm than good. Paul became extremely upset at seeing his mother behind bars and Molly became terribly worried about his health.

Ruth and Ilse managed to draw media attention to the detentions. One Saturday morning Ilse and other children of detainees arranged a demonstration on the Johannesburg City Hall steps. The children held up placards demanding the release of their parents. Ilse, Toni Bernstein, and Mark Weinberg entered the City Hall to present a petition to the mayor. A large crowd, including both domestic and overseas news reporters, had gathered to watch the demonstration. The police arrived and "arrested" the children, taking them off to the police cells at Marshall Square. Ilse alerted Bram as soon as she emerged from her meeting with the mayor. Bram accosted the police at Marshall Square and, after a fiery exchange of words, the children were released. The newspapers reported that the police had only acted in this way to "protect" the children. The next day Ruth led a deputation to the parliament buildings in Cape Town to deliver a letter of protest to the Minister of Justice. Ruth and Ilse were both prominently splashed across the front pages of the newspapers. Ruth standing outside parliament and Ilse standing on the City Hall steps with the mayor.

Molly and the other detainees were suddenly released after three months. Bram was immensely relieved but the media now drew attention to Bram. Various columnists openly referred to him as a traitor to the Afrikaner *volk*. They wrote about his eminent family background, and lambasted him for opening such a wide gulf between himself and the political credentials of his grandfather. In January 1961 Bram was issued with a further five-year banning order.

CHAPTER 10

Umkhonto we Sizwe

On 6 October 1960 South Africa held a referendum on becoming a Republic. Only white South Africans could vote. I was a British citizen and was not allowed to vote, which was trivial when you consider the millions of blacks, Coloureds, and Indians that were also denied a vote. The Nationalist government, under Hendrik Verwoerd, was staunchly determined to create an Afrikaner republic, free of any interference from Britain. Unfortunately, Harold Macmillan's "winds of change" speech had frightened many that saw Britain as abandoning white interests in Africa. Nevertheless, voting was largely split on language lines with Afrikaners voting in favour and English-speakers voting against. The result was a narrow victory for a republic. The winning margin was less than 75,000 out of a total of 1.6 million votes cast. The Afrikaners were jubilant and there was a rapid removal of British symbols in South Africa. The currency was changed from the British pound to the Rand, the Queen's picture was removed from public buildings, and new stamps were issued that no longer carried the Queen's image. The South African flag however, that had been adopted in 1928, was not changed. Many Afrikaners argued for the removal of the miniature Union Jack that, together with the flags of the Transvaal Republic and Orange Free State, were placed in the centre of the flag. South Africa asked to remain a member of the British Commonwealth, but the other members were hostile to apartheid and denied South Africa's request. Verwoerd wanted South Africa to be a white, Christian national country and he hastened his grand apartheid vision with determination and viciousness. He promoted the idea of homelands or Bantustans. Blacks could provide their labour but were otherwise to be relegated to Bantustans, which were economically unviable dumping grounds.

In 1960 the ANC, PAC, and many other organisations were banned. These organisations were now forced to operate through underground structures. Nelson Mandela feared that he would soon be banned or arrested again, and so he decided to go into hiding. The police issued a warrant for Mandela's arrest, but he avoided capture. Ruth First arranged for Brian Widlake, a television reporter with Independent Television News, to interview Mandela. It was Mandela's first television interview and the last he would give for thirty years. Mandela appeared stiff and formal but he made the telling point that the ANC might have to reconsider its policy of non-violence if the government continued to crush them with blunt force.

Mandela involved himself in promoting a three-day stay-at-home strike to commence on 31 May 1961, the day South Africa was to become a republic. Mandela popped up frequently to speak to newspaper editors to galvanise support and allay fears that the ANC was a communist party proxy. The stay-at-home campaign gained momentum and Mandela began to receive wide coverage in both domestic and foreign newspapers. The government responded to the 31 May 1961 stay-at-home strikes by calling out the army to patrol townships and making dozens of arrests. The ANC called off the strike after just one day. The prime minister, Hendrik Verwoerd, boasted that the strike had been a failure.

The reality though was that the strike was more successful than imagined and it raised a wide awareness that blacks were going to maintain their resistance to oppression.

Nelson Mandela issued a public statement saying that the strike had been a resounding success and most inspiring. He claimed that the stay-at-home campaign had caused the Nationalist government to mobilise the entire resources of the state, military and otherwise, to counter the massive public support for the strike. He noted that it was not the republican celebrations that dominated the news, but rather the strike. Mandela warned that the strike would be followed by other forms of mass pressure to force the government, who he labelled race maniacs, to make way for a democratic government of the people. Mandela stated that the aim was to make government impossible through a countrywide campaign of non-cooperation. He described non-cooperation as a dynamic weapon that could be used to send the Nationalist government to its grave. He wanted blacks to withdraw all co-operation and he called upon international bodies to expel South Africa and asked all foreign nations to sever economic and diplomatic ties with South Africa. Mandela declared that he would not leave South Africa or surrender. He had to separate himself from his family and live as an outlaw, but he believed that freedom could only be won through hardship, sacrifice, and militant action. In this last public statement before his incarceration, Mandela finished with these words: "The struggle is my life. I will continue fighting for freedom, until the end of my days."[28]

In June 1961 Nelson Mandela met with the ANC leadership in Durban and argued for the end of passive resistance. He wanted to violently overthrow the government through acts of sabotage. The ANC president, Chief Albert Luthuli, was a pacifist and strongly committed to maintaining the policy of non-violent protest. Mandela and Luthuli reached a compromise. The ANC would maintain its pacifist stance but Mandela would set-up a separate, autonomous organisation to conduct an armed military struggle. The new organisation was called Umkhonto we Sizwe (The Spear of the Nation). The SACP immediately threw itself into supporting Umkhonto we Sizwe. Nelson Mandela, Walter Sisulu, and Joe Slovo formed the High Command. They recruited other communists such as Rusty Bernstein and Jack Hodgson, who was a demolitions expert.

Umkhonto we Sizwe was not alone in embarking on a sabotage campaign. There were other organisations that resorted to sabotage out of frustration at the intransigence of the government. One of the most significant was the National Committee of Liberation, which was later named the African Resistance Movement. This movement was formed by certain members of the Liberal Party. It started off through helping young people flee the country but soon changed to engaging in acts of sabotage to make the country ungovernable. The PAC set-up a group known as Poqo, which attacked whites that were suspected of being brutal towards blacks.

The SACP received funding from Moscow and other sympathetic foreign sources. The SACP treasurer was Julius First, Ruth's father, but Bram was also very involved with handling party funds. In July 1961 they used some of their funds to purchase Liliesleaf farm in the northern Johannesburg suburb of Rivonia. Michael Harmel found the property and Harold Wolpe handled the conveyance. They placed the property in the name of Vivian Ezra, a SACP member that was unknown to the security police. Liliesleaf was to be the secret headquarters of the SACP. It was essential to preserve tight security precautions over the existence and location of this property. Bram devised elaborate security protocols but Liliesleaf would eventually be exposed through lax security.

It did not take long before Mandela started to use Liliesleaf farm as his hideaway. Bram went there frequently to meet with Nelson Mandela, other communists, and leaders of Umkhonto we Sizwe. Mandela adopted the alias David Motsayami and pretended to be the caretaker. There were numerous workers on site as the various buildings were renovated. The workers left in the late afternoon and during the evening Mandela was able to meet and plan with his Umkhonto we Sizwe colleagues. After the renovations were completed Arthur Goldreich and his family moved into the main house. Goldreich was a dedicated communist and member of Umkhonto we Sizwe, but he was unknown to the police. It was thought that his presence created a sense of normality, which allowed his fellow communist and Umkhonto we Sizwe leaders to meet, in what they thought, was relative safety. Bram was not a member of Umkhonto we Sizwe and he was hesitant about the merits of armed resistance. Bram felt that they did not have the resources to engage in open revolution. He agreed though with acts of sabotage, provided they avoided harming individuals. It was also the easiest to implement with minimal resources. Umkhonto we Sizwe planned to attack infrastructure such as military installations, power lines, and telephone lines. The idea was to frighten the public, weaken the economy, and make the state willing to negotiate.

There was a general election in October 1961 and the Nationalist government was easily returned to office. The main opposition, the United Party, lost eleven parliamentary members who resigned to form a more liberal party called the Progressive Party. These eleven members and fifteen others contested seats in the 1961 general election, but they only won one seat. This was Helen Suzman who won the seat of Houghton. Bram was pleased but not terribly enthused because he felt that the parliamentary opposition was ineffective and irrelevant.

In early December 1961 Chief Albert Luthuli, the president of the ANC, went to Oslo to receive the Nobel Peace Prize for his non-violent struggle against apartheid. He was a deserving winner but it was a little ironic that at the exact time he was receiving his prize, his ANC colleagues were initiating a programme of armed struggle. On 16 December 1961, the day on which whites celebrated the defeat of the Zulu chief, Dingaan, Umkhonto we Sizwe exploded a series of bombs in Johannesburg, Port Elizabeth, and Durban. On the same day, Umkhonto we Sizwe announced its existence through distributing pamphlets throughout the country.

In these pamphlets Umkhonto we Sizwe noted that liberation movements in South Africa had followed a policy of non-violence regardless of government attacks and persecutions upon them, and despite all government-inspired attempts to provoke them to violence. The people however, had only had two choices: submit or fight. Umkhonto we Sizwe refused to submit and the time had now come to hit back with all the means within their power in defence of their people, their future, and their freedom. The government had interpreted the peacefulness of the liberation struggle as weakness; the people's non-violent policies had been taken as a green light for government violence. Refusal to resort to force had been interpreted by the government as an invitation to use armed force against the people without any fear of reprisals. Umkhonto we Sizwe was going to break with that past and adopt new methods. They were going to strike out along a new road for the liberation of the people of South Africa. The government policy of force, repression and violence would no longer be met with non-violent resistance only.

Umkhonto we Sizwe announced that it was going to be the fighting arm of the people against the government and its policies of race oppression. Nevertheless, they still hoped to achieve liberation without bloodshed. They hoped their actions would awaken everyone to the disastrous consequences of the government's apartheid policies and that it would bring the Nationalist government and its supporters to their senses before it was too late to avoid a civil war. Umkhonto we Sizwe declared that it was working in the best interests of all the people of South Africa – black, brown, and white – whose future happiness and well-being could not be attained without the overthrow of the Nationalist government, the abolition of white supremacy and the winning of liberty, democracy and full national rights and equality for all the people of South Africa.

Bram had reservations about violent resistance, but he seemed convinced that the end was nigh for the apartheid government. I did not argue with Bram, but I could see no reason why the government was going to capitulate. It seemed very naïve to imagine that a few bombs and threatening pamphlets were going to bring the government to its knees. The government was determined to stifle Umkhonto we Sizwe immediately and it began to hunt down its leaders with a ruthless determination. Nelson Mandela was the man they wanted most but he had gone underground. The newspapers called him the Black Pimpernel as he eluded the police.

I noticed that when I visited Bram there was almost always a police car parked outside their home. Bram and Molly's socialising was severely curtailed because of their banning orders and instead of attending raucous parties I simply enjoyed a quiet drink with Bram in his study. Bram also had this incredible optimism that the South African government could not last for much longer and that its demise was imminent. I was not convinced that communism was the answer to the injustices in South Africa and attempted to argue with Bram.

"Bram," I said one evening, "South Africa is vilified throughout the word because of its apartheid policies. There is no other country in the world today where racial oppression is practiced so nakedly and shamelessly, with such systematic brutality and disregard of human rights and dignity. But surely, we should seek a change whereby we adopt the values of capitalist western democracies rather than the totalitarian policies of communist regimes."

Bram shook his head vigorously and replied, "It is the capitalists that play upon race and national antagonisms. Capitalism is a means of dividing the working classes. European capitalists developed vicious racial theories to justify their subjection of African, Asian, and Latin American people to slavery. The system of race domination and oppression has origins far back in South African history. However, it has developed into its present, extreme form with the development of capitalism and especially because of the great diamond and goldmining monopolies. It is capitalists that cultivate racial differences and prejudices as an instrument in their insatiable drive for cheap labour and high profits."

I countered, "We have witnessed post-colonial African countries promote communist ideology and it does not appear to have been to their benefit."

"It is quite to the contrary my dear fellow, said Bram. "Capitalists raped African countries. Colonialism facilitated the maximum exploitation of labour. Racialist and colonialist theories and practices have been discredited and condemned throughout the world. Hundreds and millions of people in Africa and Asia have gained independence and self-government."

"Quite" I said," But most of these countries have not done very well under their attempts to adopt socialist systems."

"I disagree," said Bram, "The liberation of these nations has put an end to racial discrimination and privilege. In these post-colonial countries land and wealth has been restored to the people. The destruction of colonialism and the winning of national freedom is the essential condition to laying the foundations of a classless, communist society."

"But Bram," I complained, "People do not like seeing what is happening in Africa. The fear of communism is playing into our government's hands."

"You misunderstand communism," said Bram as he got up to refill our glasses. "The ideas of communism, of Marxism, of Leninism, are true and answer the needs and aspirations of people. They correctly explain the world we live in and show mankind the way forward to a better world: a world without wars and racialism, without poverty and exploitation. The Communist Party of South Africa has marched at the head of the freedom struggles of the workers and oppressed peoples. It is no accident that the Nationalist government has targeted the South African Communist Party and sought to destroy us. We are the main obstacle in their plan to subjugate and exploit the masses, the blacks, in this country. Communism stands for the direct opposite of the theories and practices of the Nationalist Party. Communism stands for the rights of the workers and oppressed people – against all forms of racialism, privilege, colonialism, and exploitation of man. Communism stands for peace, freedom, democracy, and national independence."

Bram had a passionate conviction in the merits of communism and I knew that I did not have the ability to change his mind. I was unconvinced that communism was the answer. I disliked communist ideology and states like the Soviet Union and China that were its exponents. The Cold War had descended upon the world and I associated communism with autocratic regimes. In late 1961 East Germany had built the Berlin wall and this served to enhance my fear of communist regimes. Dwight Eisenhower had spoken about the domino theory: as one country succumbs to communism, so the next falls. I started to suspect that the communist rhetoric in opposing apartheid was aiding rather than harming the Nationalist Party government. The Nationalists labelled practically all opposition to their apartheid policies as communist-inspired. They claimed that South Africa was a capitalist Western country that was at the forefront of resisting the spread of communism in Africa. They inculcated a fear of a communist revolution and associated the idea of black government with the evils of communism.

In February 1962 Mandela secretly left the country to attend a conference in Addis Ababa, which had been organised by the Organisation of African Unity. Mandela was reluctant to leave South Africa but anxious to meet with leaders of other liberation movements to seek military support for Umkhonto we Sizwe. Mandela visited many countries and met various heads of government. He also caught up with Oliver Tambo in London. After Mandela's trip abroad, he went to Durban to consult with Chief Albert Luthuli, the President of the ANC. Cecil Williams, a white communist activist, had spirited Mandela back into South Africa across the Bechuanaland (now Botswana) border. Williams drove his Austin Westminster car to Bechuanaland and Mandela had then driven the car back posing as his chauffeur. Williams and Mandela used the same *modus operandi* for the Durban trip. In Durban Mandela met up with Chief Albert Luthuli, Ismail Meer, and other ANC leaders. On 5 August 1962 they set off on their return journey to Johannesburg. Police stopped Williams and Mandela near Howick (about one-hundred kilometres north of Durban) and arrested them. It seems very likely that the police had been tipped off. Bram told me that no-one had any idea as to who was responsible for the betrayal, but he suspected that it may have been the American CIA because the Americans believed that Mandela was part of the rapidly emerging communist threat in Africa.

Mandela was charged with inciting workers to strike and leaving the country illegally. Bram was very relieved over these charges because it meant that the State did not have sufficient evidence to identify Mandela (and others) as the leaders of Umkhonto we Sizwe. Bram offered to represent Mandela at his trial but Mandela decided to represent himself and used Joe Slovo as a legal advisor. The State transferred the trial from Johannesburg to Pretoria. Joe Slovo could no longer act for Mandela since he was banned from leaving the magisterial district of Johannesburg. Bob Hepple instead took up the duties of legal advisor. On 15 October 1962 Mandela entered the court on the first day of the trial dramatically dressed in a traditional Xhosa leopard skin. He applied for the recusal of the magistrate on the grounds that he did not consider himself bound by the laws of a parliament that only represented whites. Mandela made this statement: "Why is it that in this courtroom I am facing a white magistrate, confronted by a white prosecutor, escorted by white orderlies? Can anybody honestly and seriously suggest that in this type of atmosphere the scales of justice are evenly balanced? Why is it that no African in the history of this country has ever had the honour of being tried by his own kith and kin, by his own fresh and blood? I will tell Your Worship why: the real purpose of this rigid colour bar is to ensure that the justice dispensed by the courts should conform to the policy of the country, however much that policy might be in conflict with the norms of justice accepted in judiciaries throughout the civilised world...Your Worship, I hate racial discrimination most intensely and in all its manifestations. I have fought it all my life. I fight it now, and I will do so until the end of my days. I detest most intensely the set-up that surrounds me here. It makes me feel that I am a black man in a white man's court. This should not be."[29]

The State called over a hundred witnesses to prosecute their case. Mandela cross-examined some of these witnesses but declined to call any of his own witnesses. Mandela was found guilty and sentenced to five years in prison. It was an exceptionally harsh sentence given the relatively minor charges. Mandela made a lengthy speech in mitigation but since he was a banned person, nothing he said in court could be published in the newspapers. Some newspapers protested by leaving large blank spaces in their reports in place of quoting Mandela's words. The left-wing newspaper, the *New Age*, defied the government and printed an uncensored report on the trial. The government promptly closed the newspaper permanently.

Nelson Mandela was in prison but this did not deter Umkhonto we Sizwe from pursuing acts of sabotage. White activists belonging to the Armed Resistance Movement also engaged in acts of sabotage. John Vorster, the Minister of Justice, was determined to break all subversive activity with an iron fist. In 1963 he succeeded in passing the General Law Amendment Act, also known as the Sabotage Act. Under this Act the police were empowered to arrest any person and detain them for ninety days. The period could then be extended indefinitely. Helen Suzman was the sole member of parliament to oppose the Ninety-day detention law. She declared that it was ironic that the government was adopting measures to combat communism that were indistinguishable from measures taken in totalitarian communist countries. As Suzman pointed out, this legislation overrode every single principle of the rule of law. John Vorster responded to her objections with these words: "What does she want? Why does she use long sentences and pious words? Why does she not tell us straight out that it is the policy of herself and her party that the black man should take over in South Africa."[30] When it came to the vote, Helen Suzman called for a division. The United Party voted with the Nationalist government, and Helen Suzman cast the only vote against the law. The South African parliament had voted to make South Africa a police state.

CHAPTER 11

Rivonia

I did not see a great deal of Bram during the first half of 1963 because he was frequently away in Rhodesia on legal business. Bram remained hesitant about the use of violence, but Joe Slovo and Govan Mbeki were pushing the Umkhonto we Sizwe leadership to go much further than sabotage. They wanted to engage in guerilla warfare and gave this proposal the code name Operation Mayibuye (The Return). Fidel Castro had inspired them and they believed they could emulate his feats in South Africa. Most of the Umkhonto we Sizwe and ANC leaders enthusiastically supported the idea, but there were others, such as Bram, Rusty Bernstein, and Walter Sisulu who saw engaging in warfare against the powerful South African state as a mere fantasy. Documents were drawn up to identify military targets, define command structures, and detail the arsenal required. Oliver Tambo was asked to source arms and equipment.

Joe Slovo wanted to press ahead with Operation Mayibuye but Rusty Bernstein and Walter Sisulu objected. They insisted that the ANC leaders should approve the plan. Joe Slovo agreed to go abroad to present his arguments in favour of Operation Mayibuye to Oliver Tambo and other ANC leaders in exile. As a banned person Joe did not have access to a passport and he had to leave the country secretly. Certain newspapers however, picked up on his travels abroad and it was widely reported. Joe Slovo was now liable to arrest and imprisonment if he returned to South Africa. As it turned out Joe Slovo was most fortunate to be out of the country at this time.

Umkhonto we Sizwe was successful in conducting small acts of sabotage and the police were anxious to capture the saboteurs. Nelson Mandela was behind bars and even though they had caught various saboteurs, they had no strong evidence about who was orchestrating the acts of sabotage, and nothing more than suspicions about the leadership of Umkhonto we Sizwe. They did know though that Walter Sisulu was one of the leaders. Sisulu had already been arrested and charged with organising political protests and furthering the aims of the ANC. He was sentenced to six years in prison but was let out on bail pending an appeal. Sisulu immediately went into hiding and began to make illegal radio broadcasts stating that he had gone underground to pursue the freedom struggle.

The police were growing increasingly frustrated, but then they hit upon some extraordinary luck. They arrested a saboteur that claimed to know the whereabouts of Umkhonto we Sizwe's headquarters. The police agreed to free the prisoner and give him a substantial payment in return for this information. The trouble was that he had trouble remembering the location of the headquarters at Liliesleaf farm. Lieutenant Willem van Wyk drove the informant around the northern suburbs for days and began to suspect that his story had been fabricated, but eventually they came across Liliesleaf farm.

On 11 July 1963 Van Wyk decided to raid the farm with police concealed in a dry-cleaning van so that they could approach the farm buildings without raising an alarm. He was ready to conduct his raid at 1.00 pm but he faced a two-hour delay as a more senior officer demanded that they first obtain a search warrant. At 1.00 pm Ahmed Kathrada was the only person at Liliesleaf farm but by 3.00 pm Ahmed Kathrada, Walter Sisulu, Rusty Bernstein, Bob Hepple, Govan Mbeki, Raymond Mhlaba and Denis Goldberg were all there. The police pulled up in their dry-cleaning van and had little difficulty in catching them all. The police were able to retrieve a mass of incriminating documents, including copies of Operation Mayibuye, communist literature, maps detailing sabotage targets, and manuals on explosives. The police arrested all the farmhands and domestic servants and posted guards near the front gate. They arrested Arthur Goldreich, when he drove up to the farm house later that afternoon, and his wife, Hazel, when she arrived a few hours later.

Harold Wolpe was the lawyer that had completed the conveyancing for the Liliesleaf farm purchase. He was also a member of the SACP, a frequent visitor to the farm, and deeply involved in Umkhonto we Sizwe's activities. As soon as he heard about the Rivonia raid, he contacted his legal partner Jimmy Kantor, who was also his brother-in-law, and told him that he needed to go into hiding. Kantor was aware that Harold Wolpe was a communist but he had little idea about the extent of his involvement with Umkhonto we Sizwe and no knowledge of the Liliesleaf farm transaction. Harold Wolpe told Kantor that he needed to warn others and skip the country immediately.

Kantor was shocked and offered Wolpe the use of his holiday home just north of Johannesburg, A few hours later Kantor received a telephone call from Hazel Goldreich's mother, Maimie Berman. She had heard about the arrest of Arthur and Hazel and was worried about who was now caring for their two children. Kantor had never been to Liliesleaf farm before but he agreed to go there with Maimie Berman to find out what had happened to the children. When they arrived at Liliesleaf they were confronted with dozens of Special Branch police. They allowed Maimie Berman to enter the house to collect the children and pack their belongings. Kantor wandered around outside and fed some of the farm animals. This was enough to make the police suspicious that Kantor was familiar with the farm.

I went to Beaumont Street to hear Bram's reaction to the Rivonia raid. He was deeply shocked, and angry because security had grown so lax. He told me that he had just come back from visiting Harold Wolpe who was hiding in Jimmy Kantor's holiday house. Bram feared that there would be many more arrests and he was gravely concerned about the documentation that the police had found at Liliesleaf farm. I had never heard of Liliesleaf farm before and I asked Bram if he had ever heard about the farm. He looked at me incredulously and murmured, "Of course, I have been their countless times. I could be in real trouble here." I was taken aback and realised that I knew very little about Bram's political involvements.

Later that night Bram asked me to drive him to a house in the suburb of Mountain View, which was very close to Houghton. I was surprised because I thought that Bram could drive himself. Nevertheless, I was happy to oblige and we got there in less than quarter of an hour. Bram went into the house and emerged a minute later wearing gloves and brandishing a set of car keys. He opened the garage door and reversed out a bright red Chevrolet. He wound down the window and said, "Please follow me." He drove north along Louis Botha Avenue. We were halfway to Pretoria before he indicated that he was turning left into a side street. I followed him down this street for a few minutes before he stopped. He got out of the car, tossed the keys into a bush, and got into my car. He started pulling off his gloves and said quietly, "Okay. Let's turn around and go home."

I kept very calm and simply murmured, "Bram, may I ask what is going on?"

"I am sorry to do this to you. It is best that you forget where you have been tonight."

"Bram, this is all very unusual," I said.

"Yes, yes. I owe you an explanation."

"I am all ears."

"Okay, but forget about all this. The house is a safe house and that car belongs to Denis Goldberg. If the police find it at that house our cover will be blown. The police will find the car, but now the safe house will remain secure. I wore gloves so they won't find my fingerprints."

During the July school holidays Bram and Molly took Ilse and Paul on a camping holiday to the Blyde River canyon in the eastern Transvaal. Upon their return they were rattled to learn that Ruth was engaged. Ruth had completed her degree in psychology at the University of Cape Town. She intended to carry on with a Masters degree but Bram had encouraged Ruth to take a year off and go to London. Ruth had met Anthony Eastwood, who was from Zimbabwe, at university. Anthony followed Ruth to London and proposed. Bram and Molly had never met Anthony and were understandably surprised and slightly concerned at this unexpected news.

While Bram was on their camping holiday, Harold Wolpe attempted to flee across the border into Bechuanaland. His escape effort though was rather amateurish and a border policeman arrested him. Harold Wolpe was placed in the Johannesburg prison at Marshall Square. Arthur Goldreich and two Umkhonto we Sizwe saboteurs of Indian descent, Abdullah Jassat and Mosie Moola, were in the same prison. Ruth First was also at Marshall Square. She had been arrested under the Ninety-day detention law. She was kept in the women's section with Hazel Goldreich but they had no contact with the men's section. The idea of escaping seemed implausible but Wolpe, Goldreich, Jassat and Moola began to groom Johannes Greeff, a young warder. Wolpe's wife, Anne Marie, was able to secrete money into the prison in food hampers. The men then bribed Greeff to facilitate their escape. In a harebrained scheme Greeff agreed to pretend that Goldreich had knocked him out and tied him up as they stole his keys and made good their escape. It all seems breathtakingly unbelievable but their bribery plan worked and all four of these men, facing a lifetime in jail, simply walked out of Marshall Square one night.

Jassat and Moola used their Indian connections to escape South Africa but the police were more interested in tracking down the big fish of Wolpe and Goldreich. The escapees were desperate to get out of the country but they had to proceed cautiously and went into hiding in Johannesburg. The police arrested Anne Marie Wolpe but found that interrogating her was fruitless and so they let her go. Their escape was widely reported in the newspapers. Bram confided in me that he was aware of their escape plans but he thought it entirely unrealistic. He was massively delighted in their success and to my astonishment he let slip that he had visited Wolpe and Goldreich in their hideout. I implored Bram to be careful but he simply declared it his duty to help. Eventually they hid in the boot of a car and were driven across the border into Swaziland.

Their escape was huge news. It infuriated the government and the police were severely embarrassed. In their fury the police raided the legal offices of Kantor and Wolpe. They found plenty of incriminating evidence against Harold Wolpe. Jimmy Kantor was irritated but not surprised at the police raid. Kantor was even bold enough to lodge a complaint about the treatment of Anne Marie Wolpe during her detention. Then to Jimmy Kantor's huge surprise he was arrested. Kantor was married to Harold Wolpe's sister, he was in partnership with Harold Wolpe, and the police believed that Kantor was familiar with Liliesleaf farm. Kantor would end up facing all the same charges as the other Rivonia triallists. It was a cruel error on the part of the police and prosecution. Kantor suffered grievously through his incarceration and trial. The judges eventually dismissed all the charges against him. Kantor left South Africa and went to live England, but he was a broken man.

On 9 October 1963 the State brought charges against eleven people. These were the seven men caught at Liliesleaf farm: Walter Sisulu, Rusty Bernstein, Bob Hepple, Denis Goldberg, Govan Mbeki, Ahmed Kathrada, and Raymond Mhlaba, plus Nelson Mandela, Elias Motsoaledi, Andrew Mlangeni, and Jimmy Kantor. Bram Fischer led the defence and he was assisted by Joel Joffe, Vernon Berrange, George Bizos and Arthur Chaskalson. Jimmy Kantor was represented by a separate team led by George Lowen. The prosecutor was Percy Yutar, the Deputy Attorney General. The Presiding Judge was Justice Quartus De Wet, who had a reputation for impatience. Bram expected that Ruth First would also be charged. She had been detained for one-hundred-and-seventeen days and then released. Bram speculated that Ruth had not been charged because the State was reluctant to seek the death sentence against a white woman. Bram, of course, was acutely aware that he himself could well have been included as one of the accused.

Percy Yutar wanted to start the trial immediately but Bram obtained a three-week delay. Jimmy Kantor immediately applied for bail. His lawyers argued that his arrest was a grave miscarriage of justice. The State though was embarrassed by the escape of his brother-in-law, Harold Wolpe. Yutar argued that Kantor was the money-man behind Umkhonto we Sizwe. His bail was denied. Bob Hepple told Bram and his co-accused that he had been offered indemnity from prosecution if he turned State witness. Bram was furious and vented his anger in no uncertain terms.

Just two days after the start of the trial Bram was very excited to read newspaper reports about a United Nations resolution condemning the Rivonia trial and demanding its abandonment. He felt that the State dare not pass the death sentence in the face of this unanimous disapproval from the United Nations. The vote was 106 in favour and just one vote, that of South Africa, against. George Bizos gave copies of these newspaper reports to the accused. George noted that it buoyed their spirits but they also pointed out that the Nationalist government had shown nothing but contempt for the United Nations.

The court resumed on 29 October 1963. Yutar declared that he was withdrawing all charges against Bob Hepple who was going to be a witness for the prosecution. Hepple was allowed to walk out of the courtroom. Bob Hepple immediately fled the country. He gave an interview to the *Rand Daily Mail* from Tanganyika and denied that he was ever going to testify against his colleagues.

Bram attacked the indictment as being vague. He noted that the indictment did not specify who had carried out acts of sabotage and that Nelson Mandela had even been charged with 156 acts of sabotage while he was in jail. Percy Yutar attempted to defend the indictment but Justice De Wet sided with Bram and dismissed all the charges. The defendants were not free to leave the court however, because a Special Branch policeman immediately leapt to his feet and re-arrested each of the accused on a charge of sabotage.

Two weeks later the defendants were taken back to court and presented with new charges. It was a lengthy document that detailed 193 acts of sabotage. Bram argued that the indictment was deficient because it did not disclose exactly who had committed the acts of sabotage. Jimmy Kantor's defence team were outraged and argued that the indictment did not disclose any crime committed by Kantor. The judge however, dismissed all the arguments and ordered that the indictment stand. Yutar had to advise the court that Bob Hepple had fled the country and was now no longer able to appear for the prosecution. It was rather bizarre. Wolpe, Goldreich, and Hepple had all managed to flee South Africa. These embarrassing escapes was one of the main reasons why none of the accused had much chance of getting bail. Bram knew that the charges were very serious. The accused, other than Jimmy Kantor, were probably guilty and the defence's main pre-occupation would be in avoiding death sentences. The defence team congregated at the Fischer home each evening to discuss the case and tactics for the next day. They usually worked in the garden because the police had almost certainly installed listening devices in the house. Molly attended court each day, making copious notes, which she handed over to Bram. The trial proper commenced on 3 December 1963. The accused all pleaded not guilty with most of them following Nelson Mandela's lead of declaring that it was the government that should be in the dock.

Bram's defence colleagues had no idea how deeply involved he was with the accused. It would surprise them greatly as the case unfolded. One of the first steps of the prosecution was to bring Liliesleaf farmworkers into court to identify the accused and confirm their frequent presence at the farm. Bram carefully absented himself from court on these days because he feared being identified by the farmworkers. His absence did not go unnoticed by either his defence colleagues or the prosecution. When George Bizos, Arthur Chaskalson, and Joel Joffe examined some of the documents the State had found at Liliesleaf farm they saw that they were in Bram's handwriting. When these documents were tendered in court a handwriting expert testified that Harold Wolpe had written them, Bram remained dead calm as the prosecutor handed him a copy of these documents. Fortunately, his defence colleagues were able to remain equally unruffled.

The trial dragged on as the State produced witness after witness. Many of these witnesses had been arrested and held in solitary confinement under the Ninety-day detention law. They knew that their path to freedom lay in tailoring their testimony in favour of the State. The defence barristers had little difficulty in destroying their credibility. These efforts though were largely futile because the evidence against the accused, other than Jimmy Kantor, was overwhelming. Jimmy Kantor repeatedly applied for bail and it was denied each time. He feared that he would spend the Christmas behind bars but then the day before the Christmas recess the judge granted him bail. The police were convinced that Jimmy would attempt to flee the country and so they kept him under surveillance for twenty-four hours a day. There was even a bizarre evening when Jimmy and his wife, Barbara, went to the movies. A special branch policeman and his girlfriend sat virtually beside them as the policeman maintained his watch while enjoying the same movie. In late February the police claimed they had new evidence and his bail was revoked. He was not detained for long though because on 29 February 1964 Justice De Wet announced that he found Jimmy Kantor not guilty on all charges. It was a just outcome for a man that had been unjustly accused and imprisoned.

Bram met up with Ruth First to discuss her situation. She was distressed by her banning orders and seemingly hopeless predicament. Her husband, Joe Slovo, had fortuitously avoided arrest because he was in London at the time of the Liliesleaf farm raid. Her father, Julius First, had recently fled the country. Julius First was a member of the SACP. His name was splashed all over the newspapers in late 1963 as one of South Africa's most wanted men. Julius First had purchased a boat to ferry Umkhonto we Sizwe recruits in and out the country for military training. The police searched the boat one night, discovered the plans for its use, and traced the ownership back to Julius. The police attempted to arrest Julius at his workplace but he was quick-witted enough to slip off and make a hurried departure abroad. Ruth was under constant police surveillance and she became increasingly depressed. She was refused a passport but in March 1964 she was granted an exit permit.

I joined numerous relatives and friends at the airport to say farewell to Ruth, and her children, Gillian and Robyn. The eldest child, Shawn, stayed behind with her grandmother and was going a little later via boat with friends to join her mother and sisters in the United Kingdom. I was incensed at being photographed by a security policeman as I kissed Ruth goodbye. Hilda Bernstein also came to the airport to say goodbye but as a banned person she was not allowed to talk to Ruth. The security police were monitoring Ruth's every movement and I quietly suggested that they say goodbye in the ladies' toilet. The next day the front pages of newspapers were emblazoned with a picture of Ruth, Gillian, and Robyn boarding the aeroplane. I was sad but secretly relieved at their departure.

On 20 April 1964 Bram opened the defence in the Rivonia trial. His four major points were: an acknowledgement that most of the accused had participated in Umkhonto we Sizwe but not all of them were members of the High Command and that Kathrada and Bernstein were not even Umkhonto we Sizwe members; the accused would dispute that Umkhonto we Sizwe was a wing of the ANC; the accused would dispute that the ANC was a tool of the Communist Party; and, the accused would deny that Umkhonto we Sizwe had adopted Operation Mayibuye. Guerilla warfare had been contemplated but would not be launched until they were convinced that the sabotage campaign could not succeed. Bram then announced that Nelson Mandela would commence the defence case with a statement from the dock. The statement did not carry the same weight as evidence subject to cross-examination but Mandela made a lengthy and powerful statement that kept the entire court spellbound for almost five hours. Nelson Mandela admitted that he had helped form Umkhonto we Sizwe and that he had played a prominent role in its affairs. He challenged the suggestion made by the State that the struggle in South Africa was being orchestrated by foreigners and communists. He had done the things he did because he was a proud African. Mandela stressed that he had not advocated violent action without careful thought and that there had always been a priority on avoiding harm to human life. He emphasised that the ANC and Umkhonto we Sizwe were separate organisations and rejected the notion that the ANC and the SACP had the same aims and objectives. He detailed the lack of dignity blacks experienced in South Africa and how blacks wanted equal political rights. He concluded his speech with words that would become immortal: "During my lifetime I have dedicated myself to this struggle of the African people. I have fought against white domination, and I have fought against black domination. I have cherished the ideal of a democratic and free society in which all persons live together in harmony and with equal opportunities. It is an ideal which I hope to live for and to achieve. But if needs be, it is an ideal for which I am prepared to die."[31]

Mandela's address received wide coverage in the international press. As a banned person no-one was supposed to quote Mandela in South Africa but the *Rand Daily Mail* simply ignored this prohibition and quoted large extracts from Mandela's statement. Bram did not want Mandela to say the last sentence because he thought this could provoke the judge into passing the death sentence, but Mandela could not be deterred.

Bram decided to use Walter Sisulu as the main witness. One of the key issues was to persuade the judge that Operation Mayibuye had not been launched. All the other accused also entered the witness box. Walter Sisulu was probably the most impressive and acquitted himself very well despite Percy Yutar's aggressive cross-examination.

On 11 June 1964 Justice De Wet delivered his judgment. He found all the accused guilty, except for Rusty Bernstein who he found not guilty on all charges. Bernstein was immediately re-arrested on charges of violating his banning order and belonging to the banned Communist Party, but he was given bail and was free to go home. De Wet adjourned the court stating he would pronounce the sentences on the following day. The verdicts, while not entirely unexpected, left Bram and the other defence lawyers devastated. They feared that the judge would impose death sentences. Nelson Mandela and the other defendants though insisted on not appealing any sentence. They argued that any appeal would undermine the moral stance they had taken. They wanted to send a clear message that no sacrifice was too great in the struggle for freedom.

Bram had difficulty in finding prominent people to appear before the court in sentencing mitigation because they feared becoming political targets. Bram did succeed in getting Alan Paton, the former Liberal Party leader, a devout Christian, and renowned author, to speak to the court. Alan Paton detested apartheid but he disagreed with violence, including sabotage, and he was opposed to communism. Paton was also an ardent critic of capital punishment. Bram asked Harold Hanson to handle the plea in mitigation. He called Alan Paton to the witness stand and the first question he asked was why Paton had agreed to give evidence. Paton answered: "Because I was asked to come. But primarily because having been asked, I felt it was my duty to come here – a duty which I am glad to perform, because I love my country. And it seems to me, My Lord, with respect, that the exercise of clemency in this case is a thing which is very important for our future."[32]

In his final remarks Harold Hanson reminded the court that Afrikaner nationalists had opposed oppression. These nationalists had not been punished severely and went on to become future leaders. He called for understanding and compassion and stated that it was not reprehensible or immoral for leaders to desire the advancement of all people. Justice De Wet barely seemed interested in these representations. As soon as Hanson finished, the judge ordered the accused to stand. He noted that the accused were essentially guilty of treason but they had not been charged with this crime and so he was not going to impose the death penalty. Instead, he sentenced all the accused to life imprisonment. The judge stood up and abruptly left the court. The accused all smiled with relief and Denis Goldberg was heard shouting to his mother. "Life! Life! To live!" Bram's defence team had saved the lives of the accused. Bram was hopeful that international outrage would eventually lead to their release. He was also convinced that the apartheid regime could not last and the life sentences would never be fully served. The international press condemned the verdicts and sentences. The South African newspapers expressed relief that there were no death sentences but they were also pleased that these dangerous saboteurs were behind bars.

The government was determined to keep the Rivonia trialists out of the media. They wanted them to rot in jail and be forgotten. Denis Goldberg was sent to a whites-only prison in Pretoria but all the others were sent to Robben Island. This desolate windswept island off Cape Town that I had seen on that very first day of my arrival in South Africa. The government wanted to keep them out of sight and out of mind, and in this the government was quite successful.

There has been an international clamour for Nelson Mandela's release in recent years but this should not obscure the many years he was quietly forgotten. In the early 1980s Rian Malan, a young Afrikaner journalist, wrote reviews for a Los Angeles music magazine. He used the nom de plume Nelson Mandela and noted that this barely raised an eyebrow.

CHAPTER 12

Dark days of 1964

Ilse was studying at the University of Cape Town and it was her 21st birthday on 16 June 1964. Molly and Bram were anxious to join Ilse for her birthday. A trip to Cape Town would also allow Bram to visit Nelson Mandela and the others imprisoned on Robben Island. Paul was in his final year at St. John's College and stayed at home to study. Liz Lewin joined Bram and Molly on their trip. Liz worked for the Defence and Aid Fund, an organisation that assisted political prisoners and their dependants. She had got to know Bram because she had been a Liberal Party member and had helped Bram approach Alan Paton about speaking in sentence mitigation at the Rivonia trial. Liz was in the process of divorcing her husband, Hugh Lewin. I put two and two together and figured that Hugh was the boy from my house at St. John's College.

On 13 June 1964, the day after the Rivonia trial sentencing, Bram, Molly and Liz set off for Cape Town. Liz drove and Bram had a snooze in the backseat. After a few hours they switched around. Bram drove with Liz beside him, while Molly took a nap in the backseat. It was dusk as Bram approached the Sand River bridge. Suddenly a cow walked out into the road. The cow was startled as a motorcycle came from the opposite direction and it reversed direction. Bram swerved to miss the cow but went off the road and into a riverbed. It was winter and the river should have been dry but the car landed in a deep pool of water. Bram and Liz managed to roll down their windows and get out of the car. Molly was trapped in the backseat and drowned.

Other cars eventually stopped, the police were called, and Bram and Liz were taken to the nearby Winburg hospital. Bram's brother, Paul, rushed from Bloemfontein and took them back to Johannesburg that same night. Bram wanted to be the person that told his son but by the time they got back Paul had already heard the news. Bram immediately called Ruth in London and Ilse in Cape Town. They caught the first available flights back to Johannesburg. I went to Beamont Street to express my grief and sorrow. The house was filled with people that had come to offer condolences. Bram's brother, Paul, left Johannesburg and went back to Winburg where he identified Molly's body. He also went with the police to salvage the car. He retrieved suitcases, other belongings, and, at Bram's request, a box of tissues from the glove box.

The funeral service was held on the following Friday. I joined hundreds of people, of all races, at the Johannesburg crematorium. Bram did not want a religious service but he did allow his brother Paul to say the Lord's prayer. I was standing alone afterwards when Liz Lewin approached.

"Hullo," I said, "I am so sorry to hear that you were caught up in this terrible accident. I hope that you are okay."

"I am shocked but otherwise fine. It all happened so quickly."

"It is so crazy. I understand that Bram swerved to miss a cow."

"It seemed to happen in slow motion. Bram swerved to miss the cow and we landed in this riverbed. I thought the car was sitting on sand. I tried to open my door but could not do so. Bram started to open his window. He said that he would climb out the window and then open my door. I wound down my window and realised that the car was floating. I managed to climb out the window. I was in water and I could not stand. The car headlights were on and I could see that we were in a pool of water beneath a bridge. I was aware that Molly was on my side of the car and I wanted to open her door to get her out. The door would not budge and I shouted out to Bram. He said he was coming around to my side of the car. I attempted to push the car towards the riverbank. Then the car suddenly disappeared beneath the water."

Liz started to cry. She wiped her eyes with the back of her hand. I promptly offered her my handkerchief which she gratefully took and wiped her eyes. "The water was freezing. I clambered onto the bank. Bram pulled off his coat and dived into the water to try free Molly from the car. Bram would come up for air and then dive down again. He kept doing this over and over."

Liz paused, took a deep breath and continued, "I scrambled up the riverbank. A car had already stopped as they had seen the accident happen. A young man joined Bram in trying to save Molly. This Good Samaritan even climbed onto the bridge to enable him to dive deeper. But neither he nor Bram could get down deep enough to reach the car. Bram did not want to stop but eventually they drove us to the Winburg hospital and reported the accident to the police."

Bram's brother Paul joined us. Liz sighed and said, "I am so sorry. I have just been telling Henry about the accident." She looked at me and said, "I cannot thank Paul enough for everything he did for us after the accident." Liz was anxious to greet others and politely excused herself.

I looked at Paul and said, "What a tragedy. I am so shocked."

Pull nodded and said, "It is terrible. Moly was such a wonderful, courageous person."

"Molly will be so dreadfully missed, I said, "Bram, Ruth, Ilse, Paul – how are they going to cope without her?"

"I am very worried about Bram", said Paul. "His political involvements are placing him in great danger."

I thought it was poor timing to start talking about politics at this juncture but Paul lowered his voice to a whisper and said, "A man has just come up to me." Paul flicked his head sideways. "He said to me that Bram needs to get out of the country immediately because 'they' are out to get him. I keep warning Bram to stop. He is an Afrikaner and the government see him as a traitor to the *volk*. Please persuade him to stop." I nodded helplessly. Then Paul pulled out some papers and said, "This was in a tissue box in Bram's car. You can give it to Bram if you like, but I think it would be safer if you burnt them."

I suppose Paul gave these documents to me because he had an exaggerated impression of how closely I was connected to Bram. I studied them when I got back to my rooms. They were maps which seemed to be marked up with sabotage targets. I tore the maps into small pieces and flushed them down the toilet.

Bram never forgave himself for Molly's death. He constantly berated himself, he began to drink excessively, and grew reckless in his behaviour. Molly's death left a monumental void in the Fischer family and Bram's life would spiral, dangerously out of control.

The week after Molly's funeral Bram flew to Cape Town so that he could consult with those convicted in the Rivonia trial. Bram thought that a couple of them had a good chance of getting reduced sentences, but they all refused an appeal. None of them expected to be in jail for very long because they thought that the Nationalist Party would not stay in power for much longer. Bram thought that ten years was about the longest time they could possibly serve. He was so wrong.

Paul did not return to school for the remainder of the Easter term and at the end of June we broke-up for the winter holidays. Bram wanted to get away so that the family could have a quiet period of grieving together. Bram borrowed Ivan Schermbrucker's car and set off on a trip via the Garden Route to Cape Town with Ruth, Ilse, Paul, and Ilse's boyfriend, Sholto Cross. As the leading defence counsel during the Rivonia trial Bram had in a sense been immune from prosecution, but in the trials' aftermath the police had Bram in their sights. Bram and his family were under close surveillance. The police stopped Bram as he drove through the town of George. They wanted to search the car but Bram said it would be better if he followed them to the police station. On the way there he gave a wad of documents to Ruth and Ilse who promptly stuffed them into their underwear. The police searched the car and found a document on how to make a bomb but they could not prove that it belonged to Bram. It is possible that the police only wanted to scare Bram but it was clear that the net was closing.

Bram and his family arrived back in Johannesburg on 8 July 1964. Bram knew that he faced imminent arrest and that night he started destroying incriminating documents. At 5.00 am the next morning there was loud knocking on the door. Paul went to investigate and was bowled over by Special Branch detectives who made a bee line for Bram's bedroom. They ordered him to dress and advised that they were arresting him under the Ninety-day detention law. The police held Bram for three days, barely interrogated him, and then released him. Bram was a hugely respected barrister and was now well-known internationally. Bram may have been released because of his almost celebrity status but it could also have been because the police wanted to give the impression that Bram had done a deal and was co-operating with them.

The Rivonia trial had done little to abate the sabotage bombings around the country. The police now unleashed a new wave of arrests. They rounded up communists and saboteurs with ruthless efficiency. The new High Command of Umkhonto we Sizwe was shattered when Wilton Mkwayi, Dave Kitson, John Matthews, Mac Maharaj, and Laloo Chila were arrested. The Armed Resistance Movement (ARM) was destroyed when police swooped upon its members in early July 1964. Its leader, Adrian Leftwich, was detained and the police found a mass of documentation at his home detailing ARM activities. Leftwich cracked in detention and turned state witness. He helped the police with details about the whereabouts of ARM members and the police rapidly rounded them up.

I went to see Bram as soon as I heard that he had been released from Ninety-day detention. Bram was defiant and I begged him to think about his family. Bram was clearly piqued when I hinted that his family should take precedence. Bram stated quite calmly that he had a duty to fight the oppressive government without fear of consequences. Ilse was very upset because her boyfriend, Sholto Cross, had also been detained under the Ninety-day law and was still in prison. Ruth and Paul were calm, but a little rattled. They were all grateful though for having Pat Davidson with them in the house. Pat was the same age as Ruth and was the daughter of one of Molly's close friends. Pat had studied law in Cape Town and hoped to become a public prosecutor in Johannesburg. Her mother encouraged her to contact Molly. Pat soon gave up any notions of working for the state and instead worked with Liz Lewin in providing legal assistance to political detainees. Pat took over a bedroom at Beaumont Street and was a tower of strength in assisting with the domestic chores of running the household. The police arrested more and more ARM members and Ilse was soon distressed to hear that her Cape Town friend, Stephanie Kemp, had been arrested. Pat Davidson then told me that Liz Lewin's estranged husband, Hugh, had also been arrested.

On 25 July 1964 I woke up to read that a member of ARM had planted a bomb in the Johannesburg railway station. It had gone off during the evening commuter rush hour, killed one person and seriously injured almost two dozen others. I was very upset to read these reports. Apartheid was wickedly wrong, but saboteurs had no right to kill innocent bystanders. The police tortured the ARM members they had in custody, including Hugh Lewin, and quickly discovered that John Harris was the perpetrator. Harris was arrested, beaten-up, tried, and hung five months later. Police torture and beatings were not entirely hidden from the public. In September 1964 there was a huge outcry over the death of Babla Saloojee. He had been arrested on suspicion of assisting banned persons escape the country. The police threw him out a seventh-floor window of the Special Branch headquarters. At the inquest the magistrate exonerated the Special Branch police and described the cause of death as unknown.

Rusty Bernstein was on bail awaiting trial under the Suppression of Communism Act. His wife, Hilda, an active communist, feared arrest and had gone into hiding. When the police raided the Bernstcin's house in the Johannesburg suburb of Observatory, Hilda slipped out a basement window and hid at a friend's house. The police returned again and again looking for her. Hilda and Rusty had four children. The eldest, Toni, had left school and was married. The other three Patrick, Frances and Keith were still at school. The Bernstein's feared that they would both be imprisoned and were very worried about what would happen to their children. They decided to get out of the country but this was no longer easy to do. The police had arrested many of the escape accomplices and Rusty had to report to the Marshall Square police station every day. Rusty however, eventually found a man that would drive Hilda and himself to the Bechuanaland border. One night in early August 1964 Rusty and Hilda said goodbye to their children and set off. Toni was going to look after her brothers and sisters until they could be re-united with their parents. Rusty and Hilda had to walk through the bush until they found the border fence. They made their way to the border town of Lobatse. From there they planned to catch a train to Palapye, about three-hundred kilometres north, where the ANC had arranged for a small aeroplane to pick them up. At the last moment they were warned not to get on the train because South African Special Branch agents were planning to kidnap them. Instead, they hitched a ride to Palapye on a truck and made good their escape.

On 23 September 1964 Bram was arrested and charged under the Suppression of Communism Act. Eleven other people were charged with the same offence: Eli Weinberg, Jean Middleton, Ann Nicholson, Paul Trewhela, Florence Duncan, Norman Levy, Esther Barsel, Hymie Barsel, Sylvia Neame, Costa Gazides, and Pixie Benjamin. They were all white and members of the SACP. Bram immediately applied for bail because he needed to attend a hearing at the Privy Council in London on behalf of a client. The prosecutor opposed bail, arguing that Bram was a flight risk. Bram outlined his family history, his membership of the Johannesburg Bar Council, his commitment to South Africa, and belief in his innocence. Bram was granted bail and given a passport. On the day that Bram was arguing his bail application two brothers were brought before a Regional Court on charges under the Suppression of Communism Act. They had to apply for a postponement because of the absence of their defence counsel, who was none other than Bram Fischer!

I can only speculate as to why the government allowed Bram to travel overseas. It could be that the government respected Bram's professional need to represent his client at the Privy Council and that they believed Bram's promise to return and face trial. It is also possible that they wanted Bram to remain in exile. He came from an esteemed Afrikaner family and it may have been preferable to avoid the publicity associated with prosecuting him.

If he fled, the government could label him a coward and avoid the embarrassment of imprisoning a prominent Afrikaner and an internationally respected barrister.

Ruth had already returned to London with her husband Anthony and was able to meet Bram when he arrived. Bram's presence in London did not go unnoticed and he was soon featured in various newspapers. The *Observer* published a photograph of a stern-looking Bram sitting on a park bench. Bram met with Lord Caradon, the British ambassador to the United Nations, and his brother Michael Foot, who would later become the leader of the Labour Party. Bram spent some time meticulously preparing his Privy Council case and won. He was now faced with returning to South Africa. Ruth and Anthony did their very best to persuade Bram to remain in London. Bram listened attentively but wanted to consult with his SACP comrades. Bram met with Joe Slovo, Yusuf Dadoo, Michael Harmel, Rusty Bernstein, and others. His comrades urged him to remain in London. Bram argued that he was honour bound to return because he had given his word to the court. He also believed that the country needed political activists to remain in the country and it was demoralising for those remaining in South Africa to see so many of their comrades flee. He dismissed the futility of going to jail and said he would go underground if his trial looked hopeless. He argued that he could do more for the cause of fighting apartheid from underground within South Africa than anything he could achieve outside the country. He wanted the oppressed to see that communists were on their side and prepared to make personal sacrifices. Bram had this optimistic belief that the demise of the apartheid was imminent. He was convinced that the Nationalist Party would soon fall and that a new dawn was just around the corner.

In late 1964 Hugh Lewin, Baruch Hirson, Raymond Eisenstein, and Fred Pager were charged with sabotage. The evidence against them was overwhelming. Adrian Leftwich had been the best man at Hugh and Liz's wedding but he testified against Hugh and provided very damaging evidence. Hugh was just twenty-four years old: his father had died, his mother had gone back to England, and his wife Liz was in the process of divorcing him. I could not condone his acts of sabotage but he was so young. I attended his trial and hoped that the judge could find it in his heart to show leniency. Hugh made a statement from the dock. He told the court that he was the son of an Anglican priest, that he had boarded at St. John's College, and gone to Rhodes University with the intention of moving on to theological college in England. He stated that he had been brought up to believe that all people were equal in the eyes of God. When, as a schoolboy, he had gone with Father Trevor Huddlestone to Sophiatown he saw the unjustness of the laws governing black lives. He began to believe that those who accepted the situation were as guilty as those that governed and he felt a powerful need to change the situation. He stated that he wanted to focus attention on unjust laws. He was invited to join the ARM and undertake sabotage activities. He was instinctively opposed to all forms of violence but he decided to join because he thought sabotage acts might shock whites into an awareness of the oppressive laws. He believed that the ARM would only select targets that did not endanger human life. Hugh politely thanked the judge for listening to him. Hugh Lewin and Raymond Eisenstein were sentenced to seven years in jail, while Baruch Hirson was given a nine-year sentence. Pager was found not guilty.

At the same time five other ARM activists were tried in Cape Town. Stephanie Kemp, Eddie Daniels, Guy (Spike) de Keller, Tony Trew, and Alan Brooks. The trials were separated with Daniels, a Cape Coloured, and De Keller charged with sabotage, while Kemp, Trew, and Brooks were charged with the less serious offence of belonging to an illegal organisation under the

Suppression of Communism Act. The Judge President of the Cape, Justice Andries Beyer sentenced Daniels to fifteen years jail on Robben Island. De Keller was given a two-year sentence. In their separate trial the others all received sentences of between one and two years. The traitorous Adrian Leftwich was the star witness for the state in all these trials.

The sabotage trial of Wilton Mkwayi, Dave Kitson, John Matthews, Mac Maharaj, and Laloo Chila achieved far greater publicity and was soon called the Little Rivonia trial. After Mandela and Sisulu were arrested Wilton Mkwati was entrusted with reconstituting the Umkhonto we Sizwe high command. Joe Slovo was still on the high command but he was now in exile. Mkwayi recruited Dave Kitson, Laloo Chila, and Lionel Gay to form the high command. Matthews and Maharaj were active members of Umkhonto we Sizwe. Their trial commenced on 18 November 1964. I attended with Ilse Fischer on that first day. There were about forty Special Branch police officers packed into one side of the court. The public gallery was divided with blacks on one side and whites on the other. The prosecutor immediately rose to ask for the case to be remanded. At this juncture Mac Maharaj shouted out loudly that he wanted the court's protection because he had been tortured. He looked at the Special Branch policeman and said that his torturers were present in the courtroom. The judge, Justice Wes Boshoff, pounded his gavel, ordered that the police investigate, and promptly adjourned the court. George Bizos and Joel Joffe were the main defence lawyers and they soon realised that convictions were inevitable. Once again, their major concern was to avoid death sentences. Lionel Gay decided to give evidence for the state in a deal for immunity. Piet Beyleveld, who was a member of the Central Committee of the Communist Party, also decided to betray his comrades and become a state witness. The defendants declined to go into the witness box and said that they preferred to give statements from the dock. George Bizos briefed Bram on their intentions. Bram reacted negatively and quickly penned a note for Bizos to give his clients. It read as follows: "This is not the time for heroics. It is important for the movement that you be quiet; less fanfare, no drama. Try to minimise your sentences. Your job is to survive and get out of prison as quickly as you can. It's going to be a long struggle, and you'll be needed in the fight. It's enough for you to say you're a part of the struggle. Our leaders in the Rivonia Trial have made the political statement, you don't have to repeat it."[33] The judge, Justice Wes Boshoff, had been a pro-Nazi sympathiser and ardent supporter of apartheid. He found all the accused guilty, and in his judgment, he took pains to refer to Bram Fischer in the most damning way possible, even though Bram was not one of the accused. Wilton Mkwayi was sentenced to life in prison, Dave Kitson was sentenced to twenty years, and the others were given twelve-year sentences.

In early December St. John's College had its speech day. After the speeches and prize presentations, the parents and schoolboy were invited to have tea in the David quadrangle. The headmaster and staff, appropriately decked out in academic gowns, circled amongst the parents and their offspring. I noticed Paul Fischer walking through the David quadrangle and made a beeline to intercept him.

"Paul how are you?" I exclaimed.

"Very good, Sir," he replied.

"This is it. Last day of school," I remarked.

"Yes, it is kind of sad to be leaving" Paul replied.

Paul had hardly attended school at all since his mother's tragic death. He had only appeared at school on the days he had to sit examinations.

"How did you find the matriculation exams?" I asked.

"Not too bad I suppose. I do not have high expectations."

"To the contrary, Paul. You are a very good student and I am sure that you will have done very well." Then I added as quietly as I could, "I do understand how difficult it must have been to study after your Mum's death. Your Dad's trial must also be difficult for you."

Paul nodded but said with a shrug, "I am fine. In a funny way the house has been so quiet these last few months. I was able to pretty much study without disturbance. Don't worry, I was never alone. Pat was always at home with me."

I continued, "How are Ruth and Ilse?"

"I think Ruth and Anthony are pleased to be in London. Pa stayed with them and said they seemed happy. Pa wants me to go to Oxford and he has been running around trying to get me a place there."

"What course"

"Probably PPE. You know Politics, Philosophy and Economics. I think it might be better though to go to Oxford after doing an undergraduate degree at Cape Town."

"I am sure that you will do well. I would go to Oxford if you get the chance," I said encouragingly.

"I shall see what happens. As you know, I am a bad student."

"Quite the reverse, I retorted.

"What about Ilse?"

"She is still upset with Sholto being in jail. She went to Cape Town but she is back again now."

"Yes'" I said, "I hope she is okay."

"She is strong. I shall spend Christmas with Pa and Ilse at home and then I am going to London to stay with Ruth and Anthony."

"How long?" I asked.

"Probably for the whole year. I shall either go to Oxford in September or come back to study at Cape Town." He paused, fiddled with his glasses, and continued, "I am worried about Pa going to jail though."

I tried to be reassuring and said, "Your father is so respected. He will be fine." I had a heavy heart as I said these words because I knew that the evidence was stacking up badly against Bram.

Paul shook his head and said, "I think Pa is in big trouble. The police have always been pestering him. They are going to put him in jail because he is a commie."

"Fischer, your Pa is an honourable man. He has done nothing wrong."

"They just want to put all commies in jail."

"Fischer. listen to me. He is a man of principle. A highly respected advocate. They can't touch him."

Paul held my eyes with his piercing blue eyes and said, "Thank you, Sir. Thank you for everything. I need to go now."

I shook his hand and said, "I will keep in touch."

I watched Paul as he walked out of the quadrangle and out of the school. He cut a solitary figure amidst the melee of parents and schoolboys. I had a lump in my throat. This young man had endured such trauma. He had lost his mother, his father faced a prison sentence, and he had to monitor his own poor health with daily insulin injections and regular eye specialist appointments. I feared that the tragedy and stresses of the last six months would reflect in poor examination results. These fears were ungrounded and Paul achieved a first-class matriculation. I still marvel at how he managed to acquit himself so well. Paul was an impressive young man, but no-one his age should have to endure so much.

In late November 1964 Bram Fischer and twelve others were tried on charges of being members of the Communist Party, participating in activities of the Communist Party, and furthering the aims of the Communist Party. Ivan Schermbrucker and Lewis Baker were added to those arrested in September, but the charges against Pixie Benjamin were dropped. The charges were relatively mild and the maximum sentence for a guilty finding on each charge was three years in prison. Bram and Hymie Barsel were the only two of the accused out on bail. Piet Beyleveld and Gerard Ludi were two glaring omissions from the accused. Both had been in the group of SACP members that met secretly in Jean Middleton's Hillbrow flat. The reason they were not charged was because they were appearing as witnesses for the state.

Piet Beyleveld was a trade union official. He was the President of the Congress of Democrats and the President of the South African Congress of Trade Unions. He was attracted to socialism and joined the Communist Party. Beyleveld was arrested under the Ninety-day detention law immediately after the Rivonia trial. He was kept in solitary confinement and subjected to brutal interrogation. He cracked and agreed to give evidence for the state. He gave evidence in the Little Rivonia trial and was called again to give evidence in the Fischer trial. Bram was aware that Beyleveld was intending to testify and sent messages, via his wife, begging him not to do so. Beyleveld was clearly motivated to save his own skin. His testimony was not excessively damning but he would forever be held in contempt by his former communist comrades.

The next witness was Gerard Ludi and he stunned everyone with his evidence. Ludi was introduced to the court as Security Branch police officer agent Q-018. He immediately boasted of successfully penetrating the SACP. It was an enormous shock to all the accused. Ludi was born in Johannesburg in 1938 to a German father, a Nazi sympathiser, and a Czech mother. When Ludi went to the University of the Witswatersrand he was recruited as an undercover Security Branch police agent. Ludi joined the Congress of Democrats and through this he met Toni Bernstein. Ludi pursued Toni and they started dating. Ann Henderson proposed Ludi for membership of the SACP. Ludi had become friendly with Rusty and Hilda Bernstein and this connection was probably the main reason why no-one did a careful membership background check. In March 1962 Ludi was arrested together with other political activists for putting up posters encouraging people to overthrow the government. Ludi's arrest was partially a police set-up for the purpose of enhancing his credibility within the SACP. He was charged with eleven others under the Suppression of Communism Act and with furthering the aims of the ANC. Ludi and three others were acquitted, and the rest were given short prison sentences. In July 1962 the World Peace Conference took place in Moscow. The passports of most South African communists had been confiscated, but Gerard Ludi and Toni Bernstein went to the conference since they both had passports. Logically Ludi's passport should have been cancelled after his arrest. His acquittal and fact that he still had his passport should have raised his communist comrades' suspicions. Toni Bernstein's passport was confiscated three days after her return. Toni found that travelling with Ludi was an unpleasant experience and their romance ended. Ludi however, had successfully used her to infiltrate the SACP. Piet Trewhela was a member of the same communist cell as Bram, Jean Middleton, Florence Duncan, Costa Gazides, Piet Beyleveld, and Gerard Ludi. During his police interrogation Trewhela became convinced that Ludi was the only person that could have provided so much information about their cell. He managed to send a message to Bram from prison warning him about Ludi but it was all too late. Bram asked Toni Bernstein to attend court and stare at Ludi to unnerve him. Ludi did not look at Toni while he presented his damning evidence.

I was now Hill House housemaster and Craig Williamson was one of the boys in my house. I worried about him because he was a chubby fifteen-year-old that struggled to fit in with his peer group. His classmates called him Bunter after the comic book character Billy Bunter. Williamson's father, Herbert, was a dour Scotsman that had little sympathy for his son's unhappiness. Herbert had spent three years in a Japanese prisoner of war camp and was not interested in his son's complaints about boarding school hardships. Craig Williamson went to the University of the Witswatersrand and became a Special Branch agent. He infiltrated left-wing politics through getting elected to the Student Representative Council and the National Union of South African Students (NUSAS). After university Williamson assisted in spiriting activists out of the country and managed to infiltrate the ANC in Europe. He later boasted of recruiting an entire Umkhonto we Sizwe cell of saboteurs comprised entirely of Special Branch policemen. In 1980 he was exposed when the London *Guardian* newspaper ran a headline story on the apartheid spy. Williamson promptly returned to South Africa where the government openly praised his undercover work. Unlike Ludi, Williamson did not retreat into obscurity, but continued to work for the Special Branch.

CHAPTER 13

The Security Branch

Bram started planning to go underground after listening to the evidence of Beyleveld and Ludi. He conferred with Violet Weinberg who strongly opposed the idea. She pointed out, almost certainly correctly, that he only faced a short jail term under the present charges. If he went underground and was captured it was likely that he could face far worse charges and a much longer prison sentence. But Bram obtained the agreement of other SACP members to going underground and he began to draw up plans. He identified safe houses, obtained advice from theatre make-up artists on how to disguise himself, and designed methods of communicating with his London comrades through coded messages. During January 1965 he collaborated with Mary Benson, an anti-apartheid activist and author, on an article in the London *Observer*. In this article Bram stated that the Nationalist government could not maintain white supremacy in the face of an increasingly violent and chaotic struggle. He argued that the struggle for freedom could not be smothered and that it was in the whites' interests to extend rights to everyone and to negotiate with the leaders in exile and in prison on Robben Island.

Bram did not appear in court on the morning of 25 January 1965. Instead, Harold Hanson, his defence counsel handed the court a letter from Bram. In this letter Bram explained his reasons for going missing. He emphasised that he was not skipping the country but he was going underground to oppose the monstrous policy of apartheid. He stated that there was an urgency because so many opponents of the government were in jail and the cruel discriminatory apartheid laws were causing bitterness and hatred to multiply each year. He wrote that unless this whole intolerable system was changed radically and rapidly, disaster would follow. Appalling bloodshed and civil war would become inevitable because oppression would be fought with increasing hatred. As an Afrikaner he saw it as his supreme duty to fight apartheid, because it was largely representatives of his fellow Afrikaners that were responsible for these discriminatory laws. He accepted that his punishment could be increased by taking this action, but he meant no disrespect to the court, and hoped that his conduct would encourage some people to think about, to understand, and to abandon the policies they now so blindly followed. His letter concluded with these words: "Finally, I would like to urge upon the court to bear in mind that if it does have to punish any of my fellow accused, it will be punishing them for holding the ideas today that will be universally accepted tomorrow."[34]

The next day Bram's disappearance was in all the newspapers. Ilse was not answering the telephone and so I went to Beamont Street after school. There was an unmarked police car parked opposite the house, no doubt monitoring who was coming and going. Ilse and Pat Davidson greeted me but they put their fingers to their lips motioning me not to talk. I followed them out into the garden and blurted out, "I read about Bram's disappearance. I am worried about you. Is there anything I can do to help?"

Pat replied, "We need to talk, quietly, out here in the middle of the garden away from listening devices. I am sure that the police have bugged the house."

"I understand. What has happened to Bram?"

"We don't know'" said Pat.

"Seriously," I responded.

Ilse then intervened and said to Pat, "It is okay we can confide in Henry. Pa has gone underground. He hid in the back of my car last Friday evening. Pat and I drove around until we were sure that no-one was tailing us. Then we dropped him off in Killarney. Pa was picked up there and has been taken to a safe house."

"Do you know where?"

"We really do not know," said Ilse.

Pat continued, "We spent the whole weekend pretending Bram was at home. We pretended to have conversations with him and even pretended to be having dinner and lunch together. All for the benefit of the listening bugs."

Ilse chuckled and said, "We told the police and media that he simply disappeared on Sunday night. The police have already raided us. I was sure that we were going to be arrested but obviously not."

Pat interrupted, "I am sure that we have not been arrested because the police think that Bram will contact us soon. The police have found two letters from Bram telling Ilse about his plan to go underground."

"Yes," said Ilse, "Pa wrote the letters fully appreciating that the police would find them. I think these letters have helped in convincing the police that we knew nothing about his disappearance."

I assured Ilse and Pat that they should not hesitate to contact me if I could be of any help. Ilse was only twenty-one and Pat was barely much older. These very young women were caught up in a highly stressful situation. Yet they were calm and stoic. They fortunately really did not know Bram's whereabouts and so, even if they had been arrested, they could not have disclosed Bram's hiding place.

In April 1965 Bram's co-accused were convicted. Eli Weinberg and Ivan Schermbrucker were given five-year sentences and all the others received sentences from between one and three years. It seems likely that Bram would have received a sentence of no more than five years, but now that he had gone underground, it was highly probable that he would face a far greater sentence if captured. I could never fully comprehend why Bram took the dramatic step of going underground. So much had happened in little more than half a year and it is possible that Bram simply lost perspective. He had led the defence in the Rivonia trial, Molly had died in a tragic accident, he had been detained under the Ninety-day detention law, he had been arrested and charged under the Suppression of Communism Act, he had travelled to London, and he had listened to former comrades give evidence against him. Many of his comrades had been arrested and instead of fearing the government, Bram was naively convinced that the government's end was nigh. He went underground in the mistaken belief that he could successfully prosecute their downfall.

John Vorster, the Minister of Justice, immediately asked the legal profession to act against Bram. Two days after Bram went into hiding the Bar Council applied to the court to have Bram's name struck from the roll. Bram wrote to the Bar Council to defend himself. The application only came before the Supreme Court months later and Sydney Kentridge and Arthur Chaskalson appeared on Bram's behalf. Quintus De Wet (the Rivonia trial judge) presided and ruled that Bram was guilty of dishonourable and deplorable conduct and struck his name from the roll. It was a decision that greatly upset Bram because he was not an unscrupulous lawyer and had only ever acted in the best interests of his clients.

The rugby season started after Easter and I was appointed coach of the Under 14 C team. The younger teams' matches were all completed in time for the entire school to attend the 1st XV game at 3.00 pm. One Saturday we were playing against King Edward VII School. This was a government school (set up by Lord Milner) situated less than a kilometre away from St. John's College. King Edward's boasted powerful sporting teams and any contest against them was usually tough work. The St. John's loose forward, Ray Dearlove, was injured during the match. Our legendary coach, Maxie Burger, rushed on to the field and exclaimed. "Dearlove are you okay." The King Edward's players collapsed with mirth at hearing this supposed expression of endearment. Ray Dearlove had to suffer ignominious taunts for the rest of the game!

The match was played on the A rugby field. Parents and visitors sat on the amphitheatre stone steps, schoolboys watched from the opposite touch line, and many of the teachers liked to sit on the Big Walk benches with a view from on high over the entire spectacle. I was sitting on a bench with a colleague when a small man approached and asked if he might join us. He put out his hand and introduced himself as Donald Black.

"Henry Allum," and turning to my colleague I said, "and this is Michael Marais."

"How do you do," the gentleman replied. "I hope you do not mind me joining you."

"You are very welcome," I said. "Are you a parent?"

'No, no. I have daughters, I just like to watch a good game of rugby."

We continued with small chatter about the game until half time. Michael stood up and excused himself. Then this small man with a goatee beard, bald forehead, brown sideburns, rimless glasses, and a walking stick whispered quietly, "Henry, it is me."

I was totally taken aback. I looked deep into his eyes and knew that it was Bram. "My God," I exclaimed, "I cannot believe this. It is you. It really is."

"Shush," he said, "Come let's go for a walk."

We stood up and walked towards the Preparatory school. I wanted to hug him. I really did, but I dared not.

"Bram, are you okay? Where are you staying?"

"Donald," he said firmly, "Donald Black."

Then Bram began to fill me in. He avoided specific details because he thought it was safer for me not to know, He was living in a house not far from his home and claimed to be a master of disguise. I could only agree because he had sat next to me and I had not recognised him. Bram had even altered the tone of his voice and the nature of his gait. In this he was coached and assisted by professional make-up artists. He had a car and driver's licence in the name of Donald Black. He described himself as the ghost in the city in which he once lived. Bram met regularly with Violet Weinberg, Lesley Schermbrucker, Mary Benson, and Ralph and Minnie Sepel. He also admitted to seeing Pat Davidson, He proudly told me that he had approached Pat at the Old Johannian Club where she had been playing squash. Like me, Pat had failed to recognise him until he revealed his identity. His contacts only called him from public telephone boxes to prevent police finding out his whereabouts through bugging telephones. Bram admitted to seeing Ilse but claimed that he had sought to protect her by not telling her where he lived. Intermediaries would advise Ilse of a meeting point. Ilse would then hop on the back of Sholto Cross' motorbike and after ensuring that they had lost any potential police tail they would meet Bram at the designated rendezvous place. Bram mentioned that he had written to Beyers Naude encouraging him in his opposition to apartheid. Beyers Naude was a moderator in the Dutch Reformed Church but he had steadfastly refused to endorse the policies of apartheid. He resigned from his church position and established the Christian Institute of Southern Africa with the aim of promoting racial harmony in South Africa. Beyers

Naude was also seen as an Afrikaner traitor and he was ostracised and harassed. The government eventually banned Naude and closed his Christian Institute.

Ilse and Pat had moved out of the Beaumont Street house. Pat knew that she had to cut her ties with Ilse if she wanted to continue seeing Bram. Ilse moved into a small flat in the nearby suburb of Bellevue. Bram wrote Ilse frequent letters in the full knowledge that Security Branch police would intercept them. The police would have been suspicious if Bram had not written and it helped in giving the impression that Ilse had no contact with Bram. Ralph and Minnie Sepel, despite being SACP members, were largely unknown to the police. They had arranged Bram's safe house but grew angry over the visits of Violet, Lesley, and Pat. They correctly claimed that these people were all under police suspicion and they could be followed. Bram did not like the solitude of living alone and he wanted company. It was this lax security that would inevitably lead to his capture. Bram wrote letters in code to his comrades in London and was frustrated by their slow responses and lack of action. He wanted communist leaders to return to South Africa and assist in efforts to overturn the government. He even asked his daughter, Ruth, to contact his comrades to determine why they were so unresponsive. Ruth found that they were distracted, on holidays, lethargic, and lacking in any sense of urgency.

The newspapers dubbed Bram the Red Pimpernel and there were regular stories about supposed sightings, both within South Africa and in places like Bechuanaland, Zambia, and Rhodesia. The police offered a reward for his capture and this contributed to some false arrests. There was a sighting of Bram in the suburb of Greenside and so the police raided a certain house. It was rather amusing when the press discovered that this was the home of Barney Yutar, the brother of Percy Yutar, the Rivonia trial prosecutor.

The public fear of saboteurs was heightened when Marius Schoon, Raymond Thoms, and Mike Ngubeni were tried for attempting to bomb the Hillbrow police station. A security policeman had infiltrated their group, given them a bomb, and encouraged them to hatch a plot to blow up a police station. The publicity assisted in making whites sympathetic towards tougher security laws. The accused were all sentenced to twelve years in prison. As whites, Schoon and Thoms were jailed in Pretoria Local, but Ngubeni, being black, was sent to Robben Island. In September 1965 Michael Dingake, a senior member of Umkhonto we Sizwe, was arrested. The security police tracked Dingake down in Rhodesia and arrested him in Bulawayo. He was illegally deported to South Africa, tortured, and sentenced to fifteen years in prison on Robben Island. Issy Heymann had a close relationship with Dingake and the police also arrested him. Heymann' wife, Anne, protested loudly and asked George Bizos to obtain a court order securing his release. The application was successful but Heymann was not released because the government had hurriedly promulgated a new law giving the police greater powers, which included extending the Ninety-day detention law to One hundred-and-eighty days. The police simply continued to detain Heymann under the new One-hundred-and-eighty-day detention law. Heymann had previously been detained in December 1964 with the aim of forcing him to give evidence in the Fischer trial. Heymann steadfastly refused and was released. This time he was tortured and even tried to commit suicide in jail. When Anne Heymann came to visit Issy, he told her to warn Violet Weinberg that she was at great risk of being arrested. During his brutal interrogation Issy had been unable to give the Security Branch police any information about Bram's whereabouts because he truly did not know. He had broken down under torture and disclosed that Violet Weinberg was especially close to Bram. Minnie and Ralph Sepel were concerned after Anne Heymann relayed Issy's warning. They implored Violet to go into hiding or leave the country, but she chose to ignore their warnings.

I had one further meeting with Bram. He called me from a public telephone box in late October and asked if I wanted to join him at Germiston Lake for a Sunday afternoon picnic. I attended the school Sunday morning mass before asking the school kitchen manager to provide me with a packed lunch. He suspected that I had a secret date and prepared a generous lunch, which was certainly large enough for two. It was quite unnecessary because Pat Davidson was there with Bram and she had already laid out a handsome spread of food. Bram had lost a lot of weight, he looked tired, and fiddled with his pipe incessantly. He was pleased to see me and it was clear that he wanted me to do the talking while he quietly smoked and listened. I was amazed to learn that he and Pat had recently spent an entire week in the Kruger National Park. Pat was the same age as his daughter, Ruth, but they had formed a close relationship. He was curt with me just once when I used his name. "Donald," he firmly reminded me. We spent most of the afternoon speaking about cricket and rugby. South Arica had just completed a three-test cricket tour of England. South Africa won the second test, and drew the other two. I was enthralled by the exploits of the talented young side. Graeme Pollock, just nineteen years old, had scored a century in the second test, and his elder brother Peter had taken five wickets. Bram reminded me that the tour had been tainted with anti-apartheid protests. He was also pleased to point out that the Springbok rugby tour to Australia and New Zealand had attracted anti-apartheid protests, and that South Africa had their invitation to the 1964 summer Olympics withdrawn. In the next two decades sporting boycotts would increase and South Africa would be barred from virtually all international sporting events, but this did very little to deter the government from its relentless pursuit of apartheid policies.

My relaxed day with Bram and Pat was followed by the most daunting week of my life. It was the first Friday of the month, 5 November 1965, when I was woken with a loud banging on my study door. I assumed that there was a problem in the boarding house and hastily donned some clothes before opening the door. I was confronted by two Security Branch policeman. They barged into my room. One of the house prefects heard the commotion and came to investigate, but the policeman simply slammed the door.

"What on earth do you think you are doing? I demand an explanation."

"You are under arrest. One-hundred-and-eighty-day detention. Sit there."

"What?" I exploded with rage. "What nonsense is this? What on earth are you talking about?"

Lieutenant Viktor roughly shoved me back into the chair. "Quiet. Sit."

I jumped up and Lieutenant Viktor placed his hands on each of my shoulders and forced me down into the chair. "This is your last warning. Sit still."

His accomplice, Lieutenant van der Merwe, started rifling through the papers on my desk, stacking documents into a brown bag.

"That is schoolwork," I said, "nothing but schoolwork."

Viktor glared at me and said threateningly, "Still." Viktor then marched into my bedroom and I could see him opening cupboard doors and emptying out the contents of my bedside table.

Then Deane Yeates rapped on the door and burst into the room. Deane needed no introduction. He had a presence and air of authority. Viktor pulled a document out of his pocket and told Deane that he could inspect the search warrant. Deane did so with an astonished frown.

"What is this all about?" he said as he waved the warrant.

"Mr Allum is under arrest," he replied with a smug smile. "Now" he said turning to me, "Go pack a bag with some spare clothes and a washbag. No books. Do you understand, no books." He followed me into my bedroom as I grabbed a sports bag and quickly shoved in some toiletries, clean clothing, a pen, and a notepad.

"Come. Come. Let's go."

Viktor grabbed me by the arm and frogmarched me out of my rooms, down the Hill House steps, across the Pelican and David quadrangles and into an unmarked police car. By this time a dozen or more boys had gathered to watch the spectacle. Deane walked beside me the entire way. He warned Viktor and Van der Merwe that he would be briefing lawyers and that they would be held accountable. They ignored his protests and hurried me along. I was in a state of bewildered confusion.

I was put in the back seat, Van der Merwe drove, and Viktor sat beside him. He immediately turned to me and said with a sneer, "We know everything about you. You are going to sing like a canary."

"I want a lawyer."

Viktor chuckled and said, "You are going to sing beautifully. You commies all sing. You just cry like little babies."

"I am not a communist."

"Oh yes. Sure. All you commies say that."

"I demand a lawyer."

Viktor and Van der Merwe both began to laugh.

"You don't need a lawyer. You just need bird seed. You will sing like a canary and then we will crush you." Viktor held up his right arm and closed his hands into a fist before slapping it into the open palm of his left hand. I was confident that Deane Yeates would summon a lawyer but this conviction did little to squash my rising fear and anxiety.

The car stopped outside the Grays, the headquarters of the Security Branch. I was marched up two flights of stairs and into an office. There I was confronted by the notorious Captain Theunis Swanepoel, the chief interrogator of the Security Branch. He was a large man with a neck that seemed to merge with his shoulders. He had a ruddy complexion and a fixed scowl. He barely looked up as he took a sip of coffee and turned over the pages in a file on his desk. I was not offered a chair and I merely stood in the middle of the room. Viktor and Van der Merwe drew up chairs and slouched into them

"When did you join the Communist Party?" Swanepoel barked.

"I am not a communist. I demand a lawyer."

"Lawyer. You want a lawyer. You know where your lawyer is and you better tell us."

"My headmaster, Mr Deane Yates is arranging for a lawyer. In any event..."

Swanepoel cut me off and shouted, "Fischer is the only lawyer you are going to see. Where is he?"

"I have not the faintest idea."

"Listen you commie, we are going to make you talk. You all talk. Save me the trouble of making you talk. Where is Fischer?"

"I am not a communist and I don't know where he is "

We then went around in circles as Swanepoel persistently accused me of being a communist and repeatedly asked me about Bram's whereabouts. Swanepoel consulted his notes and astounded me with the dates and times of my visits to the Beaumont Street house. When I told them that I had met Bram at Oxford University it led to a farcical exchange.

"Oxford. Where is that?"

"Oxford University is in Oxford."

"Which province?"

"Province. It is in England."

"Ah yes. That is the place where they teach you to be a communist."

"I read history."

"Now you teach communism, hey."

"Nonsense. I teach the school curriculum."

"Ha, you admit, you teach communism."

"The curriculum, the approved course."

"Do you want to overthrow the government?"

"I have no desire to involve myself in politics."

"That is because you are a communist revolutionary."

"Rubbish."

"Don't talk smart to me. Call me Captain."

"Captain. I have no idea as to why I am here."

"You know very well. You just tell us where to find your commie buddy and we will let you go. No perhaps we will deport you. You are a bloody Englishman. We are just going to send you back there, back to your commie friends."

Viktor interjected, "Better if we just lock him up. Throw away the keys."

"Ja," said Swanepoel nodding in agreement, "Just leave him in detention, One-hundred-and-eighty days, then another One-hundred-and-eighty-days, forever. You will never see the sun again."

I felt tired. I had nothing to eat or drink and I held out a hand to steady myself against a filing cabinet.

Swanepoel shouted, "Stand up. Stand up straight."

Viktor then leapt to his feet and drew a chalk circle around me. "Don't move out of that circle," he bellowed.

The interrogation went on endlessly. Swanepoel reminded me of all the times I had been sighted in Bram's company. How I had attended various court trials in apparent sympathy with the defendants. He even detailed how I had visited Ilse a few days after

Bram's disappearance. Swanepoel read out names, many of which were familiar, and demanded to know if any of these people had been in contact with Bram. Strangely he never bothered to ask me if I had seen Bram. I was now getting so tired and fraught that there was every possibility that I could have confirmed our meetings.

Swanepoel suddenly stood up. He shoved a piece of paper and a pen into my hands, and said, "I want the names of everyone that is hiding Fischer. Make it easy on yourself. Don't move. Stand there."

Swanepoel, Viktor, and Van der Merwe left the room. I did not dare open the door or sit down. I simply leant against the filing cabinets and trembled with fear. After what felt like an eternity the three of them re-entered the room.

"Right let's see those names."

My piece of paper was blank and this sent Swanepoel into a blind rage.

"Ilse Fischer. You are telling me that even she does not know where he is."

"I assure you that Ilse has no idea."

"How do you know that? Of course, she knows. Who else?"

"Captain. I need to sit down. I just do not know."

"Stand. Stand straight, you commie bastard. Now talk or else we use other tactics."

"A few punches will make this *rooinek* talk. Give me five minutes," hissed Van der Merwe as he moved threateningly towards me.

"Maybe," said Swanepoel, "but we are going to lock him up until he talks. Solitary. Do you understand? Nothing. You are going to sit there until you talk. You will talk otherwise you are just going to die there."

I was too tired and demoralised to answer back. Viktor and Van der Merwe pushed me out the door, down the staircase and into their car. It was a relief to walk but I was giddy with hunger and thirst. I was driven the short distance to the Marshall Square police station. Viktor shoved my sports bag into my hands and took me into the reception area. Viktor told the duty officer that I was a detainee. The duty officer handed over a form, which Viktor began to fill in.

"Date of birth?" he asked.

"Second of January, 1913."

The duty officer told me to hold out my arms and he frisked me up and down. Then he began to go through my sports bag. "No pens." he said, and he tossed my pen into a waste paper basket. "There is too much stuff here," he said with undisguised scorn. He gave me my sports bag and told me to follow him. He escorted me through a myriad of corridors, opening and shutting iron grills as we walked. He then opened a cell door and told me to go in. The door slammed behind me and I could hear the loud grating of the key in the lock. I had never been in a prison cell before and it was a surreal experience. It was clean, it had a shiny concrete floor, and was painted light brown. There was an iron bed with a thin mattress, a pillow, two grey blankets, and a covered bucket in the corner. Mercifully there was an enamel water jug and cup on a small shelf. I drank cup after cup of water. I still had my watch and noted that it was now 4.00 pm.

I sat on the edge of the bed and stared at the wall. I was alone in the cell but surrounded by noise. There was a persistent banging of doors and the shouting of warders. Marshall Square was in the middle of the city and I could clearly hear the traffic. Then my door opened and a warder shoved a tin tray in front of me that contained a couple of sausages, mashed potato, two slices of bread and a mug of coffee. I had barely finished eating when the warder returned. He picked up the tray and shouted instructions in Afrikaans.

I said as calmly as I could, "I am very sorry but I do not understand Afrikaans."

He nodded, gave me a miniature sized towel, and stated in broken English that I should bring my toilet bag with me. I followed him to a small room that had a shower, wash basin, and toilet with no seat. I had a cold shower, and washed my teeth. I was pleased to go to the toilet for the first time that day. I was returned to my cell and locked in for the night. A dull light burned constantly in my cell and I only slept fitfully. The night dragged and I kept hoping that common sense would prevail. I was not politically active and I was not a communist. I was a good friend of Bram's but there really was no reason why I should know where he was living. I had enormous faith in Deane Yates and felt sure that matters would be resolved in the morning.

My door clanged open at 5.30 am. The warder indicated that I should bring my bucket to an ablution area where I was to empty and clean it. I had not used the bucket at all. I was pleased to use the toilet. He escorted me back to my cell. At 6.30 am the door opened again and the warder presented me with a food tray. Two boiled eggs, two hard biscuits, a mug of coffee, and a fresh jug of water. Barely half an hour later the key rattled once more in my door. It was flung open and I was confronted by the warder and the Station Commander, a small man in a smart uniform. He simply said, "Any complaints?"

"Yes," I replied. "Why am I here? I want a lawyer."

The Station Commander sniffed and said, "You are here under One-hundred-and-eighty-day detention." He turned to the warder and said, "Close up."

The door slammed and I was left in splendid isolation. I walked up and down the tiny cell, which was no more than two metres square, anxiously waiting for something to happen. There was shouting and all sorts of other noises, but no-one came for me. I lay down on the bed and pondered my predicament. I imagined the horror of being locked up indefinitely, but kept convincing myself that this was all a big mistake. At 12.00 pm my door opened and I was handed a bland cheese sandwich and an apple. Two hours later I was taken out of my cell, given an opportunity to go to the toilet, and then I was shoved into an outdoor courtyard. It was no bigger than a tennis court, it was surrounded by high walls, and there was a constant gurgling from the various plumbing pipes on the walls. I could see blue sky above and tall office buildings. I was alone and walked around like a confused rat for about an hour. The inside of the door was a bright green and detainees had scratched their names on it. Some people had written their full names, others had just inscribed their initials. The names included Ruth First, James Kantor, Wolfie Kodesh, Mosie Moolla, Abdullah Jassat, Lilian Ngoyi, Joseph Molefe, Benson Tsele, Mazisi Kunene, Nkosazana Dhlamini, Arthur Goldreich, Hazel Goldreich, and Horold Wolpe.

The routine was the same each day. The warders made a cursory inspection of my cell whenever they brought or collected my food tray. They warned me to fold my blankets and keep my cell tidy. It was hardly necessary. I kept my clothes in my sports bag and there was nothing else in the cell. One morning a warder gave me a broom and told me to sweep out my cell as he stood menacingly just outside the door. The warders could not be engaged in any form of conversation. Isolation is torture. I was surrounded by noise but I was acutely aware of my solitude. I could not speak to anyone, and I had nothing to do except thumb through a Bible that I found on the cell shelf. It was the King James version and difficult to read. I looked at it for hour after hour after hour. At times I read aloud just to have the comfort of hearing my own voice.

One day, two days, three days. Time froze. I remained alone in this cell for six days and nights. I started to hallucinate, talk to myself, and I imagined being incarcerated indefinitely. After just four days I told the warder that I wanted to talk. Please could he advise the Security Branch police. Nothing happened. There was no response. I complained to the Station Commander when he visited each morning. He said my request had been noted but said nothing more. I began to grow desperate, shouted at him, and demanded to see Captain Swanepoel. The Station Commander glared at me and said that if I threatened him again, I would be placed in a punishment cell with half rations. I just wanted to speak to Captain Swanepoel. I had no idea what I wanted to say. I was prepared to admit to anything, tell him whatever he wanted, I so badly needed relief from being locked up alone.

My cell door was opened at around midday on Thursday. I expected to receive my lunch, but the warder told me to follow him. I was shown into a room and saw a large man, with bright blue eyes, neatly dressed in a suit and tie.

He greeted me with a smile and indicated that I should sit before saying, "Ah, so this is Allum. I am General van den Bergh. Do you know who I am?"

"I think you are important."

"Exactly," he said with exaggerated pride. "I am the head of the Security Branch. So, you are that English communist."

"I am not a communist."

"You were at Oxford University."

"Yes."

"You met Fischer there?"

"Bram Fischer. Yes."

"You must be a communist,"

"I am not."

"Then why are you so friendly with Fischer?"

"He is a close friend from my university days."

"Close," he exclaimed, "How close?"

"Well, a good friend."

"So why don't you tell us where he is?"

"I don't know where he is."

"Looking after communists, hey?"

"He is a friend, but I have no idea where he is now."

"You think my men cannot find him?"

I shrugged and there was an awkward silence before Van den Bergh continued, "If I ask my men to find him, they find him. We know everything. We can find anyone."

I mumbled. "I am sure you can."

"Prove to me that you are not a communist."

"I am telling you I am not a communist."

"Then why are you always meeting Fischer and his commie friends?"

"Bram Fischer was the only person I knew in South Africa when I first came to this country."

"Yes, and we can send you back to England."

"I want a lawyer."

"Lawyer! Don't get cheeky. You are a detainee. You don't get a lawyer."

"This is ridiculous."

"This is the law."

"I demand a lawyer."

Van den Bergh sniggered. He fastened his hands together and spread his palms towards me.

"Are you a Christian?" he asked.

"Yes."

"I know about communists. They are heathens. They are not Christians."

Van den Bergh stood up and retrieved a book from the shelf behind him. It was a Bible but an Afrikaans version because the word *Bybel* was inscribed in gold letters on the black cover. Then he said, "Put your right hand on the Bible and swear that you are not a member of the Communist Party."

I put my hand on the Bible and said, "I am not a member of the Communist Party."

Van Den Bergh glared at me with his cold blue eyes and said, "If I ever find you have lied to me, I will have no mercy on you."

Van den Bergh then abruptly left the room. I heard a murmuring in the corridor outside and then the warder entered the room and told me to follow him. I was not taken back to my cell, but was taken to the reception area. Another warder gave me my sports bag, pointed to the door, and said that I was free to go. I walked out the door and into a busy street. It was if I was living on a film set. The world about me seemed unreal. I had no money. I could not make a telephone call or catch a bus. So, I simply decided to walk. I made a few wrong turnings and it took me almost two hours to reach St. John's College. It was evening, the day boys had gone home, and the boarders were in Darragh hall eating dinner. I walked up to my rooms, which still bore the scars of the police search. I immediately picked up the telephone and called Deane Yates.

Deane expressed surprise and pleasure at hearing my voice. He wanted to know my whereabouts and gave a loud sigh of relief when I told him that I had been released and had walked back to school. He quickly deduced that I was hungry and in need of company. He said he would pick me up in half an hour and take me home for supper. Deane fetched me and we drove to his Rose Road home in his mini minor. His wife, Dot, welcomed us and guided me into the kitchen where she heated up a casserole. I ate while Deane asked a few questions. Then he paused and said he had some important news. I was still shovelling food into my mouth, but stopped abruptly when Deane said, "Bram Fischer was arrested today."

I dropped my knife and fork and stared at Deane with disbelief, "Are you serious?"

"Yes. Quite serious. It has been on the news. He was arrested earlier today."

Tears filled my eyes. It is with some embarrassment that I must confess to feeling a sense of relief that the police would now probably have no interest in hounding me further. Nevertheless, I felt deeply miserable to think that Bram was in the hands of those vicious Security Branch policemen.

I wanted to return to my classes the next day but Deane refused. I did attend the Friday morning assembly though. My appearance was noticed and there was a murmuring buzz. Deane took the bull by the horns and stated I had been a victim of an atrociously wrongful arrest. He took pains to assure the school that I had done nothing wrong, I had been accused of nothing, and had probably been mistakenly arrested in connection with the police's search for Bram Fischer. He thanked God for my care, and said cheerfully that the entire school body was delighted to see me back safe and sound. When quizzed by staff and boys I simply confirmed I had been Bram Fischer's university friend. Some were impressed, some were not interested, and others frowned at my association with the notorious Bram Fischer. Most sympathised with my nasty experience, but some clearly thought that I deserved the police's attention. They figured there must be fire if there is smoke.

Deane called me to a meeting later that Friday morning in his study. Herbert Entwistle, the School Council chairman was already there. Both Deane and Mr Entwistle assured me that I had their full support and that they were outraged at my treatment. They advised that the school's lawyers would be joining us to discuss any possible course of action against the police. Two lawyers from the firm of Bell, Dewar and Hall duly arrived, and I related everything that had happened to me. They kept pressing me on how I had been treated. I soon sensed that they were trying to establish whether I had been assaulted. I had to emphasise that I had been abused but never actually physically assaulted. They wanted time to deliberate but it was clear that there was no obvious legal remedy. They picked up on the threats to deport me and cautioned that this could very well occur if I attempted to press any sort of charges.

I had been treated with kid gloves. I was not a political activist, anti-apartheid campaigner, or communist. The Security Branch police had detained me because they thought I could help them find Bram. The atrocious reality was that other political detainees were not so fortunate. Hundreds upon hundreds were tortured and locked up in solitary confinement for month after month. During the next decade over forty detainees were tortured to death. The cruelty and viciousness of the Security Branch police should never be underestimated or forgiven. General Hendrik van den Bergh reigned as the Head of the Security Branch from 1963 until 1980. John Vorster, the Minister of Justice (who was later to become Prime Minister) and Van den Bergh had both been members of the *Ossewabrandwag,* the Neo-Nazi para-military organisation that conducted acts of sabotage to undermine South Africa's involvement in the Second World War. They were both detained under wartime emergency measures. Now in their roles as Minister of Justice and Head of the Security Branch (later called the Bureau of State Security) they used their powers to incarcerate, torture, and murder their political opponents. Their names should forever live in infamy.

CHAPTER 14

Life sentence

The arrest of Bram Fischer was a big story in the weekend newspapers, but the story had to compete with news of Rhodesia's Unilateral Declaration of Independence (UDI). On 11 November 1965, the same day that Bram was arrested, the Rhodesian parliament voted to declare Rhodesia an independent sovereign state. Rhodesia (or more accurately Southern Rhodesia) was a self-governing British state. Britain had allowed British territories like Zambia (formerly Northern Rhodesia) and Malawi (formerly Nyasaland) to become fully independent. Southern Rhodesia, which had an overwhelmingly predominant white parliament, was refused independence under the NIBMAR principle ("no independence before majority rule"). There was a protracted dispute between the British and Rhodesian governments. The British prime minister, Harold Wilson, wanted significant black representation in the Rhodesian government. The Rhodesian prime minister, Ian Smith, refused to negotiate further and declared UDI. The Rhodesians fought a vicious guerilla war against black independence groups. The Rhodesians could not sustain the war and withdrew their declaration of UDI in 1979. A year later the country was granted independence and became known as Zimbabwe. The corrupt rule of Robert Mugabe did little to inspire white South Africans' confidence in black government.

I picked up a copy of the *Rand Daily Mail* that Friday morning. Despite the prominence given to Rhodesia's UDI, there was a large picture of Bram on the front page, which showed Captain Swanepoel holding Bram by the arm. Bram was wearing a jacket, he was fingering his rimless glasses, and he was still sporting his goatee beard. He looked diminutive beside Swanepoel and I felt sick as I was stared at the photograph. The article on the front page was full of praise for the police in capturing him.

George Bizos called me on Sunday evening. He had heard about my detention and was ostensibly calling to sympathise and check up on me. I suspected he may have been fishing to see if I had directly or indirectly been responsible for aiding the police in finding Bram. I expressed my shock at Bram's arrest and gave George a detailed account of my detention, my interrogation, and my inability to shed any light on Bram's whereabouts. George told me that he had visited Bram on Saturday at Pretoria Local prison. Bram had been very calm and in his typically polite manner, he had first asked after George's wife and children, before expressing concern over Paul's health. Paul had returned to Johannesburg a few days earlier. He had gone to stay with Ilse but was on his own since Ilse had gone into hiding, fearing that she too would be arrested. Ruth was arriving the following week because her husband, Anthony Eastwood, had accepted a job at the University of Natal. Bram had enquired loudly about Ilse and Pat stating that he had missed them dreadfully. George said that their conversation was almost certainly being bugged and so Bram had taken care to say this to reinforce Ilse and Pat's claims that they had no contact with him since he had gone into hiding. Bram asked George to undertake his defence. George felt that he was too junior and arranged for Sydney Kentridge to be the lead counsel. Arthur Chaskalson and George would assist.

During their meeting George had thoughtlessly asked Bram if giving up his family, his practice, and his freedom had been worthwhile. George would always regret this hurtful question. He had to bow his head in shame when Bram looked at him angrily and replied, "George, did you ask Nelson Mandela the same question? He too had a practice, a family and loved freedom. Did you ask Walter Sisulu or Govan Mbeki?"

George replied, "No Bram. I had not thought of asking them that question."

"Well, then, don't ask me."[35]

On Monday 8 November 1965 the Security Branch police detained Violet Weinberg. I had been interrogated for less than half a day. Violet was brutally interrogated non-stop for four days. She was forced to stand, denied sleep, and given few toilet breaks. The police worked in relay teams. When Minnie and Ralph Sepel heard that Violet had been arrested, they begged Bram to disappear. Bram was living in a house in Corlett Drive and the Sepel's insisted that he should move immediately. Bram agreed but fatefully delayed for one day too long. The police found that Violet was in possession of a mysterious key. Violet cracked and told her interrogators the address of the house for that key. It was Bram's house in Corlett Drive. On the morning of 11 November 1965, the Security Branch police staked out the Corlett Drive house. The police observed Bram driving off in a Volkswagen. They stopped the car near his Beaumont Street house. Bram claimed that he was Donald Black but they drove him back to the Corlett Drive house. The police opened the house and found a mass of documents and disguises. These documents were more than enough to convict him on charges of sabotage. Bram was placed under arrest.

Bram was brought into court the following Monday and had his case remanded as the State worked on the charges it wanted to bring against him. Paul and Ruth were allowed visits but Ilse preferred to lay low and stay away. Bram's brothers Paul and Gustav were also allowed to visit. Pat Davidson had frequent visits because she was an attorney and was allowed to help Bram prepare for his trial. On 26 January 1966 Bram was brought before the Johannesburg Regional Court for a preparatory examination. The police called witnesses and produced a mountain of incriminating evidence. Sholto Cross was called as a witness but expressed his annoyance and claimed that he was merely being used to embarrass Bram because he was Ilse's fiancé. Lesley Schermbrucker was also called as a witness but she refused to testify. She was sentenced to 300 days in prison for refusing, despite her husband being in jail, and having two teenage children at home. Violet Weinberg also refused to testify and she was kept in solitary detention for six months. Bram pleaded not guilty to all the charges because he said much of the evidence given against him was grossly distorted. He was committed to trial and elected to be tried by a judge alone rather than a jury.

Bram's trial commenced on 23 March 1966 before Justice Wes Boshoff in the Palace of Justice in Pretoria. Bram sat alone in the very same dock that had held the Rivonia accused. Bram was charged with being a communist and furthering its aims but now he faced additional charges of which the most serious was that of sabotage. Bartholomew Hlopane was the most damning of the many witnesses. Hlopane had been a member of the SACP and he accused the SACP of being in control of both the ANC and Umkhonto we Sizwe. He even went as far as saying that Umkhonto we Sizwe had approved Operation Mayibuye, the guerilla warfare plan. Sydney Kentridge though skilfully highlighted the contradictions and untruths in Hlopane's evidence. Piet Beyleveld and Gerard Ludi were also called to give evidence. The case took only two days before Kentridge announced that Bram would not testify but would make a statement from the dock. Bram's statement took five hours to deliver as he read calmly and patiently from his notes. His opening words were: "I am on trial, my Lord, for my political beliefs and for the conduct which those beliefs drove me to. My Lord, whatever labels may have been attached to the fifteen charges brought against me, they all arise from my having been a member of the Communist Party and from my activities as a member. I engaged upon these activities because I believed that, in the dangerous circumstances which have been created in South Africa, it was my duty to do so."[36]

Bram then set out to explain why he acted as he did. He acknowledged that laws should be obeyed but when the laws themselves become immoral and required a citizen to take part in an organised system of oppression, then a higher duty arose. Bram felt compelled to refuse to recognise unjust laws. Bram argued that the laws of South Africa had been enacted by a wholly unrepresentative parliament because three quarters of the people had no voice whatsoever. He stated that laws had not been implemented to prevent the spread of communism, but rather to silence all opposition.

Bram explained that the reason he was attracted to Marxist theory was because he saw communism as the solution to the glaring social injustices in South Africa. Bram observed that all white South Africans could see these injustices but were not moved to do anything about it. Bram explained that he grew up on a farm and that as a young boy his daily companions were black boys of the same age, and he could never remember that the colour of their skins affected their fun, or their quarrels or their close friendship in any way. As a university student Bram confessed to believing in segregation. Nevertheless, he joined the Bloemfontein Joint Council of Europeans and Africans, a body that was attempting to provide proper and separate amenities for blacks. Bram stated that he found himself being introduced to blacks and had to shake hands with them. This required an enormous effort on his part. He spent many hours thinking about why he had these feelings of revulsion at shaking hands. He had never had such feelings towards his friends. What became clear to Bram was that he had changed and it was not the black man that had changed. He had developed an antagonism towards the black man for which he could find no rational basis whatsoever. Bram realised colour prejudice was a wholly irrational phenomenon and that true friendship could extend across the colour bar.

Bram noted that the Communist Party refused to accept any colour bar and had always stood firm in the belief that everyone was equal. Bram was a communist because the South African Communist Party was committed to destroying white domination of an oppressed people. The aim of a communist revolution in South Africa was to restore the land and wealth of the country to the people and guarantee democracy, freedom and equality of rights and opportunities to all. Bram felt compelled to act because of the present dangers in South Africa. It was against his instincts as a trained lawyer to break the law but many of South Africa's kindliest, wisest, and otherwise law-abiding citizens were also doing so. The unjust apartheid laws had created an explosive situation which should cause extreme unrest. The relative calm in the country was not because of the success of the policies of segregation but because of the tolerance, understanding, and infinite goodwill of blacks. He saw it as remarkable that so far there had been little more than highly controlled and restricted acts of sabotage. Nevertheless, Bram feared that the government had set itself on a course that was destined to end in a civil war. A war which could never be won by the whites of South Africa, but the consequences would be horrifying and permanent. It was imperative to find a solution and he believed that answer lay in creating a Socialist State.

Bram stated that he and the Communist Party were rigidly opposed to acts of violence and that the Communist Party was quite separate from Umkhonto we Sizwe. It would be politically dishonest and foolish to recruit members who believed in non-violence if the Communist Party was involved in acts of sabotage. Bram declared that he was not a member of Umkhonto we Sizwe but he did not personally disapprove of this organisation. He did not believe that acts of sabotage would bring about fundamental change alone but it would highlight dissatisfaction.

Bram commented on his personal background. As young man he had believed in the policies of segregation (apartheid) and was a Nationalist Party student leader but it was Hitler's theory of racial superiority that caused him to shed his old beliefs. He said that his doubts about the merits of racial segregation first arose when he said to an ANC leader that if you separate races, you diminish the points at which friction between them may occur and hence ensure good relations. This ANC leader answered that the basis of all racism is suspicion and fear which arises when you separate people. Bram stated that he had dedicated himself to maintaining contact and understanding between the races of South Africa.

Bram concluded his statement by quoting Paul Kruger's prophetic words from 1881. These words were inscribed on the base of Paul Kruger's statue which stood in front of the Court. President Kruger's words were:

> *"Met vertrouwen leggen wy onze zaak open voor de gebeele wereld. Het zy wy overwinnen, het zy wy sterven: de vryheid sal in Afrika ryzen als de zon uit de morewalken".*

(With confidence we lay our case open before the whole world. Whether we conquer, or whether we die: freedom shall rise in Africa like the sun from the morning clouds.)[37]

Justice Boshoff adjourned the case for six weeks. On 4 May 1966 he declared Bram guilty on all charges and set Monday, 9 May 1966 as the day of sentencing. I watched proceedings from the public gallery. I arrived early so that I could claim a place inside the court. Ilse and Paul were seated in the front row. Ruth was not in court. Ruth's husband, Anthony Eastwood, had not been able to take up his post at the University of Natal because he was declared a banned immigrant and had returned to Rhodesia. On the day of sentencing Ruth was stuck in Rhodesia as she attempted to navigate the difficulties of commuting back and forth.

The judge spoke for almost half an hour before sentencing Bram to life imprisonment. Bram looked at Ilse and Paul, smiled, and then raised his right fist in the ANC salute. He was quickly taken down to the cells. I would never speak to or hear from Bram directly again. The courtroom was buzzing with anguished cries and shouts of protest. I sat in shocked silence. Outside the court Ilse and Paul were surrounded by friends. I managed to hand Paul a card that had been signed by many of the staff and boys from St. John's College. The card contained words of sympathy, understanding and friendship.

After sentencing Bram was sent to Pretoria Local prison. For the first few months, he was kept with just two other political prisoners, Harold (Jock) Strachan and Issy Heymann. Strachan had already completed a three-year sentence, but upon his release he had written a series of articles criticising the conditions of political prisoners. Strachan was charged under the Prisons Act and sentenced to another year in prison. All the other political prisoners had been sent to Pretoria Central to be confined with common criminals. Bram, Strachan, and Heymann were treated in a petty and vindictive way. The head warder, Du Preez, attempted to make their lives a misery. Du Preez took pleasure in forcing Bram to wash the toilets with nothing more than rags. He issued clothing to Bram that was too big and an oversized hat. Bram would come to wear this hat as badge of honour and as an appendage of his personality. In November 1966 the other political prisoners were returned to Pretoria Local. There were usually around twenty white political prisoners at a time in Pretoria Local. At the same time there were over a thousand black political prisoners on Robben Island.

Conditions slowly improved over the years. At first, Bram was restricted to two five-hundred-word letters (in and out) every year and one six monthly visit. By 1969 his privileges were upgraded and Bram was allowed two letters a month and monthly visits. The prisoners studied through the University of South Africa, they produced plays, they were allowed music, and they were able to watch the occasional film. They played volley ball and tennis in the exercise yard. Despite his age and damaged knee Bram soon proved to be the wiliest and most adept tennis player. They were given menial jobs and Bram was pleased to be assigned to the garden where he nurtured flowers. In May 1967 Bram was awarded the Lenin Peace Prize. Bram wrote to Ilse and described it as an award he could only accept "as a representative of people who are braver than I and who have given far more."[38]

CHAPTER 15

Funerals

The government had largely succeeded in subduing its opponents and so many powerful figures had been removed. For example, Nelson Mandela, Walter Sisulu, and Bram Fischer were serving life sentences, while Oliver Tambo and Joe Slovo were in exile. The Nationalist Party was enthusiastically supported by almost all Afrikaners and an increasing number of English-speakers. The Nationalist Party enjoyed a resounding victory in the March 1966 general election and won 106 out of 170 seats. Helen Suzman was the only member of the Progressive Party to win a seat. The United Party won the remaining seats.

The government was riding high. There was little opposition, the economy was flourishing, much of the apartheid programme was in place, and the country had just celebrated five years of being a Republic. In 1966 Senator Robert Kennedy, a staunch critic of apartheid, visited South Africa. The government banned foreign journalists from entering the country to report on his visit. His speech at the University of Cape Town on 6 June 1966 however, was widely reported in newspapers. Robert Kennedy spoke powerfully against discrimination and reminded the government that it could not stand against injustice and oppression. His speech was a tempered warning against the unfairness and inequities of apartheid, but the government chose not to listen.

On 6 September 1966 a parliamentary messenger, Dimitri Tsafendas, walked up to the South African prime minister, Hendrik Verwoerd. Tsafendas pulled out a knife and stabbed Verwoerd four times in the neck and chest. Members of parliament rushed to his aid but Verwoerd died in the ambulance on the way to hospital. After the stabbing on the floor of parliament, the Minister of Defence, P. W. Botha, came rushing past Helen Suzman. He stopped, shook his finger at her, and shouted, "It's you who did this. It's all you liberals. You incite people. Now we will get you. We will get the lot of you."[39] At his trial Tsafendas claimed that his actions were politically motivated but he was declared insane and confined to a mental institution.

Verwoerd's funeral was held on the afternoon of Saturday, 10 September 1966. I joined colleagues in the staff common room to listen to the funeral on a radio broadcast. White South Africans were in a state of shock but I and many of my colleagues were acutely aware that not everyone in South Africa was mourning. The September 1966 edition of the English satirical magazine, Private Eye, printed the word "Verwoerd" in bold on its cover. The picture below was of four Zulu warriors jumping for joy, with the words below in the same bold font: "A Nation Mourns."

After Verwoerd's assassination Balthazar John Vorster, the former Minister of Justice, was appointed prime minister. He was from the right-wing of the party, he had been a Nazi sympathiser and was interned during the Second Word War. He had been a vicious Minister of Justice and implemented the detention without trial laws. He was a dogged proponent of apartheid although he was prepared to relax certain petty laws. His only modest accomplishment was an attempt to establish diplomatic relations with other countries. Vorster did away with the One-hundred-

and-eighty-day detention law but replaced it with the Terrorism Act, which was even more draconian. The Terrorism Act made participation in terrorist activities a capital crime. The definition of terrorism was expanded to include possessing arms, ammunition, or explosives and receiving military training. Anyone suspected of endangering law and order could be detained indefinitely without trial, on the orders of a senior police officer.

The Australian cricket team toured South Africa at the end of 1966 and early 1967. After school closed for the December school holidays. I decided to spend most of my holiday following the tour. The first test match was at the Wanderers in Johannesburg. The South African wicketkeeper, Denis Lindsay, was in fine form and smashed the Australian attack to set up a South African victory. I immediately charged off to Cape Town so that I could watch the second test at Newlands. Australia won the toss and elected to bat first. Bobby Simpson and Keith Stackpole scored centuries. South Africa had to follow on and lost the match, despite Graeme Pollock's effortless double-century. Graeme Pollock had scored a first-class century when he was just sixteen, a test century at nineteen, and here he was at twenty-two years in peak form. It was self-evident that I was watching one of the great batsmen of all time. I watched the first three days of the third test at Kingsmead in Durban, before returning to school for the start of the new year. Australia won the toss and Simpson elected to field first. This decision seemed well vindicated when Graeme McKenzie had Eddie Barlow caught and bowled off the very first ball of the match. It was Mike Proctor's debut test and he would become one of the world's great all-rounders. Proctor bowled off the wrong foot but had blistering pace and the Australians were soon ducking and weaving to avoid painful blows. South Africa comfortably won the match. The fourth test in Johannesburg was drawn after lengthy rain interruptions and then in late February 1967 the South Africans won the fifth test in Port Elixabeth.

Professor Christiaan Barnard was a dashing young surgeon. He was an Afrikaner but he was not afraid to condemn apartheid. Barnard was taught open heart surgery at the University of Minnesota. When he returned to South Africa, he pioneered this technique at Groote Schuur hospital in Cape Town. On 2 December 1967 Professor Barnard performed the world's first heart transplant operation. South Africa was jubilant when the news was announced. Barnard and his team of surgeons had brought international acclaim and honour to South Africa. The first transplant recipient. Louis Washkansky, died less than three weeks later, but Barnard was able to rightly claim that the operation had been a success and could be performed again and again.

South Africa had legislated apartheid laws, but racial inequality and discrimination was not unique to South Africa. The civil rights movement in the United States was seeking to abolish segregation. Martin Luther King was one of the most visible civil rights leaders. On 1 April 1968 he was shot dead while standing on the balcony of his hotel in Memphis, Tennessee. In the wake of the war in Vietnam President Lyndon Johnson decided not to seek re-nomination in the 1968 United States presidential election. Robert Kennedy competed for the Democratic Party presidential nomination, but on 5 June 1968 a deranged young man assassinated him at the Ambassador Hotel in Los Angeles.

The English cricket team were due to tour South Africa in late 1968. I had enjoyed following the Australian tour in 1966-1967 and wanted to make a similar pilgrimage following the 1968-1969 English tour. The Marylebone Cricket Club (MCC) had selected Basil D'Oliveira, originally a Cape Coloured from South Africa in their team. The MCC realised that D'Oliveira's selection would be controversial and initially did not select him. D'Oliveria's non-selection was criticised in England as it was seen as pandering to the wishes of the South African government. Another player though was ruled out through injury and D'Oliveira was named as his replacement. South Africa objected. Vorster stated that he was withdrawing the invitation to tour because the MCC team had not been picked on merit. Vorster argued that D'Oliviera was only selected because the anti-apartheid movement had made such an outcry over his non-selection in the first place.

The MCC cricket tour was cancelled and South Africa rapidly became a sporting pariah. South Africa was excluded from the Olympic Games, the Commonwealth Games, and faced increasingly hostile international sports boycotts. The South African cricket team played a four-test series against Australia in 1969-1970, but after that they were banned from all international fixtures. I supported the international boycotts but felt sorry for the cricketers whose careers were dashed on the altar of apartheid. The South African test cricket team beat Australia 4-0 in the 1969-1970 series, but its talented players would never play international cricket again – Barry Richards, Graeme Pollock, Mike Proctor, Ali Bacher, Lee Irvine, Peter Pollock, and Eddie Barlow all had their glittering careers cut short. Eddie Barlow would later campaign against apartheid as a parliamentary candidate for the Progressive Party.

Nelson Mandela, Bram Fischer, and the many other revolutionaries, who were now either incarcerated or in exile, had mistakenly assumed that the South African government could not last long and would soon collapse. As the 1960s wore on these expectations were dashed. The South African economy grew strongly and international companies invested heavily in the country. Britain and the United States had large investments and now other countries, such as Germany and France, began to engage with South Africa. France became very important because it was

213

the South African government's main arms supplier. President de Gaulle pushed French monetary reserves into gold. De Gaulle bought more and more gold at the fixed price of USD 35 per ounce. The United States was no longer able to continue selling at this price and the gold price rose sharply to over USD 300 per ounce. South Africa was one of the world's major gold producers and the high gold price caused the economy to boom.

The United States was embroiled in the Cold War and was heavily engaged in Vietnam. Henry Kissinger was President Richard Nixon's National Security advisor. He wanted Nixon to maintain a public opposition to racial oppression, but at that the same time advocated that the United States should provide enough support to ensure that communism was not allowed to take over in southern Africa. He saw South Africa as an ally in thwarting the spread of communism. In 1969 Kissinger drew up a security assessment of Southern Africa. There were white governments in South Africa, South West Africa, Rhodesia, Mozambique, and Angola. National Security Study Memorandum 39 on the future of United States policy towards Southern Africa stated: "The whites are here to stay and the only way that constructive change can come about is through them. There is no hope for the blacks to gain the political rights they wish through violence, which will only lead to chaos and increased opportunities for the communists. We can, by selective relaxation of our stance toward the white regimes, encourage some modification of their current racial and colonial policies and through more substantial economic assistance to the black states...help to draw the two groups together and exert some influence on both for peaceful change. Our tangible interests form a basis for our contacts in the region, and these can be maintained at an acceptable political cost."[40]

Ilse broke off her relationship with Sholto Cross, and started dating Tim Wilson, a young doctor. In late 1969 Ilse went to

Cape Town to be with Tim. Paul joined her and enrolled in an Honours degree at the University of Cape Town. Paul struggled with his health but managed to complete his degree. Paul needed constant medical attention and was a frequent visitor to Groote Schuur hospital. In January 1971 Ilse and Tim went on holiday to the Eastern Cape. Paul flew to Johannesburg so that he could visit Bram and then returned to Cape Town, On 27 January 1971 Paul checked himself into Groote Schuur hospital. His lungs collapsed that night and he died. He was just twenty-three years old. B r a m was refused permission to attend the funeral. Arthur Chaskalson gave a moving obituary. He described Paul as having similar qualities to Bram, but he was not simply Bram Fischer's son. "He was Paul Fischer, a boy who grew into a young man, who lived fully, and was loved by all who knew him... He would not have wanted us to gather here today to pay tribute to him; but that is our right and he is not here to prevent it, nor to prevent our saying that we are glad that he lived and we knew him."[41]

I was filled with sadness. This fine young man had suffered so much: he was plagued with poor health, he had lost his mother as a schoolboy, and seen his father sentenced to life in prison. Yet he soldiered on. He never complained and he always had an engaging and cheerful disposition. I felt acute pain for Ruth and Ilse, who were broken-hearted, and for Bram who suffered alone in prison.

At the end of 1970 Deane Yates resigned from his position as headmaster of St. John's College. He had decided to establish an international school in Gaborone, the capital of Botswana. Deane felt that a headmaster should not overstay his welcome, he was deeply troubled by the policies of apartheid, and wanted to start a school of excellence for pupils from all racial backgrounds. The school is called Maru-a-pula which in Setswana means "clouds of rain" or "promises of blessings." Jan Breitenbach was appointed the new Headmaster of St. John's College. Deane Yates was the first lay-headmaster and Jan Breitenbach was the first headmaster with a South African heritage. He was to prove a most capable headmaster and I enjoyed working under his leadership. The appointment of the first South African headmaster was a talking point in the staff common room. I ventured to say that it had taken seventy-two years to appoint a local man and I wondered how long it would take before a black man was appointed headmaster. There was a consensus that this idea was laughable and that it would never happen!

I enjoyed watching the school cadets compete each year for the Allen Cup, which was a trophy awarded to the most efficient house. The St. John's College cadet corps was formed in 1910 and used the Union Jack as its regimental colours. In 1960 the school realised that this was no longer appropriate. The Union Jack was laid up in the chapel and the Old Johannian Association presented the school with new colours. In 1971 Witswatersrand Command advised that only boys of pure European descent could participate in cadets. This meant that Chinese schoolboys were not allowed to be members of the school cadet corps. The School Council acted promptly and correctly by immediately shutting down the St. John's College cadet corp.

Ruth and Anthony adopted a baby girl, named Gretel. Ruth and Anthony however, would divorce because Anthony had an affair. Ruth came back to live in South Africa and she, Ilse and Tim visited Bram regularly. In 1971 Ilse married Tim Wilson. Ruth and Ilse were both very active in campaigning for Bram's release. They petitioned the State President, the Prime Minister, the Minister of Justice, and numerous judges. There were others that helped in these release campaigns, and included distinguished people like Helen Suzman, Professor Christiaan Barnard, Archbishop Denis Hurley, Louis Babrow (a Springbok rugby player), and Leslie Blackwell QC.

The imprisonment of Nelson Mandela, other ANC leaders, and white political activists had created an anti-apartheid leadership vacuum. In the early 1970s however, a new generation of young black leaders emerged. Steve Biko, a medical student from the Eastern Cape, became a prominent leader and spokesman for the black consciousness movement. Biko encouraged blacks to be proud of their identity. He argued that blacks should not be submissive, and that they should celebrate their capabilities and achievements. In September 1970 he wrote the following in the South African Students Organisation journal: "The type of black man we have today has lost his manhood. Reduced to an obliging shell, he looks with awe at the white power structure and accepts what he regards as the 'inevitable position'...In the privacy of his toilet his face twists in silent condemnation of white society but brightens up in sheepish obedience as he comes out hurrying in response to his master's impatient call. In the homebound bus or train he joins the chorus that roundly condemns the white man but is first to praise the government in the presence of the police and his employers...All in all, the black man has become a shell, a shadow of man, completely defeated, drowning in his own misery, a slave, an ox bearing the yoke of oppression with sheepish timidity..."[42]

Steve Biko abandoned his medical studies and became a political activist promoting the black consciousness movement. He was fond of the slogan "black is beautiful." The government arrested and detained him repeatedly. In 1973 he was banned and confined to King William's Town. He was forbidden from speaking in public, prohibited from publishing any articles, and only allowed to gather with one other person at a time. Steve Biko received little attention but international disapproval of apartheid was growing. On 30 November 1973 the United Nations adopted the International Convention on the Suppression and Punishment of Apartheid. It passed with 91 votes in favour, 26 abstentions, and 4 votes against (South Africa, Portugal, Great Britain, and the United States). Apartheid was declared a crime against humanity. South Africa began to face economic pressures too. In 1973 Great Britain entered the European Economic Community (EEC) and this meant that Britain no longer relied on its trading relationships with its former colonies. South Africa was excluded from the beneficial EEC trading arrangements.

The government though did not let up on its relentless pursuit of political activists. They were ruthlessly detained and dozens died suspiciously in custody. The security police proffered excuses like suicide, shot while trying to escape, and even suggested someone slipped on a piece of soap in the shower. Ahmed Timol was the first political detainee killed while in custody. Timol was an Indian that distributed Communist Party literature to mobilise Indians in the anti-apartheid struggle. Timol was detained, tortured, and then dropped to his death from the tenth floor of the Security Branch headquarters in Johannesburg. His death resulted in an international outcry, but all the police were exonerated at the inquest.

In June 1973 Alex Moumbaris was sentenced to twelve years in prison for Umkhonto we Sizwe activities. Moumbaris was of Greek heritage, born in Egypt, and had worked for the ANC in London. Joe Slovo, Yusuf Dadoo, Jack Hodgson, and Ronnie Kasrils were the Umkhonto we Sizwe members tasked with training combatants and infiltrating them back into South Africa. One of their slightly hare-brained schemes was to ferry combatants into the country by boat. The ANC purchased a boat called the *Aventura* and obtained a Greek crew. Moumbaris was sent to South Africa to scout out suitable landing places. He recommended an isolated beach on the Wild Coast, somewhere near where I had walked with Father Ted on our school trip. The Greek crew refused to land when they discovered their mission. Moumbaris was caught trying to enter the country illegally and the security police unravelled his Umkhonto we Sizwe activities including the failed *Aventura* plan.

In April 1974 South Africa had a general election and the Nationalist Party retained its huge majority by winning 122 out of 171 seats. The Progressive Party however, increased its seats to 6 and then 7 after a bye-election. Their leader, Colin Eglin won the Cape Town seat of Sea Point, Alex Boraine, a former moderator of the Methodist Church, won a seat, and the star newcomer was Frederik Van Zyl Slabbert who won the Cape Town seat of Rondebosch. I would come to view Van Zyl Slabbert with the same high regard that I had for Bram. In some ways they were opposites, but in other ways they were similar. They were Afrikaners, highly intelligent, charismatic, and natural leaders. In a different time and place they would have been Prime Ministers or Presidents. Bram was a committed communist and did not associate with any parliamentary political party. Van Zyl Slabbert on the other hand attempted, at least for a while, to work within the parliamentary system. Van Zyl Slabbert's parents divorced, his mother was an alcoholic, and his grandparents brought him and his twin sister up on a farm in the Northern Transvaal. Like Bram, some of his earliest childhood friends were black farmworkers' children. Van Zyl Slabbert decided to become a church minister (or dominee in Afrikaans) and went to Stellenbosch University to study theology. One day he went with a group of students to conduct missionary work in the township of Langa near Cape Town. Van Zyl Slabbert noticed that his colleagues seemed to be more intent on defending the policy of apartheid than spreading the gospel. The crowd of listeners soon began to hurl insults and even stones, and the group had to beat a hasty retreat. Soon afterwards Van Zyl Slabbert abandoned his theological studies. He became a lecturer in sociology and wrote a doctoral thesis. Van Zyl Slabbert was strongly opposed to apartheid and decided to make a practical difference through engaging in parliamentary politics.

Helen Suzman, the Progressive Party member for Houghton, made it her business to visit prisoners. She wanted prisoners to know that someone was looking after their welfare and she wanted the government to know that she was keeping a watchful eye on their treatment. She visited Bram regularly. Bram was the spokesman for all the political prisoners and he would hand her a list of grievances. Breyten Breytenbach, a brilliant Afrikaner author and poet, was sentenced to nine years in prison for his anti-apartheid activities. This is what he wrote about Suzman's prison visits: "I don't think it will be excessive to say that the prisoners, both political and common law, consider her as Our Lady of the Prisoners. She is indeed a living myth among the people inhabiting the world of shadows. The quality of the food suddenly improves. Out of the blue a movie is shown on a Saturday afternoon. People have been sleeping for years on mats on the floor – 'sleeping camel' as we said, because the skin of the hips eventually becomes calloused- and now beds are made available. Prisoners would look at one another and nod their heads wisely and say, 'You see, Aunty Helen did it after all.'"[43]

South African whites are rugby mad and in 1974 the country was captivated by the British & Irish Lions tour. The government was delighted to host the tour because there was international pressure against playing sport against South Africa. Two Welsh rugby stars, Gerald Davies and John Taylor, declined tour invitations because of their opposition to apartheid. The Irish forward, Willie John McBride, captained the side and led the Lions on an undefeated tour. They won eighteen tour matches and the first three tests before finishing with a tied fourth test. South African whites were humiliated but enthralled by the thrilling rugby contests. I could not help observe that black South Africans seemed to celebrate the Lions' victories with unbridled joy.

In May 1974 Bram was admitted to hospital because of a bleeding ulcer. He also had a cancerous prostate removed. By September the cancer had spread and Bram was suffering from acute hip pain. The prison authorities refused to give Bram a crutch and his fellow inmates had to make one out of a broom. On 6 November 1974 Bram slipped in the shower. He requested medical attention but the prison authorities ignored him. Denis Goldberg and Dave Kitson resorted to carrying Bram around, assisting him shower, and helping him eat. Bram was eventually taken to a hospital where X-rays confirmed a fractured hip. The medical treatment was totally negligent and Bram was returned to prison. Bram was so weak that Denis Goldberg had to obtain permission to remain with Bram in his cell so that he could put him in bed and take him to the toilet. On 11 December 1974 Bram returned to hospital where he was diagnosed with advanced cancer. He was in a critical condition. Ruth and Ilse visited him every day in hospital.

The news of Bram's health spread and there were international campaigns for his release. There were letters from British politicians; Michael Foot, Lord Goodman, Neil Kinnock, and James Callaghan; American politicians, Congressman Donald Fraser and Senator George McGovern; and the Secretary-General of the United Nations, Kurt Waldheim. The government rejected all these petitions, claiming that Bram's criminal transgressions were too serious to justify his release. Ruth and Ilse made an appointment to see Jimmy Kruger, the Minister of Justice. Kruger contemptuously declined their release request and even suggested that there was no certainty that Bram had cancer, and he might recover even if he did. Then on Friday, 7 March 1975, Paul Fischer, Bram's brother, suddenly received a telephone call from the Prisons Department advising that Bram was going to be released into his care. Paul had to sign undertakings acknowledging that

Bram was still a prisoner and that no visitors, other than family, would be allowed. On the following Monday Ilse and Tim went to meet Bram at the Voortrekkerhoogte military airfield in Pretoria and accompanied him on an aeroplane to Bloemfontein. There they were met by a cavalcade of vehicles. There was an ambulance, cars filled with security policemen, and traffic policemen on motorcycles. They were driven to Paul's home with sirens wailing. Ilse, Ruth, and her daughter Gretel, were able to join Paul in caring for Bram. They enjoyed his quiet and dignified company for his remaining days. On 8 May 1975 Bram, just sixty-seven years old, passed away peacefully in his bed.

I attended Bram's funeral that was held in Bloemfontein the following week. Arthur Chaskalson delivered the eulogy and read a moving tribute from Hugh Lewin. Hugh had completed his prison sentence in November 1971. He immediately left the country and went to live in England. Pat Davidson, who had visited Hugh regularly in prison, followed him there and they soon married. These are some of the words from Hugh's funeral tribute:

> "Do not weep for Bram. He would not have you weep on his behalf. And do not weep for the recent long years in jail. That especially he would not like. For although they were long painful years away from his family and friends outside, for Bram inside they were not lost years. They meant for Bram, in a very real sense, a rounding and a completion. However full the man who first went to jail, however distinguished the lawyer, however fine the father, husband, friend, adviser, however full the man before, jail encompassed the fullness and enlarged it.
>
> In the beginning, prison stripped Bram bare, in a process which, for him, was even more severe and complete than it is for most; it stripped him of the protection of a respected position and of privilege and esteem, and denied him what had always been so dear to him, the comfort of family and friends and familiar surroundings.

But in so denuding him, prison in fact gave Bram something new. In seeking to stifle him, it gave him new vigour. It sought to maim, but it made him strong. It sought to hide him and succeeded only in revealing the simple, essential greatness of the man.

To the authorities, Bram in prison was a sort of prize exhibit, evoking a mixture of horror and respect and curiosity. It was always Bram who was picked out for inspection and nodded at, always Bram who was greeted with 'Hello, Bram' – even 'Hello, Braampie' – as if the chance to greet him with familiarity somehow enhanced their position, somehow gave them added status. And Bram, usually with his battered brown-felt prison hat in hand, would stand quietly, nod back and smile, always scrupulously polite and unbowed.

In those who sought to bait him, trying to gain something for themselves by denigrating and humiliating him, Bram's unbroken charm produced indignant antagonism. But more often his patient indulgence – and his constant refusal ever to let any situation get him down – won him the tacit admiration of all those who guarded him and came into contact with him...

In a world made up of so much triviality and tedium, there is scant scope for anything heroic, but Bram managed always to instil in those with him (some, like him, facing dauntingly long and seemingly endless sentences) a keen sense of purpose in their unchanging day-to-day lives inside. He especially kept alive their interest in everything around them and, though they were strenuously deprived of news of the outside world, Bram's achievement was always to maintain an eager and ever-searching awareness of that so-easily-forgotten world outside. And he never himself forgot – nor allowed others to forget – the deep-seated belief in and struggle for that justice and freedom which had always been his prime concern."[44]

Ruth and Ilse received letters and telegrams from around the world. Winne Mandela sent a telegram on behalf of Nelson

Mandela, and others imprisoned on Robben Island, which read: "Deepest sympathy from Robben Island. Farewell, people's hero. His spirit will live forever. Our salute, great son of Africa."[45]

As I sat at the funeral, I could only see the face of a youthful Bram. The young man that limped along the corridor of New College on his crutches, and accepted my invitation for a cup of tea. He was my friend. A man that soared, a man that made a difference, a man of honesty and integrity, a man of compassion, a man of the people. A man that the apartheid state saw as an Afrikaner traitor. He ended his life hobbling on a crutch made from a broom. He was a man that shook hands and built bridges. He was a great man.

The Prison Department's final act of bastardy was to demand the return of Bram's ashes. They never told Ruth and Ilse what they did with the ashes. They wanted to erase him, but they could never destroy his legacy or memory.

CHAPTER 16

Soweto

After Bram's funeral I returned to a very quiet St. John's College because the school had broken up for the end of Lent term holidays. I felt generally miserable and decided to attend the Sunday service at St. Mary's Cathedral in the city. The cathedral buildings were eerily like those of St. John's College. This was hardly surprising since they were designed by the same architect, Sir Herbert Baker. I found a seat towards the back and observed the congregation slide into the pews as they gathered for the Sunday morning mass. The organ was playing softly and then paused. The congregation rose and the organist began to play the processional hymn. The procession was led by a young boy, followed by the choristers, who were all dressed in blue and gold robes. Then came the altar servers, carrying candles, dressed in black cassocks and white surplices, followed by the clergy dressed in ornate robes. At the rear of the procession was the bishop, carrying a crook, wearing a mitre and clad in purple robes. I noticed that one of the priests was a diminutive man. This was Desmond Tutu, the newly appointed dean of the cathedral, and the first black man to hold this important office. I was rather pleased to discover that Tutu was going to deliver the sermon.

After the gospel reading, Tutu took up his position in the lectern and made the sign of the cross. I could see little more than his head but I shall never forget his beaming smile. He called out a cheerful good morning and announced that his sermon would consider the Jews liberation from bondage in Egypt as told in the book of Exodus. Tutu explained that the story of Exodus was a paradigm for all oppressed people and not just the people of Israel. He suggested that the children of Israel were the oppressed people everywhere. Tutu challenged the congregation to accept that religion could not be separated from politics. Tutu then leaned forward, grasped the lectern sides with both hands and said earnestly, "Our God is not a God who sanctifies the status quo. He cares that children starve in resettlement camps. He cares that people die mysteriously in detention. He is concerned that people are condemned to a twilight existence as non-persons by banning them without giving them the right of reply to charges brought against them." Tutu explained that the entire story of the Bible was about God's mission to restore the perfection of God's creation at the beginning. Man sinned and Jesus was sent to die on the cross for our sins so that we could be reconciled with God. Tutu said that apartheid was a sin and concluded with these powerful words, "So Jesus came to restore human community and brotherhood. Apartheid quite deliberately denies and repudiates this central act of Jesus, and says we are made for separateness, for disunity, for enmity, for alienation, all of which we have shown to be the fruits of sin. The only separation the Bible knows is between believers on the one hand and unbelievers on the other. Any other kind of separation, division, disunity is of the devil. It is evil and from sin."

The congregation was almost all white with just a smattering of black faces here and there. I looked around to see if there was a reaction from the congregation but there was scarcely a murmur and the service continued as everyone stood to recite the Apostle's

Creed. There was a very smartly dressed young black man alongside me in the pew. I could not help glancing at him from time to time and was forced to hastily avert my eyes when I caught him smiling back at me. At the end of the service, I nodded to him in greeting. He took a step forward, extended his hand to shake mine and said, "Peace be with you."

"And with you," I murmured. He looked me straight in the eyes and held my gaze. I continued with stutter, "It is my first visit to St. Mary's. It was a very enjoyable service."

"Well then, you must come again," he said.

"Yes indeed, I would like that." I paused and continued, "I was rather moved by the Dean's sermon."

"You should tell him."

"Yes, I should"

"Frank Chikane,"

"I am Henry Allum," I replied, "It is very nice to meet you."

I was anxious to depart but this young man would not be deterred. "Please," he said, "join me for tea."

"Thank you."

I followed him outside the church and into a hall where he shepherded me to a trestle table where a parishioner kindly offered us a cup of tea and a biscuit.

"You have an English accent," remarked Frank.

"You are quite right, but I have been here a long time. Almost thirty years now. I am a teacher at St, John's College."

"Yes, that is a very fine school. I have heard of it,"

"What about you," I asked.

"I am training to be a pastor with the Apostolic Faith Mission. It is a Pentecostal church. The services are a little different. Let's say, it is more participatory. A vibrant church."

"So, what brings you here?" I asked.

"I came to listen to Tutu's sermon. I am pleased to see a black man appointed to the high clerical office of dean of the cathedral."

"He was rather forthright in attacking apartheid."

"Did that offend you?"

"Good grief, no. I agreed with every word he said."

At this very moment Tutu approached and he greeted us both warmly.

I shook his hand and said, "It is the first time I have attended mass in this cathedral. I am normally tied up in our school chapel on Sundays."

"You are always welcome," said Tutu. "I hope you enjoyed the service."

"I particularly enjoyed your sermon," I said.

"I am pleased."

"I was glad to see that you are not afraid of criticising apartheid."

"Why should I be afraid of teaching God's Word?" said Tutu.

"I agree, but the state is oppressive and creates fear."

"Do not be afraid," he said.

I went on the defensive and said in a halting voice, "I have had some bad experiences." I swallowed hard and continued," What has happened to me though is nothing. My good friend, Bram Fischer has just died in prison. He fought so hard against apartheid."

"I know of Bram Fischer," said Tutu. "He fought without fear. We need the government to know that we do not fear them. They are trying to defend the utterly indefensible, and they will fail. They will fail because they are ranging themselves on the side of evil and injustice against the Church of God. Like others who have done that in the past – the Neros, the Hitlers, the Idi Amins of this world – they will end up as the flotsam and jetsam of history."

Tutu excused himself and drifted away to greet other parishioners. I turned to Frank said, "What a gracious and determined man." He nodded in agreement.

I then suddenly blurted out, "I would love to attend one of your services in Soweto."

Frank looked surprised and said, "I can arrange for you to visit my father's church in Naledi, Soweto. No white man has ever asked to do this."

"Is this a problem," I asked.

"Of course, not. I shall arrange a visit. How shall I contact you?"

I wrote down my telephone number on the back of the service sheet and said, "Please don't go to any trouble."

A week later Ilse Fischer was in the newspapers. The St. John's College librarian had resigned. Ilse was working as a librarian at the University of the Witswatersrand and I suggested that she apply for the position at St. John's College. Ilse was offered the job but the offer was retracted when the incumbent librarian changed her mind about retiring. The matter caused a major controversy. On 27 May 1975 there was an article about the retracted job offer in the *Sunday Times*. Father Aelred Stubbs, a member of the School Council, had got very upset. He objected to the job withdrawal and escalated his complaint to the highest levels in the Anglican Church. Timothy Bavin, the Bishop of Johannesburg and Bill Burnett, the Archbishop of Cape Town were all drawn into the affair as Stubbs publicly aired his unhappiness and demanded a full investigation. He was not successful though in restoring Ilse's appointment. Stubbs was formerly the principal of the Anglican Theological College at Alice in the Transkei, where Desmond Tutu had trained for the ministry. Stubbs was well-known for his anti-apartheid views. He championed the black consciousness movement and ministered to banned and imprisoned black political activists. The government grew tired of his anti-apartheid activism and deported him to the United Kingdom.

It was in late June when I received a call from Frank. He invited me to be his guest at a Sunday service at his father's church. I told him that I would be delighted to attend and asked for directions on how to find the church. Frank chuckled and said that I could not drive into Soweto on my own. He would pick me up and take me there himself. I knew that it was a relatively long round trip to Soweto and back and protested that this seemed to be an enormous imposition on him. Frank would not be deterred and said that this was not a problem.

I attended the Sunday mass in our school chapel, had an early lunch and waited outside the school entrance for Frank to pick me up at 1.00 pm, which he said would give us sufficient time to get to Soweto in time for the 2.00 pm service. Frank arrived in a small yellow mini. "Good morning. Are you ready to celebrate the Lord's Day, Soweto style?"

"Good morning, Frank. Thank you so much for doing this. I am very excited about visiting your father's church."

Soweto is short for South Western Townships. It is home to almost a million blacks that live and work in Johannesburg. As we drove into Soweto, I saw rows and rows of small houses, and areas that contained shacks and cheap hovels. There were some large buildings in the distance, which Frank said were dormitories for migrant workers. There were few cars and people either wobbled along on bicycles or walked. I could not help notice the litter. There were papers, bottles, and cans strewn alongside the road. Frank read my mind as I gawked at the litter and said, "It is difficult when rubbish collection is so frequent. When rubbish is not collected regularly, it is easier to just dump your rubbish on the street. Do you know why we hold our service at 2.00 pm?"

"No. I suppose it is as good as time as any."

"Our service is in the middle of the day because the church and most of Soweto has no electricity. Almost a million people without access to electricity. Our mothers cook on fires and our children study by candle light."

"That is unjust."

"The government claims that Sowetans are happy. They ignore our plight at their peril."

I unfortunately responded by saying, "Am I safe here?"

"Are you scared?"

"Should I be?"

"Do not worry. You are safe with me."

"Without you?"

"It might not be a good idea. The older generation are peaceful, but the youths are filled with anger. They seethe with discontent and advocate violent revolution."

"What do you think?"

"We are all made in the image of God. He wants us to love one another."

Frank had to gently beep repeatedly as we made drove through the narrow and congested streets. "We are here," said Frank with a smile. I could see a small white building and the words Apostolic Faith Mission in bold black letters. I opened my door and was immediately greeted by a lady, who was dressed smartly and wearing a large-brimmed hat.

"Welcome," she said, "You must be Mr Allum."

"Henry,"

"We are very pleased that you are here."

Frank appeared from the rear of the car and said "Let me introduce you. This is my mother, Erenia."

"I am so pleased to meet you," I said nodding my head vigorously.

She gently tapped my arm and said, "Follow me. Frank is late. The service is about to start,"

The congregation was already seated and there was a loud babble of conversation. As I entered the congregation fell quiet and everyone turned to stare at me. I felt very conspicuous, nodded a few times, and was relieved to sit down. There was a steady murmuring of voices and I feared that I was the subject of their whispered conversations. Frank's father James, stood up to commence the service.

James called out loudly, 'Hallelujah."

The congregation shouted back, "Hallelujah."

James continued, "We welcome our special guest today, Mr Henry Allum. Welcome,"

The congregation answered loudly, "*Yebo*." and turned to look at me. I smiled and raised my hand in an appreciative acknowledgment.

There was no organ, no hymn books, and no order of service. The congregation seemed to need no direction and simply sang hymns with gusto. Men, women, and children swayed from side to side and clapped their hands as they gave full voice to the most glorious gospel music. They sang the freedom song *Nkosi Sikelel iAfrika* (God Bless Africa). This song was a symbol of black liberation. James Chikane gave a passionate sermon in the vernacular that I could not follow, but it hardly mattered because most of the service consisted of gospel singing.

After the service Erenia invited me to join them in the rectory. Many people were crowded into the small, sparsely furnished house. I barely had a chance to talk to James because he was pre-occupied with others.

"Did you enjoy the service?" asked Frank.

"Very much so. The singing was beautiful and very joyous."

"Oh yes. We wake up the good Lord on a Sunday."

I smiled and accepted Erenia's invitation to help myself to a slice of fruit cake.

Erenia said. "You are a school teacher,"

"Yes," I said. "I met Frank at St. Mary's cathedral and expressed an interest in attending his church. I am so grateful for all the trouble he has gone to today to make this visit possible."

"It is unusual for any white to visit Soweto, let alone our church", said Erenia.

"They are the poorer for missing out on such glorious singing."

Erenia smiled and continued, "They do not want to see how we live. They want us to be out of sight, out of mind."

"Apartheid is regrettable." I remarked.

"Only regrettable," huffed Erenia, "it is a sin."

"Indeed."

Frank interrupted, "Soweto is bubbling with anger. The young will not be passive like our parents. They want a revolution."

I clasped my hands in front of me and said, "One of the reasons I came to South Africa from England was because I met Bram Fischer. He died recently. He gave his life to fighting apartheid. Bram introduced me to Nelson Mandela, Walter Sisulu, and others from the Rivonia trial. They have paid a heavy price, but in the long-run they shall overcome."

Frank said, "I read about Bram Fischer's death. I am very sorry. Mandela has suffered greatly for the people but he has achieved little."

"I hope not. He is very courageous and has sacrificed everything for the struggle."

Frank shook his head and said, "Mandela was a stooge of white communists."

I objected strongly. "That is not true. Fischer was a communist and dedicated to equality for all."

"Yes" said Frank, "But we need blacks, not whites, to stand up for blacks. I support Robert Sobukwe, He was imprisoned on Robben Island for many years. He is out now but he is a banned person and confined to Kimberley. Sobukwe argues that we should not collaborate with whites. This is still a master and servant relationship. We, blacks, must take charge of securing our freedom."

"Can you do that without resorting to violence?"

Frank replied, "I believed in violence as a young man. I was filled with hatred and wanted to participate in a violent revolution. I could have continued down that road but I joined the church. Now I try to quell black anger but I encourage blacks to be proud of being black."

"What made you become a pastor?" I asked.

"I wanted to be a physicist or mathematician and studied these subjects at the University of the North in Turfloop."

"Where is that?" I asked.

"The university is near Pietersburg in the northern Transvaal. I got involved in university politics. Many student leaders were arrested and I was heavily involved in raising funds for their defence. The stress got to me and I missed some exams because I was in hospital. I wanted to re-take my exams but the university authorities told me that I could not continue my studies, I was so angry but my father has taught me to control my anger. I realised that I could achieve more by preaching the Christian message of hope and forgiveness. I have almost finished my studies now to become a pastor."

"Was it the interruption to your studies or apartheid that made you so angry?" I asked.

"You could say so but I was very damaged as a sixteen-year-old."

"How."

"Let me explain," said Frank. "At sixteen-years old blacks must carry a pass. This evil paper confirms our servitude. I was walking down a road in Soweto when a car pulled up and three white policemen jumped out. One of them demanded to see my pass. I said, Good Morning, *Meneer*. The white policeman shouted call me *Baas*. I thought it was polite to address him as *Meneer*, but this obviously offended him. He wanted me to call him *Baas*, or Boss, because this confirms his superiority and my inferiority. He immediately punched me hard in the stomach and I fell to the ground. I was kicked on the ground and called a cheeky *kaffir*. I screamed that I could show them my pass. They kicked me again and again calling me a *kaffir* each time they kicked. I was simply left lying on the ground in a pool of blood, just because I had called a white policeman *Meneer* instead of *Baas*."

"I am so sorry."

"It is not your fault. I decided that no black should accept a status of inferiority. I try help blacks understand that we are all equal in God's eyes."

Erenia decided that it was time to change the subject and she asked me a barrage of questions about England, Oxford University, and St. John's College. Her interest was genuine but I was acutely embarrassed in talking about my life that was so clearly enveloped in privilege. Frank then announced that he should return me to St. John's College before it got too late.

On our way out of Soweto, Frank drove down Vilikazi Street. We had to travel very slowly because the street was filled with people. He stopped outside a small red brick house and said that this was the home of Nelson and Winnie Mandela. He stated that Winnie was probably inside the house. She was a banned person, who was prohibited from meeting more than one person at a time. We proceeded a little further and he pointed out another house, the home of Desmond Tutu.

In November I learnt that the headmaster, Jan Breitenbach, had invited Beyers Naude to deliver the Sunday Evensong sermon in the St. John's College chapel. Beyers Naude was once the moderator of the Dutch Reformed Church and a member of the Broederbond, the exclusive society that sought to promote the

Afrikaner people. After the 1960 Sharpeville massacre, Naude resigned from the Dutch Reformed Church and formed the Christian Institute of Southern Africa, an ecumenical organisation that aimed to promote racial harmony. Naude was seen as a traitor to the Afrikaner cause and the security police persistently harassed him. In 1977 he was banned and subjected to house arrest for seven years.

Beyers Naude, like Bram Fischer, was a privileged Afrikaner from an elite family. These two men could have been embraced by their fellow Afrikaners as leaders, but instead they courageously joined the anti-apartheid movement. I wanted Frank Chikane to appreciate that not all white opponents of apartheid were focused on a communist revolution. There were whites, like Beyers Naude, that were prepared to make great sacrifices in fighting against apartheid. I asked Jan Breitenbach, if I could invite Frank to the service. Breitenbach encouraged me to do so. I called Frank and to my pleasant surprise he accepted my invitation. I asked Frank to join me for an early tea in my rooms before the 6.00 pm evensong service.

At around 5,00 pm there was a gentle knock on my door. I was at my desk marking essays and I called out, "Come in."

A prefect from my house opened the door and said, "There is a boy here who wants to see you."

I replied, "Well, let him come in."

"Fine'" he said, "you can go in."

I looked up to see Frank as he entered my study. He turned to the prefect and said, "Thank you."

I blurted out, "I am so sorry. He called you a boy."

"I am used to that," replied Frank.

"I shall speak to him. You are an adult. It is so disrespectful to be called a boy."

"You should not be surprised," said Frank, "black men are called that all the time. It is better than some of the other things I have been called."

I was acutely aware that referring to black men as boys was very common. I made a mental note to speak to this schoolboy. He, like so many others, commonly referred to black men as boys. It reflected a deeply ingrained belief in racial superiority.

I put the kettle on and asked Frank to make himself comfortable on the sofa. He did so and said, "Please do not be angry with that young man."

"It is just ignorance," I said.

"He is a very privileged young man going to a school like this. I guess you are teaching them to be the masters."

"I hope not. I hope we are teaching them to serve rather than be served."

Frank scoffed, "A white man in Africa serving?"

"We can but try, "I replied, "At any rate that young man will be conscripted into the army next year to do his national service."

"Whites only. They get trained to fight for apartheid," said Frank.

"Yes, but many of them are now getting caught up in this dreadful war in Angola."

"Fighting communists?"

"Of course, but it is more than that. The South African government is terrified at seeing states to our north acquire black governments. They like to argue that we are fighting communists. I think we are really fighting to preserve the status quo."

"All the black youths want the South African army to lose," said Frank.

"The South African army is very powerful, but they cannot stop black governments taking over from their former colonial masters."

"Indeed," said Frank, "we need to remove all colonial governments. The whites in South Africa must also go."

"Where to?" I asked.

"Back to Europe. Back to where they came from,"

I thought for a moment and said, "I am pleased you have come to listen to Beyers Naude. His family has been here for hundreds of years. He is not a colonialist, he is an African, He believes in equality and that everyone can live here in harmony."

I am here to listen," said Frank.

Frank and I finished our tea and sandwiches. I realised that evensong was about to start and I told Frank that we needed to hasten to the chapel. I donned my academic gown and guided Frank to the chapel. Jan Breitenbach and Beyers Naude were standing in front of the main doors. I approached Jan Breitenbach and introduced Frank. Breitenbach greeted Frank warmly then introduced us both to Beyers Naude. Little did they realise then that they would develop a very close relationship. Beyers Naude would, many years later, recommend that Frank succeed himself as the general secretary of the South African Council of Churches.

Naude preached to the schoolboys and kept his message relatively simple. He warned that the boys would face great challenges in South Africa and encouraged them to remember that the highest authority was God. He asked them to think about what Jesus would do when faced with the situations they encountered in their lives. Frank was keen to get back home as soon as possible after the service. He was impressed with Beyers Naude and very complimentary about the magnificent singing of the school choir. I said farewell and then walked across the rugby fields to the headmaster's house. Jan and Rose Breitenbach had laid on a tea for Beyers Naude, the Second Master, the three boarding housemasters, and six school prefects. It was all very pleasant and Beyers Naude did very well in engaging the boys in conversation.

He turned to one of the prefects and said, "Would it worry you if blacks attended this school?"

The prefect barely paused and answered, "No, I think that would be fine, provided they behaved like us."

I was proud of his affirmative answer but cringed at his proviso. I knew though that in the context of white South African society this young man had at least opened his mind to racial mixing. The government's apartheid policies had so segregated South Africa that boys of his age had never mixed at all with blacks. Beyers Naude simply smiled and I realised that he was prompting them to think about a future South Africa where apartheid did not exist.

As I listened to these young men talk to Beyers Naude it worried me that most of them would be conscripted in just a few months. The South African Defence Force had recently invaded Angola. Many of these conscripts would find themselves fighting in Angola or the neighbouring state of South West Africa. We all knew about the invasion of Angola but the government was silent. South Africa denied its involvement and the newspapers were banned from publishing anything about it.

In April 1974 there was a military coup in Lisbon. The Portuguese abandoned their African colonies of Angola and Mozambique and black Marxist governments came to power in these countries. This had a huge impact in South Africa. Whites felt threatened and blacks felt empowered. Portuguese troops withdrew from Mozambique and Frelimo freedom fighters poured into the country. In September 1974 Portugal handed over power to Frelimo. The Frelimo leader, Samora Machel, set out to transform Mozambique into a Marxist state. He nationalised farms and industry, reduced the power of local chiefs, and attacked the church. Machel declared that his aim was "to win total independence, to establish people's power, to build a new society without exploitation for the benefit of all those who consider themselves Mozambican."[46] His policies would leave the economy in ruins.

In Angola the transition to black rule was a mess. There were three factions that competed for power. The first faction was Holden Roberto's FNLA, which received military support from China. The second faction was Agostini Neto's MPLA, which received military supplies from the Soviet Union. The third faction was Jonas Savimbi's Unita, which received some arms from China but little other foreign support. Roberto, Neto, and Savimbi agreed to form a temporary coalition government prior to a general election in November 1975. Whites fled the country and the coalition soon began fighting amongst themselves. The MPLA received arms from the Soviet Union and imported Cuban military instructors. The MPLA was soon able to drive the FNLA and Unita out of Luanda and seize control. The United States had recently suffered a humiliating defeat in Vietnam and it feared the expansion of communism in southern Africa. Henry Kissinger, the United States Secretary of State, persuaded President Ford to support both the FNLA and Unita through supplying them with arms.

South Africa was feeling tvulnerable as the white governments to its north fell. In November 1974 South Africa's membership of the United Nations was suspended. South Africa was desperate for international alliances and the government felt that it could enhance its relationship with the United States through demonstrating a strong opposition to communism. South Africa supplied the FNLA and Unita with arms and in October 1975 launched an invasion into Angola. The South Africans advanced to the outskirts of Luanda from both the south and the north. The MPLA received massive assistance from the Soviet Union and Cuba. Soviet tanks and thousands of Cuban troops were flown in and they abruptly stopped the South African advance. On 11

November 1975 Agostino Neto proclaimed the People's Republic of Angola, while in the Huambo highlands, Jonas Savimbi announced the Democratic People's Republic of Angola. The civil war would continue for years. South Africa had charged into Angola to curry favour with the Americans. United States lawmakers however, soon became opposed towards ploughing funds into Angola and on 19 December 1975 the United States Senate voted to shut down all funding for Angola. The South African government began to see the folly of its Angolan adventure. Even if they captured Luanda, how would they govern the country? It would be like another Vietnam. Nationalist independence movements could not be thwarted indefinitely. South Africa had no option but to withdraw its troops. Nevertheless, South Africa would continue to fight against Swapo (South West Africa People's Organisation) guerillas that operated from Angola.

At the end of the First World War the League of Nations gave South Africa possession of South West Africa in terms of a mandate. In 1945 the United Nations superseded the League of Nations. Despite various United Nations resolutions South Africa refused to relinquish control of South West Africa. In 1969 the United Nations declared South Africa's occupation of South West Africa illegal, but South Africa would not budge. Swapo fought a guerilla war against South African occupation. Swapo based themselves in Angola, obtained assistance from Cuban troops, and relied on the Soviet Union for arms and ammunition. These communist alliances alienated Swapo from western support. The South African military were committed to keeping Swapo at bay and in 1977 compulsory national service (for white young men) was increased to two years to provide the required military manpower. The government imposed harsh sentences on those young men who refused to serve.

The demise of Portuguese rule in Mozambique and Angola made the continuation of white government in Rhodesia untenable. The South African government realised that Smith's Rhodesian government only served to destabilise the region. Guerillas fighters against the Smith regime were now able to operate freely from both Angola and Mozambique. Rhodesia was being propped up with South African military support and a negotiated settlement was needed. Henry Kissinger was concerned that if the position in Rhodesia remained unresolved it could widen the opportunities for the Soviet Union to expand its influence in southern Africa. Kissinger attempted to force Smith into accepting a settlement. Smith resisted and Rhodesia continued to fight an ugly guerilla war until they were forced to capitulate. In the 1980 election Robert Mugabe won an overwhelming victory. Mugabe commenced his rule with the spirit of reconciliation but would soon reduce the country, renamed Zimbabwe, to poverty, through corruption, greed, and mismanagement.

In 1976 Soweto exploded. The rise of the black consciousness movement and the collapse of colonial governments in Mozambique and Angola had contributed to black South Africans growing anger over the inequities of apartheid. The fuse that lit the powder keg was the government's decision to regulate that school children be taught half in Afrikaans and half in English. Very few blacks spoke Afrikaans and it was seen as the language of the oppressor. There were efforts to make the government change its mind but they adamantly refused. On 16 June 1976 students in Soweto organised a protest march. They carried banners, shouted slogans, and sang freedom songs. The government sent in armed police who fired tear gas. The crowd responded angrily and hurled stones at the police. The police fired indiscriminately. Sam Nzima, a photographer from *The World* newspaper, captured the tragic consequences of this murderous shooting in an epic photograph that went around the globe. The photograph shows eighteen-year-old Mbuyisa Makhubo carrying a thirteen-year-old boy, Hector Pieterson, who had had been shot dead. Pieterson's sister is running alongside them. The rioting spread and soon all of Soweto was aflame. Policemen were lynched and two white government employees were dragged onto the streets and killed.

Frank Chikane, now a newly ordained pastor in the Apostolic Faith Mission, had been sent to a congregation at Kagiso, a little to the north west of Soweto, one month before the outbreak of the Soweto riots. The residents of Kagiso went on the rampage. They smashed and set fire to buildings. The police responded by arresting scores of residents. It was a baptism of fire for Frank as he was thrust into the role of confronting the police and demanding to know the whereabouts of people they had detained. I called Frank to check that on his well-being. My calls were not answered but when he did call back, I could detect that he was exhausted, emotional, and slightly irritated by the supposed concern of this white school teacher who was largely oblivious to the realities of the turmoil in the black townships.

In December I wanted to wish Frank all the best for Christmas. I tried unsuccessfully to contact him and decided to call his mother, Erenia, who told me that Frank had been in prison for the past six months. On 6 June 1977 the police had arrested Frank because they believed he was a communist stooge. During his interrogation the security police demanded the names of his communist masters. Frank steadfastly maintained that he was nothing more than a servant of God. Frank was interrogated for four days and deprived of sleep. He was shackled and hung upside down, he was burnt with cigarettes, and suffocated under water. Frank refused to buckle and his interrogators gave up. He was taken to a police cell in Rustenberg and left in solitary confinement for six months. He was then brought before a magistrate and charged with public violence. It was an absurd charge and Frank was released on bail.

We had just returned to school in January 1978 when Erenia called me. "Henry", she said, "I thought you would be pleased to know that Frank has been released on bail."

"I am so pleased. Is he okay?"

"I don't know," replied Erenia. "He seems to be well but I fear that he has been treated very badly. The ordeal is not over though because he must return to the Krugersdorp courts on Tuesday."

The police arrested Frank in the early hours of the morning on the day he was due to return to court. James and Erenia Chikane, friends, and members of Frank's congregation, were packed into the courtroom. I sat in the separate area of the public gallery, reserved for whites only. In the whites only gallery there were some church clerics, a court reporter, and a handful of others. The black section was crammed and many of those who had come to the court were forced to wait outside. Everyone was asked to stand as the magistrate entered the court. Then Frank was led in. He had been brutally assaulted and was in a mess. He stooped, his head hung down, one eye was closed, and blood oozed from his head where clumps of hair had been pulled out. The gallery broke out into cries of "Shame, killers, torturers, murders." The magistrate demanded silence and court officers glared menacingly at those shouting in the public gallery. The prosecutor stood and declared that the Reverend Frank Chikane was being charged with inciting public violence and disorder. The magistrate asked for the police report and flipped rapidly through the pages. He then looked sternly at the prosecutor and declared that there was no charge against this man. He ordered that Frank be released immediately and the trial closed. There were shouts of jubilation. Frank was mobbed and I could not get near him. I caught his eye from a distance. He nodded and mouthed "thank you,"

One of the most disgraceful things about the Soweto uprising was that the government ministers responsible for imposing the Afrikaans language, M. C. Botha and Andries Treurnicht, made no effort to rectify their heinous education policies. The government simply responded with force and resorted to detaining black leaders, both young and old. This included Percy Qobozo, the editor of the *Sowetan* newspaper, and Dr Nthato Motlana, a respected civic leader and physician. The violence spread throughout the country and over the next two years the police killed over seven-hundred protesters. There was an entire generation of schoolchildren that lost out on an education. They adopted the motto of "Liberation before education" and thousands of schoolchildren fled the country to join the ANC. They would receive military training and infiltrate back into the country to conduct acts of sabotage. Although many of the schoolchildren that joined the armed struggle found themselves simply languishing in ANC training camps.

CHAPTER 17

Enemies of the State

The South African government were ruthless in acting against perceived enemies. Political opponents were viewed as being dangerous terrorists and communists. The government doggedly pursued political activists and used the courts to impose harsh sentences for relatively trivial offences.

Raymond Suttner, a lecturer at the University of Natal in Durban, joined the ANC. From 1971 to 1975 he produced anti-apartheid pamphlets which he distributed in letter-boxes in Durban and Pietermaritzburg. The security police imagined that he had done far worse things and tortured him during interrogation. George Bizos represented Suttner at his trial but two ANC colleagues had become state witnesses and the outcome was never in doubt. Justice Neville James sentenced Suttner to seven-and-a-half years in prison.

In September 1976 David Rabkin and his wife, Sue, were sentenced to ten years and one year respectively for publishing and distributing ANC and SACP pamphlets. David Rabkin was a journalist at the *Cape Argus* newspaper. David and Sue had two children and Sue was pregnant when sentenced, but she only served one month before being released. Sue and the children immediately left South Africa. David joined Umkhonto we Sizwe after his release, but was killed in Angola during a training accident. Jeremy Cronin, a lecturer in philosophy at the University of Cape Town, was tried at the same time as David and Sue Rabkin, on the same charges. He was sentenced to seven years in prison. In November 1976, Tony Holiday, a journalist with the *Cape Times,* was sentenced to six years in prison for publishing ANC literature.

International criticism of apartheid hardened but within the country the government faced little opposition. The government used their powers of detention to silence opponents. In parliament the Progressive Party fought valiantly but they were too small to make a difference. Harry Schwartz resigned from the United Party and formed the Reform Party. In 1976 the Progressive Party and Reform Party merged to become the Progressives Reform Party. Then in 1977 they were joined by other disaffected United Party members to form the Progressive Federal Party. In the 1977 general election the Progressive Federal Party became the official opposition but held only 17 seats against the Nationalist Party's 134 seats.

Steve Biko continued to write and campaign against apartheid. In August 1977 he travelled to Cape Town, despite his banning orders. On his return to King Williams Town he was arrested at a police roadblock. He was thrown into a police cell, kept naked, and savagely beaten. A doctor called to examine him reported that he could see no injuries. When the security police noted that he was unconscious they decided to move him to a hospital in Pretoria over one-thousand kilometres away. He was thrown naked into the back of a prison van and driven to Pretoria. On 12 September 1977 he died from his head injuries. He was just thirty years old. The Minister of Justice, Jimmy Kruger, announced that he had died from a hunger strike and callously made this comment at the Transvaal congress of the Nationalist Party: "I am not glad and I am not sorry about Mr Biko. It leaves me cold."[47] One of the delegates frivolously congratulated Kruger on being so democratic that he allowed prisoners the democratic right to starve to death. Kruger enjoyed the attention of the laughing delegates and confirmed that this was very democratic. He continued, "Of course one feels sorry about any death – I suppose I would feel sorry about my own."[48]

Donald Woods, the editor of the Eastern Cape newspaper the *Daily Dispatch*, had befriended Steve Biko to understand the black consciousness movement better. Woods hired black journalists and was very critical of the government. Woods was outraged when he heard about Biko's death. He challenged the starvation story as implausible nonsense and publicly demanded that Kruger release the results of the post-mortem. Kruger backed away from the starvation story, and began to depict Biko as a violent terrorist, from whom the police had successfully protected the public. The coroner's post-mortem report stated that Biko had died of brain damage. Woods managed to inspect Biko's body in the mortuary and saw for himself that Biko had not starved to death and had suffered head injuries. There was widespread rioting and, as usual, the government responded with force. They detained hundreds and flooded the townships with riot police. Over fifteen thousand attended Biko's funeral and thousands more were prevented from attending as the police set up roadblocks. Bishop Desmond Tutu delivered the eulogy. He drew a parallel between Steve Biko and Jesus Christ and said, "We, too, like the disciples of Jesus, have been stunned by the death of another man in his thirties. A young man completely dedicated to the pursuit of justice and righteousness, of peace and reconciliation."[49] Tutu urged the angry mourners to pray for whites who had lost their humanity. He concluded with a blunt message for the government: "Please, please, for God's sake listen to us while there is just a possibility of reasonably peaceful change."[50]

The outcry over Biko's death forced the government into holding an inquest. The presiding magistrate concluded, "The cause or likely cause of Mr Biko's death was a head injury, followed by extensive brain injury and other complications including renal failure. The head injury was probably sustained during a scuffle with the Security Police... The available evidence does not prove that death was brought about by an act or omission involving an offence by any person."[51]

The government responded to Donald Woods' vocal criticisms by banning him. In terms of his banning order Woods was forbidden "to write; to be quoted; to be with more than one person at a time; to speak with more than one person at a time; to communicate with any other banned person; to leave the magisterial district of East London; to enter harbour premises there; to enter printing or publishing premises of any kind; to enter any factory or school or other educational institution."[52] Woods could no longer work although his newspaper employers continued to pay his salary. At the end of 1977 Woods made a daring escape across the Lesotho border and obtained asylum in the United Kingdom. He published a book on Steve Biko and continued to criticise the apartheid government.

Tim Jenkin and Stephen Lee met at the University of Cape Town. They treated their university courses cynically but read voraciously and decided that white superiority was a racist and fascist indoctrination. Jenkin identified four great white myths that were widely disseminated. The first was that whites had a historical claim on the land because most of it was unoccupied when they trekked into the interior. This was not true and blacks had occupied the land for hundreds, or even thousands, of years before white settlers arrived. The second was that there were no majorities only minorities. South African whites argued that there were multiple ethnic black groups and that no one group could claim a right to South Africa. A cornerstone of apartheid policy was to segregate black groups and despatch them to live in unviable independent homelands. The third was that blacks in South Africa were better off than anywhere else in Africa. Blacks were supposed to be grateful for living under apartheid rather than under a black government in some other African country. The fourth was that the white government was invincible. The security forces were so strong that opposition was futile. Tim Jenkin recognised that students tended to espouse liberal politics until they entered the workforce. They found well-paying jobs and enjoyed their luxurious lifestyles given the advantages of white privilege. In his opinion doing nothing was the same as condoning the system and emigrating was copping out. He thought that the parliamentary opposition was ineffectual, and he saw the ANC as the only organisation that stood for a democratic South Africa without any reference to race. Tim and his friend Stephen Lee went to London and offered their services to the ANC. They were trained in the art of writing political propaganda, how to use duplicating machines, and how to distribute the pamphlets using letter-bombs. These were not real bombs but explosive devices that dispersed bundles of pamphlets over a large area. Tim Jenkin and Stephen Lee went back to South Africa and they embarked on writing and distributing pamphlets using the letter-bomb technique. They carried out this task successfully for almost four years until the security police caught up with them. On the charge of disseminating seventeen pamphlets with the intention of undermining law and order, Tim Jenkin and Stephen Lee were sentenced to twelve years and eight years in prison respectively.

They were incarcerated with the other white political prisoners at Pretoria Local. Jenkin, Lee, and Moumbaris though would create dramatic headlines eighteen months later when they staged a remarkable prison escape on 11 December 1979. They had made wooden keys in the prison workshop. After elaborate planning and practice they managed, in the dead of night, to open nine doors before finding their way barred by a final tenth door. Their escape plan was almost foiled but they managed to chisel out the final lock and walk out of the prison. The front pages were filled with reports of their escape. They were described as dangerous terrorists and the police assured the public that they would be caught. The escapees luck held and they managed to get out of the country through the Swaziland border. On 2 January 1980 the three escapees gave a press conference in Lusaka, to the dismay of the South African government. South African newspapers suggested wild theories about the escape. One newspaper stated that Joe Slovo had planned the escape, while another claimed it was the work of the Soviet KGB.

It was not unsurprising that South Africa suffered from an exceedingly poor international image. Eschel Rhoodie became the secretary of the Department of Information after working in various South African embassies as a press attaché. He convinced the Prime Minister, John Vorster, that the government's image could be improved if they conducted an international campaign to highlight South Africa's strategic importance to the west. Vorster gave him access to unlimited secret funds to wage this campaign. Vorster kept this funding secret. He did not advise the Department of Foreign Affairs or even all the members of his cabinet. Rhoodie decided that foreign journalists were obtaining too much of their input from anti-government English language South African newspapers. He set up an English language newspaper called *The Citizen* whose editorial policy was to cast the government in a favourable light. He attempted to take over media organisations in Europe and the United States. His only real success though was in acquiring a Californian newspaper, the *Sacramento Union,* and a half share in a television station. Rhoodie spent lavishly on foreign politicians who undoubtedly enjoyed his largesse. Rhoodie's extravagant expenditures were noticed and the Department of Information came under scrutiny. The *Sunday Express* exposed the expenditures on its front pages and the secret funding became known as the Information Scandal. Vorster was widely criticised and he was forced to sack Rhoodie and restructure the Information Department. The Information Scandal had severely damaged Vorster and on 20 September 1978 he resigned, citing ill health.

There were three candidates to take over as Prime Minister: P W (Pieter Willem) Botha, Connie Mulder, and Pik (Roelof Frederik) Botha. Vorster wanted Connie Mulder to succeed him. Mulder was the most right-wing of the candidates and he enjoyed the support of the Nationalist Party base in the Transvaal. Mulder however, had been the Minister of Information and the persistent scandal surrounding this department damaged his political career. Pik Botha was the youngest and most enlightened of the candidates. He was the Minister of Foreign Affairs and easily commanded the popular support of the white public. The Nationalist Party caucus though would not support him. P W Botha was the Minister of Defence and the most senior cabinet minister. On 28 September 1978 P W Botha narrowly beat Mulder in a caucus ballot to become Prime Minister. P W Botha attempted to soften the image of apartheid through moving away from petty apartheid policies but he was a belligerent man that would remain resolutely committed to maintaining white rule.

P W Botha removed Hendrik van den Bergh from the Bureau of State Security and renamed it the Department of National Security. He then transferred the main power for protecting the state to the military. He described South Africa as facing a total onslaught from enemies both within and outside South Africa's borders. He believed that the Soviet Union had a plan for global domination. He argued that the armed struggle against South Africa had little to do with its apartheid policies, but it was because there were communist forces marshalling to take over South Africa.

International pressure continued to build against South Africa. The United Nations imposed an arms embargo, OPEC imposed an oil embargo, and major oil supplies were cut off following the 1979 revolution in Iran. In 1977 Jimmy Carter became the President of the United States and he adopted a far less conciliatory attitude to South Africa than his predecessors. There were growing anti-apartheid campaigns pushing for economic boycotts, trade sanctions, and disinvestment. South Africa was excluded from the Olympic Games and other international sporting events. In 1977 the Commonwealth Heads of Government met at the Gleneagles Hotel in Scotland. They resolved to discourage sporting contacts between their countries and South Africa. Despite this agreement the New Zealand Prime minister, allowed the Springbok rugby team to tour in 1981. There were huge protests. The game against Waikato had to be called off because the ground was invaded by hundreds of protesters. The All Blacks won the three-test series 2-1 but a massive police presence was needed to combat protesters. During the third test a light aircraft dropped flour and smoke bombs on the Eden Park ground in Auckland.

I called Frank Chikane occasionally. He was very busy looking after his congregation. The concern that I expressed from the comfort of my secure home in a plush white suburb hardly resonated with this man that dealt with the harsh realities of apartheid every day. Frank saw politics as meaning different things for whites and blacks. Frank noted that whites saw politics as being about different political parties. Blacks however, were accused of being involved in politics for opposing apartheid policies. Frank was arrested again in 1980 and the Apostolic Faith Mission removed him from his congregation because he was too heavily involved in politics. The white leaders of the Apostolic Faith Mission were un-Christian in their behaviour and were even so cruel as to evict Frank's wife and child from their church-provided home. Frank appealed his suspension but was never reinstated. Frank moved on to work for the South African Council of Churches. He remained deeply committed to the anti-apartheid movement and in 1983 he became an important leader in the United Democratic Front.

In June 1980 Joe Slovo successfully used Umkhonto we Sizwe operatives based in Mozambique to blow up two power plants and an oil refinery in the Transvaal. On 30 January 1981 the South African Defence Force struck back and attacked an Umkhonto we Sizwe base at Matolo in Mozambique. During the raid they shot and killed fourteen Umkhonto we Sizwe comrades, including the respected Communist Party Leader, Motso 'Obadi' Mokgabudi. They also killed an innocent Portuguese civilian in the mistaken belief that he was Joe Slovo. They kidnapped Vuyani Mavuso, an Umkhonto we Sizwe soldier, and interrogated him. He refused to supply information about his comrades and was later executed.

The military mindset dominated all government decision-making and hit squads were emboldened. In July 1981 Joe Gqabi, the ANC representative in Zimbabwe was gunned down in front of his house in Harare. Gqabi had once worked closely with Ruth First as a photographer and reporter for the *New Age* newspaper. In June 1982 Petros Nyawose, the ANC representative in Swaziland, and his wife, Jabulile, were blown up by a car bomb outside their home.

In 1974 St. John's College played a rugby game against Hilton College, an excellent school based just outside Pietermaritzburg in Natal. Charles Yeats was their head boy and captain of rugby. I saw a lot of good schoolboy rugby players but you only remember the names of those very few that are truly exceptional, Charles Yeats was one of those extraordinarily talented players that left a lasting impression. I was the master on-duty when he led his team into Darragh Hall for the evening meal. It was evident that Yeats was a natural leader of men. He did not hold court but quietly drew everyone into the table conversation. In mid-1981 Yeats received much publicity in the newspapers because he refused to serve in the South African Defence Forces. His refusal might have gone unnoticed but his rugby talents, in a country besotted with rugby, meant that the media picked up his case. Yeats refused to serve in the army but offered to serve in a non-military capacity. He stated that his refusal was because of his belief in the injustices of apartheid, the illegality of South Africa's occupation of South West Africa, and because he was a Christian pacifist. Denis Hurley, the Catholic Archbishop, Philip Russell, the Anglican Archbishop, and Professor John Dugard an expert on international law, provided testimony in his support. Yeats was found guilty and sentenced to a year in military detention barracks. He refused to wear a military uniform in the detention barracks and for this he was sentenced to a year in prison where he was incarcerated with common criminals.

Yeats was not the first, or last, young man to refuse military service. In the 1950s a group of liberal women formed an organisation called The Women's Defence of the Constitution League, but it became known as the Black Sash because the women wore black sashes when they demonstrated. In 1983 the Black Sash began an End Conscription Campaign. They supported conscientious objectors and argued for alternative forms of military service. The government detained many Black Sash members and many conscientious objectors were jailed.

Dr Neil Aggett was a medical doctor and trade union organiser. In November 1981 the security police detained Aggett and his partner, Elizabeth Floyd. After seventy days in detention Neil Aggett was found hanging in his cell at John Vorster Police Station in Johannesburg. The police announced that Aggett had committed suicide. His funeral received huge publicity and thousands attended. His father, Aubrey Aggett, refused to accept the suicide explanation and he approached attorneys to investigate. The attorneys briefed George Bizos who discovered a written statement from Neil Aggett to a police officer complaining about being tortured. Bizos also obtained affidavits from other detainees concerning ill treatment and systematic torture. A magisterial inquest was held into the death. Bizos interrogated the police who claimed that Aggett was well treated and appeared normal, but Bizos presented affidavits from detainees that described beatings, electrical shocks torture, and sleep deprivation. Elizabeth Floyd described hearing detainees screaming while they were being interrogated. The magistrate disbelieved all the detainee's evidence and accepted no criticisms of the security police. The magistrate concluded that another detainee was to blame for Aggett's death because he had failed to report his suicidal state to authorities. The media mocked the magistrate's findings as lacking all credibility. The government was deeply embarrassed by the deaths of Steve Biko and Neil Aggett, but instead of modifying their treatment of detainees, they adopted even more draconian measures. The security police were allowed to form death squads to kill their enemies.

Ruth First had found it difficult to be a stay-at-home mother, especially while her husband, Joe Slovo, was so engrossed with ANC and Umkhonto we Sizwe affairs. Ruth and Joe both had affairs. It was reasonably common knowledge that Joe had an affair with Stephanie Kemp who was married to Albie Sachs, the son of the well-known trade unionist Solly Sachs. Kemp had first met Albi Sachs during her trial when he acted as junior counsel for her defence. Sachs was subsequently detained twice under the Ninety-day detention law and decided to go to the United Kingdom. Kemp applied for an exit visa immediately after her release from prison and married Albi Sachs in London shortly afterwards. Sachs and Kemp had two children but Joe Slovo had fathered one of them. In 1980 Sachs and Kemp divorced. Ruth First and Joe Slovo managed to stay married despite their separate lives. Ruth obtained a lecturing job in Durham, but in 1976 she went to Maputo, Mozambique to take up a position as a research director at the Eduardo Mondlane University. Ruth was no longer actively involved with the ANC, but she was married to one of the most hated men of the South African state. In August 1982 the security police intercepted a letter addressed to her in Maputo. The security police inserted an explosive device into the envelope. Ruth opened it and was blown to pieces. Thousands attended her funeral in Maputo where she was buried in the national cemetery alongside the slain Matolo fighters. I wrote to Gillian Slovo to express my condolences. She thanked me and forwarded a newspaper cutting of her, her sisters Robyn and Shawn, and her father, Joe Slovo, standing next to Ruth's grave.

After completing his twelve-year prison sentence Marius Schoon went into exile and joined the ANC and SACP. He was working as a lecturer in Lubango, Angola. The security police tracked down his address and sent him a letter that contained an explosive device. The letter arrived on 28 June 1984, Marius Schoon was not at home, but his wife Jeannette opened the letter. The resulting explosion killed both her and their six-year-old daughter, Katryn. South Africa had lost its moral compass.

CHAPTER 18

The darkest hour is before dawn

In November 1978 Frederik Van Zyl Slabbert replaced Colin Eglin as the leader of the Progressive Federal Party. Van Zyl Slabbert was hugely competent and a marvellous parliamentary debater. He was charismatic, intelligent, and a natural leader. In the April 1981 general election, the Progressive Federal Party increased its number of seats to 26 and consolidated its position as the official opposition. The Nationalist Party still won an overwhelming majority, winning 131 out of 165 seats. It is easy to imagine that opposition to the Nationalist Party would build on the left. This was not the case and despite the descent into a police state, white opposition to the government grew on the right.

P W Botha realised that South Africa had to do something to justify the continuation of the apartheid state. He adopted the slogan 'adapt or die' and embarked on a programme to reform the constitution. The grand policy of apartheid was to have no black citizens in South Africa as they were to be given citizenship rights in independent black homelands. The democratic rights of Indians and Coloureds were more problematic and the government recognised the need for constitutional change. Chris Heunis was appointed to the position of Minister of Constitutional Reform. He led a commission to devise a new constitution and came up with the idea of a tricameral parliament. The tricameral constitution excluded blacks but incorporated a form of power sharing with a White, Coloured, and Indian chamber elected on separate rolls on a fixed ratio of 4:2:1 that corresponded to the population size of each group. It was transparently obvious that the whites could not be outvoted by the Coloureds and Indians. Andries Treurnicht led a large right-wing Nationalist Party faction that would not tolerate any form of power-sharing. On 24 February 1982 Andries Treurnicht and twenty-nine other members of parliament, including Connie Mulder, left the Nationalist Party and formed the Conservative Party.

In November 1983 the government held a white-voters only referendum to approve the new constitution. It was rather bizarre because both the Conservative Party and the Progressive Federal Party campaigned for a no vote. The Conservative Party believed that any form of power-sharing would lead to the demise of white government. Frederik Van Zyl Slabbert led the Progressive Federal Party in campaigning against the new constitution. Van Zyl Slabbert articulated his reasons very succinctly: "It was one party's solution imposed on the rest of the country; it excluded blacks from its workings, and therefore would polarize black/white and promote conflict and dissatisfaction; it entrenched racial laws which lay at the heart of apartheid as we and the rest of the world came to know it; and it gave too much power to the new executive President."[53]

The government unleashed a massive marketing campaign to promote the new constitution. It was thoroughly depressing to see how the white electorate bought the government line that this was progress towards a more democratic society. There were some exceptions and four significant business leaders voiced their opposition: Harry Oppenheimer, Gordon Waddell, Tony

Bloom, and Clive Menell. The Afrikaans press had always taken a pro government line, but the English press, with the obvious exception of *The Citizen,* had generally supported the government's opponents. It was enormously disappointing therefore to see the English newspapers come out in favour of the referendum. The *Sunday Times* and the *Financial Mail* urged its readers to vote yes because they saw the new constitution as a step in the right direction. *The Star* took the cowardly position of recommending that its readers abstain from voting. The government carried the referendum with almost two-thirds of the vote and the new constitution came into effect in September 1984. It was impossible to determine exactly who had voted no because of the opposition of both the Progressive Federal Party and Conservative Party. Van Zyl Slabbert was very upset by the yes vote which he described as "thumb sucking and wishful thinking on an impressive scale."[54]

In terms of the new constitution, P W Botha became the President. P W Botha immediately ensured that the State Security Council (SSC) became more powerful than the cabinet. The SSC comprised the President, the Minister of Defence, the Minister of Foreign Affairs, the Minister of Law and Order, the head of the National Intelligence Service, the Chief of the South African Defence Force, the Commissioner of Police, and the Directors General of Foreign Affairs and Law and Order. P W Botha argued that a total strategy was required to combat the total onslaught that the country faced. The ANC was now operating within all South Africa's border countries. There was no possibility of the ANC defeating the South African military but they continued to launch sabotage attacks. The most devastating was a car-bomb outside a military building that killed sixteen people and injured almost two hundred others.

The government attacked military targets in neighbouring countries. South Africa increased its support of Unita in Angola, it gave arms and ammunition to Renamo, the Mozambiquan rebel group that was attempting to topple Samora Machel's Frelimo government. It attacked Swapo bases in Angola and ANC targets in Lesotho and Mozambique. The South Africa government placed economic pressure on its neighbouring states through trade restrictions. This forced them to fall into line and expel the ANC. Swaziland and Lesotho signed agreements and then Mozambique also signed an agreement. This agreement was known as the Nkomati Accord and was signed by P W Botha and Samora Machel in March 1984 on the bank of the Nkomati River, which marked the border between South Africa and Mozambique.

Allan Boesak, a Cape Coloured, was a minister in the Coloured branch of the Dutch Reformed Church. In 1981 he became the chairman of the Alliance of Black Reformed Christians in Southern Africa. In August 1982 he attended a meeting of the World Alliance of Reformed Churches (WARC) in Canada. He successfully persuaded WARC to declare apartheid a heresy, have the membership of South Africa's Dutch Reformed Church suspended, and get elected as WARC's president. Boesak called for a united front to oppose the proposed tricameral parliament reforms. This led to the formation of the United Democratic Front (UDF), an umbrella organisation for civic groups, trade unions, and students. The UDF opposed the participation of Coloureds and Indians in the tricameral parliament elections and over eighty percent of Coloureds and Indians boycotted the elections. The UDF soon became a legal front for the banned ANC and it adopted a charter that closely resembled the ANC's Freedom Charter. Frank Chikane became the national vice-president of the UDF. Frank gave the opening address at the launch of the UDF at a rally in Cape Town on 20 August 2983. Chikane promoted the UDF slogan "UDF Unites, Apartheid Divides." Allan Boesak also spoke and captured the mood of the movement with one brief sentence: "We want all our rights, we want them here, and we want them now."[55]

In 1976 Desmond Tutu was appointed Bishop of Lesotho. In 1978 he returned to Johannesburg to become the General-Secretary of the South African Council of Churches (SACC). The SACC was an ecumenical organisation of churches in South Africa. Under Tutu's leadership the SACC grew increasingly critical of apartheid. The government accused the SACC of being an instrument of foreign organisations trying to foment a communist revolution in South Africa. The government tried various ways of shutting down the SACC and in 1981 they appointed Justice Christoffel Eloff to investigate SACC's activities. The government was severely embarrassed when he reported that he could find no evidence to substantiate the government's claims. The government then had to suffer the indignity of learning that Tutu had won the 1984 Nobel Peace Prize. This gave him a world platform and as Tutu himself said so vividly, "One day no one was listening. The next I was an oracle."[56] In 1985 Tutu was elected Bishop of Johannesburg and the Anglican archbishop of South Africa the following year. There was some irony in Tutu moving into the archbishop's palatial home in Cape Town called Bishopscourt. It was once the home of Jan van Riebeek and a mere stone throw away from the residence of President P W Botha.

The tricameral parliament was a divide-and-rule strategy. The whites had tried to co-opt Coloureds and Indians in a fraudulent power-sharing scheme which served to alienate blacks even more. The government wanted to consign all blacks to homelands but they had a problem with the large numbers that lived on the fringes of urban cities. Piet Koornhof, the Minister of Cooperation and Development, designed a system whereby black municipal councils ran the affairs of urban townships. Permanent urban status was only given to those who had jobs and approved accommodation in urban areas. Koornhof boasted that this was a great reform that recognised the permanency of urban blacks in South Africa. Popo Molefe, who was the Secretary General of the UDF in the Transvaal, described the municipal council system as follows: "We saw it as a substitute for political participation in central government. It was a clever way of denying black people, the African people, the right to participate in the government of the country at a time when the Coloured and Indian people were offered a vote in the tricameral system. Our reaction was one of anger."[57]

The municipal councils were not autonomous. The minister had the power to remove members, appoint others, or even dismiss the entire council. This made the councils responsible to the government rather than their electorates. Even worse was the policy that the councils should be self-supporting. They had to collect their own revenue through imposing housing rents. The UDF campaigned against participation in the municipal council elections. Few respectable black leaders stood for election and the polls were only supported by less than ten percent of eligible voters. The result was that deeply unpopular councils were elected. Many of the councillors were corrupt. They increased rents, gave themselves loans, granted themselves liquor licences, and built themselves magnificent homes that stood out provocatively against the shanty homes of the residents. There were huge tensions in the townships as residents demanded explanations for the rent increases. On the night of 2 September 1984, the police placed barricades across the road between the township of Bophalong and the white city of Vanderbijlpark. A skittish police officer fired a shot and killed Reuben Twala, a Bophalong township soccer hero. This caused an explosion of anger. Youths attacked the houses of the councillors and killed three of them. An Anglican priest, Father Geoffrey Moselane, attempted to lead a peaceful protest march the next day against the rent increases. He was confronted by a large police contingent, who panicked and opened fire with shotguns, rubber bullets, and tear gas. It fuelled the fires of anger. Black youths went on a rampage. They roamed the streets, burning cars, liquor stores, and council buildings. The police over reacted and killed thirty people. The rioting spread throughout the country: to Soweto, the Cape, Durban, the Orange Free State, and even into the homelands of the Ciskei, Bophuthatswana, and KwaZulu. The townships became ungovernable and the government declared a state of emergency.

The ANC leaders, in Lusaka, wanted to ensure that the ANC was associated with the spontaneous uprisings. In January 1985 Oliver Tambo announced that the ANC had embarked on a strategy to render South Africa ungovernable. The ANC also focussed attention on promoting an international demand for the release of Nelson Mandela. The pressure to release Mandela grew and P W Botha thought he had come up with a master stroke to thwart this campaign. On 31 January 1985 P W Botha announced that he was prepared to release Mandela if he unconditionally rejected violence as a political instrument. He saw this as a perfect solution because if Mandela refused his offer, then the entire world would understand why he was being kept in prison. Nelson Mandela however, deftly turned the tables on P W Botha and in doing so the prisoner, not the jailer, became the master of his destiny. Mandela, rather than the government, now held the keys to his freedom. On 10 February 1985 his daughter, Zindzi Mandela, read out a statement to a packed crowd at the Jabulani stadium in Soweto. It was the first time that the people had heard a word from Mandela in over twenty years. The crowd was mesmerised and ecstatic over what they heard. This is the last part of what Zindzi said:

"My father says: I am a member of the African National Congress.
I have always been a member of the African National Congress

and I will remain a member of the African National Congress until the day I die. Oliver Tambo is much more than a brother to me. He is my greatest friend and comrade for nearly fifty years. If there is anyone amongst you who cherishes my freedom, Oliver Tambo cherishes it more, and I know that he would give his life to see me free. There is no difference between his views and mine.

I am surprised at the conditions that the government wants to impose on me. I am not a violent man. My colleagues and I wrote in 1952 to Malan asking for a round table conference to find a solution to the problems of our country, but that was ignored. When Strijdom was in power, we made the same offer. Again, it was ignored. When Verwoerd was in power, we asked for a national convention for all the people in South Africa to decide on their future. This, too, was in vain.

It was only then, when all other forms of resistance were no longer open to us, that we turned to armed struggle. Let Botha show that he is different to Malan, Strijdom, and Verwoerd. Let him renounce violence. Let him say that he will dismantle apartheid. Let him unban the people's organisation, the African National Congress. Let him free all who have been imprisoned, banished, or exiled for their opposition to apartheid. Let him guarantee free political activity so that people may decide who will govern them.

I cherish my own freedom dearly, but I care even more for your freedom. Too many have died since I went to prison. Too many have suffered for the love of freedom. I owe it to their widows, to their orphans, to their mothers and to their fathers who have grieved and wept for them. Not only I have suffered during these long, lonely, wasted years. I am not less life-loving than you are. But I cannot sell my birthright, nor am I prepared to sell the birthright of the people to be free. I am in prison as the representative of the people and of your organisation, the African National Congress, which was banned.

What freedom am I being offered while the organisation of the people remains banned? What freedom am I being offered when I may be arrested on a pass offence? What freedom am I being offered to live my life as a family with my dear wife who remains in banishment in Brandfort? What freedom am I being offered when I must ask for permission to live in an urban area? What freedom am I being offered when I need a stamp in my pass to seek work? What freedom am I being offered when my very South African citizenship is not respected?

Only free men can negotiate. Prisoners cannot enter into contracts. Herman Toivo ja Toivo, when freed, never gave any undertaking, nor was he called upon to do so. I cannot, and will not give any undertaking at a time when I and you, the people, are not free. Your freedom and mine cannot be separated. I will return."

The UDF, the ANC front, became very active. The UDF drove out corrupt councils and replaced them with UDF organisational structures that effectively took over the townships. Residents stopped paying rents to councils and ad hoc UDF committees were set up to create a semblance of administrative control. There were peoples' courts that administered harsh justice to criminals and collaborators with whites. Umkhonto we Sizwe began to infiltrate operatives into the townships to ferment insurrection. A tragedy was the unnecessary savagery of certain youths. In their revolutionary zeal they resorted to barbaric behaviour. They attacked anyone they suspected of violating boycotts, forcing them to eat purchases from white shops such as soap and washing powder. They resorted to the ghastly murderous system of necklacing, which involved placing a car tyre around a victim's neck, filling it with petrol, and then setting it alight. The funerals of those killed in the rioting became massive political rallies. The funerals were often held in football stadiums. There would be rows of brown coffins for adults and white coffins for children, adorned with the yellow and black colours of the UDF, or the green, black, and gold of the ANC, or even communist red. Speakers would fire up the crowd, and then the people would sing and dance (toyi-toyi) as they carried the coffins to the graveyard.

The police grew increasingly exasperated in their efforts to quell the insurrection and decided to use more force. General Hendrik de Witt, the deputy commissioner of police, authorised the police to use automatic weapons and to kill rioters throwing acid or petrol bombs. On 21 March 1985 there was a large funeral in the Langa township, near Uitenhage, in the eastern Cape. The Uitenhage police commander, Lieutenant-Colonel Frederik Pretorius, ordered that there would be no more rubber bullets or tear gas. He armed his police officers instead with semi-automatic rifles and shotgun cartridges. The night before the funeral the police realised that the 21 March was the anniversary of the Sharpeville massacre. An order was obtained from a magistrate prohibiting the funeral. The next morning people began to arrive at Maduna Square to board buses to take them to the football stadium for the funeral, but they were unaware of the order prohibiting the funeral. The police arrived and ordered the people out of the buses. The people were confused, but they got out of the buses and began to walk to the stadium. The police set up a road block with their armoured Hippo vehicles. The crowd continued marching and singing funeral songs. In a repetition of the Sharpeville massacre, exactly twenty-five years earlier, the police commander, Lieutenant John Fouche, gave the order to shoot. The police killed twenty people and wounded twenty-seven. This is how Eric Thembani, one of the wounded victims, described the scene: "A man on top of the Hippo is moving from one side to the other, shooting all the time. I see people falling in front of me and I grab one of them and hold him against me. I stagger backwards holding him against me like a shield. Then I am hit by a shot on top of my head and I let go of this other person and fall down. I fall face down in the road and lie there dazed. I hear more shots and then a policeman's voice in a mixture of Xhosa and Zulu that they should finish off the people lying there because they may bring claims later. I lie there still, pretending to be dead. Someone near me says, "Here's the leader." There is a shot and I think they have shot the [man] lying behind me because the bullet hits me in the sole of my foot."[58]

Louis Le Grange, the Minister of Law and Order, claimed that the police had acted in self-defence. At the subsequent inquiry, Judge Donald Kannemeyer found that Le Grange had lied to parliament and that the police had fabricated the attack to justify their shooting. He noted that thirty-five of the victims had been shot in the back as they attempted to flee. His extraordinary conclusion though was that no-one was to blame for the massacre. This did nothing to quell black anger and the country descended into a virtual state of civil war. The government reacted to the enormous influence of the UDF by detaining all members of its national executive.

South Africa received a great deal of attention in the international media and there were loud calls for economic sanctions and disinvestment. It was very fortunate for the South African government that there were friendly conservative leaders in three major countries. Ronald Reagan was the President of the United States, Margaret Thatcher was the Prime Minister of the United Kingdom, and Helmut Kohl was the Chancellor of West Germany. They all shared the view that radical black political activists were communist backed, that sanctions would hurt blacks more than whites, and that South Africa was making tentative progress towards abandoning apartheid. Reagan favoured a policy of constructive engagement which was a policy of quiet encouragement. Reagan branded Mandela a terrorist and had the

ANC listed as a terrorist organisation. Pragmatists in the South African cabinet, such as Pik Botha, the Minister of Foreign Affairs, and Chris Heunis, the Minister of Constitutional Affairs, persuaded P W Botha that a statement of reform intent would put it beyond doubt that South Africa was reforming its apartheid policies. They saw this as an essential step in keeping the growing sanctions pressures at bay. Pik Botha paved the way and told international diplomats to expect a major announcement from President P W Botha at the Nationalist Party congress on 15 August 1985.

The United States was keen to prove that its policy of constructive engagement was working. Pik Botha was eager to impress Western diplomats. The press sensed a dramatic story. There was speculation that Nelson Mandela would be released, that all apartheid laws would be scrapped, and that there would be a national convention to devise a new constitution. *Time* magazine wrote that P W Botha was about to make "the most important statement since Dutch settlers arrived at the Cape of Good Hope 300 years ago."[59] P W Botha was unimpressed and decided to show that he was not weak and not afraid of international pressure. In what became known as the Rubicon speech he waved his finger belligerently and made it clear to the entire world that he refused to be forced into doing anything because of outside pressures. He called Mandela a violent revolutionary and said that he would only consider releasing him if he gave a commitment to reject the use of violence. He stated that the government was considering further constitutional amendments, but he flatly rejected the principle of one-man-one-vote in a unitary system. He claimed this would lead to the domination of one over the other and it would lead to chaos. He said defiantly, "I am not prepared to lead white South Africans and other minority groups on a road to abdication and suicide. Destroy white South Africa and our influence, and this country will drift into faction strife, chaos, and poverty."[60] The speech was a disaster and calls for economic sanctions reached new highs. Banks in the United States, Britain, Germany, and Switzerland refused to roll over loans and demanded repayment. South Africa's currency collapsed and the government was forced to impose stringent foreign-exchange controls as the economy went into free fall. Living standards dropped dramatically as the country was starved of foreign capital and loans.

The government continued its strongarm measures and repressive tactics. In October 1985 the state charged sixteen people with high treason and incitement to overthrow the government. The case was the largest political trial since Rivonia and became known as the Pietermaritzburg treason trial. Frank Chikane, now the vice president of the UDF, was one of those arrested. The accused included four more members of the UDF, four members of the South African Allied Workers' Union, three members of the Natal Indian Congress, two members of the Transvaal Indian Congress, and two members of the Release Mandela Campaign. Frank Chikane, Curtis Nkondo, Archie Gumede, and Albertina Sisulu were the members of the UDF that were charged. Albertina Sisulu was the wife of Walter Sisulu who had been sentenced to life in prison at the Rivonia trial. Alan Boesak did not hold a position on the UDF executive and was not charged. Five of the defendants were arrested outside the British consulate in Durban in rather bizarre circumstances. Archie Gumede, Billy Nair, Mewa Ramgobin, George Sewpershad, MJ Naidoo, and Paul David became known as the Durban Six. On 13 September 1984 the Durban Six walked into the British consulate requesting protection. They remained in the British consulate for several weeks and were eventually persuaded to leave after unsuccessfully applying for sanctuary in Britain, the United States, France, the Netherlands, and Germany. Five of the six were promptly arrested as soon as they walked out of the consulate.

All the accused faced the death penalty if found guilty. I had not kept in contact with Frank over the past few years, but I was well-acquainted with his growing political stature as a UDF leader. Frank was kept in jail for three months until he was released on bail. He returned to his family in Soweto and the very next night his home was attacked with petrol bombs and set alight. His neighbours rushed to douse the flames. I managed to speak to Frank just once before he was consumed with his trial. Frank thanked me for my call and remarked, "They accuse us of being communists and doing all sorts of evil things. It is in fact the government that is causing us to suffer under their evil satanic system."

Justice John Milne, the Judge President of Natal, presided over the Pietermaritzburg treason trial. Ismail Mahomed was the chief counsel for the defence. Isak de Vries, a lecturer in politics at the Rand Afrikaans University, appeared as an expert witness on revolutionary warfare. Ismail Mahomed tore De Vries to shreds during cross examination. De Vries was forced to concede that the Natal Indian Congress and Transvaal Indian Congress followed the guidance of their founder, Mahatma Gandhi, who advocated non-violence. Mahomed got De Vries to acknowledge that he was a theoretician who had insufficient background knowledge to make factual statements. The state was forced to withdraw all the charges against twelve of the accused and only proceeded against the four South African Allied Workers' Union members: Thozi Gqweta, Sisa Njikelana, Sam Kikine, and Isaac Ngcobo. The defence received another blow when Judge Milne ruled that much of the State's evidence, audio, and video recordings were inadmissible as evidence. There were suspicious gaps in the recordings and Milne argued that the State could not prove that the tapes had not been tampered with. There was also doubt over the identity of the speakers and where and when they were speaking. The State withdrew the charges and all the accused were acquitted.

I was delighted at their acquittal and called Frank to express my congratulations. I could not get in touch with him because he immediately went into hiding. He feared being arrested again and lived underground for the next year. In early 1986 he slipped out of South Africa and took refuge in Europe.

At the same time as the Pietermaritzburg treason trial the State charged twenty-two men in the Transvaal with treason, terrorism, and furthering the aims of unlawful organisations. They named hundreds of co-conspirators, such as Archbishop Desmond Tutu, Beyers Naude, and all the UDF leaders, for conspiring with the ANC and SACP to bring about a revolution. The indictment alleged that this conspiracy had caused the violence in the Vaal triangle and other parts of the country. The accused included three high ranking UDF leaders: Patrick Lekota, Popo Molefe, and Moses Chikane (Frank's cousin). Arthur Chaskalson, George Bizos, Karel Tip, and Gilbert Marcus were the main counsel for the defence. The judge, Justice Kees van Dijkhorst, transferred the case to the small town of Delmas because he believed that the facilities there were better suited to a trial of this size.

After the failure of Isak de Vries at the Pietermaritzburg treason trial, the State decided to use a different expert witness. They called upon Andre Pruis, a political scientist from the University of the Orange Free State. George Bizos was able to thoroughly discredit Pruis under cross-examination. Bizos tackled all the state witnesses and got most of them to agree that the local councillors were corrupt. Bizos questioned one of the accused, Peter Mokoena, about a table he had placed outside his shop inviting people to sign the 'million-signature petition' against the tricameral parliament. One of the judge's assessors, Professor Willem Joubert, remarked that he could see no problem with this because he had also signed the petition. The presiding judge, Kees van Dijkhorst, was furious and dismissed Professor Joubert from the trial. Chaskalson argued that this was highly irregular, but Van Dijkhorst ordered the trial to continue, and threatened to charge Chaskalson with contempt of court. The trial dragged on month after month as the defence called the accused and other witnesses to take the stand.

Margaret Thatcher resisted the international call for sanctions. She was pressured on the topic at a Commonwealth heads of government meeting and she suggested that before sanctions were applied a committee of eminent Commonwealth representatives should visit South Africa to see if there was any prospect of initiating change through a dialogue between the South African government and black leaders. This committee became known as the Eminent Persons Group (EPG) and was chaired by Malcom Fraser from Australia and General Olusegun Obasanjo from Nigeria. During 1986 the EPG visited South Africa and held discussions with the ANC in Lusaka. The EPG concluded that there was sufficient goodwill to negotiate a new constitution. They recommended the unbanning of the ANC, and the release of Mandela and other political prisoners. In turn the ANC was asked to renounce the use of violence. The ANC was sceptical but prepared to consider entering negotiations.

During the EPG process Winnie Mandela, Nelson Mandela's wife, caused a public relations disaster for the ANC. Winnie never held back in criticising the government and she was treated extremely harshly. Winnie was arrested, detained, and banned many times. For eight years from 1977 to 1985 she was banished to live in Brandfort, a small agricultural town in the Orange Free State, but in 1986 she returned to her home in Soweto. She did not have the statesmanlike qualities of her husband, and she was aggressively defiant. She wore a khaki uniform and was militant in her behaviour and speeches. She did the liberation movement few favours as her behaviour became increasingly erratic. On 13 April 1986 she severely embarrassed the ANC when she said: "We have no guns- we have only stones, boxes of matches and petrol. Together, hand in hand, with our boxes of matches and our necklaces we shall liberate this country."[61]

In May 1986 P W Botha's cabinet rejected the EPG's proposals. The government proceeded to launch military raids against ANC bases in Zimbabwe, Botswana, and Zambia. The military hawks under the sway of General Magnus Malan, the Minister of Defence wanted to show that they were tough and would not cede power. Another state of emergency was declared. South Africa was now a country governed under virtual martial law. The government projected the view that they were protecting South Africa from a communist revolution. They never entertained the possibility that the oppressed people of South Africa sought equality, justice, and democratic rights. The government adopted a total revolutionary counter-strategy. They gave the military and security police sweeping powers. The press was muzzled, there were bannings and detentions. Thousands were arrested, including women and children. The security forces fuelled tensions between rival organisations such as the UDF, the Azanian People's Organisation, and Inkatha. They armed black *kitskonstabels* (instant constables), set them loose in the townships, and then stood aside as black on black violence escalated. The police would periodically barricade certain townships and launch raids, detaining anyone who appeared to be a political activist. The securocrats in the cabinet held on to the delusion that if they wiped out the revolutionaries, all the moderates would be won over to negotiate a peaceful settlement. The revolutionaries did not have the military might to overthrow the government, but the South African government could never shut down the revolutionary struggle. Sanctions were hurting and the country was practically ungovernable.

I was very disturbed by a white vigilante group called the *Afrikaner Weerstands Beweging* (Afrikaner Resistance Movement). Their leader was Eugene Terreblanche, a former police officer.

They reminded me of the Nazis as they paraded around in khaki military uniforms and displayed a red and white flag which had an emblem of three sevens that looked like the swastika. They wanted to deport all blacks to homelands, expel all Jews, and return all Indians to India. They were never more than a superficial threat, but they were not without support. They were however, at the extreme end of white opposition to any form of negotiation and constitutional change.

In October 1985 Frederik Van Zyl Slabbert, the leader of the Progressive Federal Party, took executives from his party to Lusaka, where they met with leaders of the ANC. These leaders included Thabo Mbeki, Mac Maharaj, and Barbara Masekela. Thabo Mbeki told Van Zyl Slabbert that the ANC was committed to an armed struggle, which Van Zyl Slabbert thought was naive since he knew that the South Africa could not be defeated militarily. Mbeki however, conceded that talking was better than killing. Upon his return to South Africa Van Zyl Slabbert publicly declared that there could be no negotiated resolution in South Africa without involving the ANC. He also pleaded with P W Botha in private to release Nelson Mandela unconditionally. P W Botha refused and absurdly claimed that he enjoyed the support of most blacks. In December 1985 Van Zyl Slabbert flew to Maputo to meet with Samora Machel, the president of Mozambique. Machel presented him with detailed information that confirmed South Africa was violating the Nkomati Accords through repeated military raids.

Van Zyl Slabbert recognised that the country had reached a stalemate between the politics of repression and politics of revolt. On 11 February 1986 he stood up in parliament and resigned. He described the tricameral parliament as a complete waste of time. He saw the white opposition as passive spectators in a game in which they could not participate. White liberals were furious and felt that he had undermined the opposition. He was seen as an Afrikaner glamour boy and traitor to the liberal cause. Thabo Mbeki's responded to his resignation with these words: "Never in the history of our country has a white establishment political leader confronted the iniquity of the system of white domination as Dr Slabbert has today. We salute his courage, his honesty, and his loyalty to a common South African nationhood... Today millions of our people, of all races, will acclaim Dr Slabbert as a new Voortrekker."[62]

I had placed huge faith in Frederik van Zyl Slabbert and held on to the vain hope that he could be instrumental in bringing about a better future for all South Africans. His resignation crushed me. I had always hoped that there would be a peaceful resolution in South Africa but now I feared a violent conflict. In September 1986 I resigned from my role as an administrative assistant at St. John's College. I decided to leave South Africa and return to the United Kingdom. The South African government was not going to be defeated militarily, but the country had become ungovernable. The black townships were in flames, and the country was dissolving into civil unrest.

It took me little time to sell my meagre possessions and prepare for my departure. I had been in South Africa just under fifty years. I had arrived as a young man filled with enthusiasm. Now I was leaving as an old man that cried for a country that was destroying itself. I flew out of South Africa on a cold day. I had a panoramic view as the aeroplane took off from Jan Smuts airport. I could see the smoke-filled haze over the township of Alexandra, then I could see the St. John's College clock tower, the busy centre of town, and finally the huge tailings dams from the gold mines on the city outskirts. Blacks called Johannesburg Egoli (the "City of Gold"). It was gold that had created so much wealth, but South Africa had been shaped by greed and fear. It was bleeding to death. The joy of seeing Table Mountain as I sailed into Cape Town a half-century ago was a distant memory.

As the aeroplane climbed higher and higher I saw the blood-stained red of the dusty landscape. I loved St, John's College, the splendour of the Cape, the sun-drenched beaches of Natal, the majestic Drakensberg mountains, the wild game reserves, and a Sunday *braai* in the company of interesting people. Bram was dead. I thought of his comrades and other noble revolutionaries rotting in prison cells. I was running away. The future looked bleak, but I did not appreciate that the darkest hour is always before dawn.

Postscript

T he Delmas treason trial wound its way to a weary conclusion in November 1989 after four years. Charges were dropped against six of the accused, five were acquitted, six received suspended sentences, and five received lengthy jail sentences: Patrick Lekota (twelve years), Popo Molefe (ten years), Moses Chikane (ten years), Tom Manthata (six years), and Gcini Malindi (five years). A year later the Appeal Court acquitted all the accused. The higher court found that Justice Van Dijkhorst had erred in sacking Professor Joubert and the trial court was no longer properly constituted. The Delmas trial was a flagrant miscarriage of justice.

P W Botha's security state strategy failed. Alister Sparks, the former editor of the *Rand Daily Mail,* explains why: "Essentially, the Afrikaner securocrats had read too much foreign military literature and too little of their own history. Their ethnocentric minds were unable to project into the black situation and to recognise that the blacks would respond exactly as they had done when their own revolution was on the rise. They had never abandoned Afrikaner nationalism for the 'moderate' compromisers and dealers. They had never been prepared to settle for less than full power. And the more they had felt themselves persecuted and oppressed, the more politicized they had become and the more committed to their Nationalist cause. Yet somehow, they expected the blacks to do all the things they themselves had scorned. Part of the reason for this failure was that they were so conditioned to thinking of blacks as 'different' that they could not imagine them reacting in the same way as themselves. But a more important reason was that they had become victims of their own propaganda, and believed that a black revolution really was being directed from outside and that the uprisings had nothing to do with an oppressed indigenous people yearning to be free. Thet is why they could follow so literally a strategic blueprint designed to counter a revolutionary war rather than a liberation struggle."[63]

South Africa had descended into violence and Mandela took the initiative. He sent a message to the Commissioner of Prisons stating that he needed to speak to the government on a matter of national importance. The message was passed on to the Minister of Justice, Kobie Coetsee, who had over a dozen meetings with Mandela. Coetsee brought in the head of the National Intelligence Service, Dr Niel Barnard, to join him in the talks. Barnard was a young, intelligent, and a competent man that had long believed in opening negotiations with the ANC. Barnard repeatedly made the point that it was impossible for P W Botha to release Mandela if he refused to reject the use of violence. Mandela stuck to his argument that the government had to renounce the violence of apartheid first. In July 1988 there was a huge rock concert in London to celebrate Mandela's 70th birthday. The performers included Stevie Wonder, Harry Belafonte, Whitney Houston, and Roberta Flack. The concert was televised to a worldwide audience and cries for Mandela's release reached a crescendo. In August 1988 the government got a fright when Mandela was taken to hospital suffering from a lung infection. Mandela was given the best medical care possible because the government was all too aware that a dead Mandela would be worse than a free Mandela. It took until July 1989 for Coetsee to engineer a meeting between P W Botha and Mandela. The meeting was little more than a courtesy call. P W Botha was extremely courteous and respectful. Both Botha and Mandela committed themselves to finding peaceful solutions to South Africa's problems.

Six months earlier however, P W Botha had a stroke and stood down as the leader of the Nationalist Party. The apparently conservative Frederik Willem De Klerk was elected leader. P W Botha thought he could remain State President but De Klerk was working to undermine him. On 14 August 1989 P W Botha was forced to resign and F W De Klerk became State President. In September 1989 De Klerk called a snap general election to shore up the support of the white electorate. De Klerk had been a staunch supporter of apartheid, but he was a pragmatist and was quick to understand that the privileged position of South African whites could not be preserved without making significant concessions.

In 1985 Mikhail Gorbachev became the leader of the Soviet Union. He initiated a policy of *glasnost* (openness) and *perestroika* (restructuring) with the intention of resolving Cold War hostilities. It would set in motion a series of events that led to the demise of communism and the dismemberment of the Soviet Union. On 9 November 1989 the Berlin Wall collapsed. This extraordinary event heralded the collapse of communism and its timing was extremely fortuitous for South Africa. In many ways De Klerk was South Africa's Gorbachev. He realised that South African whites could no longer hold on to the belief that they were part of a global struggle against communism. The demise of communism was a major reason why the South Africa government was willing to pursue a programme of reform. Although like Gorbachev, De Klerk set in motion reforms that went further than he intended. The ANC dropped its communist rhetoric and quickly discovered that it was no longer perceived as a communist-terrorist organisation.

On 2 February 1990 De Klerk made a momentous speech in parliament. He announced that he was unconditionally releasing Nelson Mandela and other political prisoners, unbanning the ANC and other political organisations, ending the state of emergency, and placing a moratorium on the death penalty. On 11 February

1990 Nelson Mandela walked out of Victor Verster prison, hand in hand with his wife Winnie. There were four years of protracted negotiations, frequently punctuated with violence, before a national convention agreed on a new constitution. South Africa held its first democratic elections and on 10 May 1994 Nelson Mandela was sworn in as South Africa's first post-apartheid president.

It was the end of over three centuries of white rule in South Africa. On inauguration day De Klerk said, "Mr Mandela has walked a long road and now stands at the top of a hill. A man of destiny knows that beyond this hill lies another and another. The journey is never complete. As he contemplates the next hill, I hold out my hand to Mr Mandela in friendship and cooperation."[64] Mandela's response was equally generous: "We enter into a covenant that we should build a society in which all South Africans, both black and white, will be able to walk tall, without fear in their hearts, assured of their inalienable right to human dignity – a rainbow nation at peace with itself and the world."[65]

Mandela had a saintly quality of forgiveness and a desire to bring about a reconciliation between all races. His magnanimity of spirit was enormous. He invited Quartus De Wet and Percy Yutar, the Rivonia trial judge and prosecutor, to attend his inauguration. He visited Betsie Verwoerd, the widow of Hendrik Verwoerd. He wore the Springbok rugby jersey at the final of the 1995 rugby world cup in Johannesburg, which was an amazing gesture, given how closely the Springbok rugby team was associated with apartheid. There were many others though that were baying for vengeance. They wanted to set up Nuremberg-style trials to prosecute the criminal acts of the apartheid regime. Nelson Mandela and Desmond Tutu came up with an extraordinary idea. They decided to set up a Truth and Reconciliation Commission (TRC) to investigate apartheid crimes and grant a pardon to all who were prepared to confess their crimes. Desmond Tutu was appointed chairman with Alex Boraine as deputy chairman. The TRC commenced its work on 16 December 1995 and over seven thousand people registered a petition for clemency, The TRC operated for almost four years and submitted its report to Nelson Mandela on 29 October 1998. The TRC heard confessions of terrible brutality. There were some who saw the TRC as allowing the guilty to get away with their crimes, while others saw the TRC as a witch-hunt against people that were only carrying out orders. Tutu provided the moral compass and ensured that the TRC focused on its objective to establish the truth as basis for a process of national reconciliation. During the hearings Tutu and other commissioners would frequently break down in tears as apartheid victims recounted their stories. The TRC deserve high praise for their work in exposing the truth and effecting reconciliation.

The South African security police had an undercover counterinsurgency unit, or death squad based at Vlakplaas, a farm near Pretoria. The unit was the idea of Brigadier Johan Viktor, a notorious security branch policeman. The unit captured liberation movement activists, tortured them, and turned them into 'askaris." These askaris were then sent back into the townships to sow havoc. Captured activists that refused to becomes askaris were killed. Captain Dirk Coetzee, a former Vlakplaas commander, applied to the TRC for amnesty. Coetzee confessed to murdering a young activist, Sizwe Kondile. They burnt his body in an open fire to destroy the evidence. He ghoulishly described how it took seven hours of burning to make sure that not even bones or teeth could be identified. Colonel Eugene de Kock succeeded Coetzee as the Vlakplaas commander. He could not recall how many activists he killed. He said he often disposed of bodies by blowing them apart with dynamite. He admitted to bombing the SACC offices in Johannesburg and the ANC offices in London. De Kock claimed he was acting on orders and tried to implicate P W Botha and F W De Klerk. The TRC refused to give him amnesty and at his subsequent trial De Kock was sentenced to over two-hundred years in prison. Craig Williamson applied for amnesty and described how the police had mailed poisons and letter-bombs to activists in foreign countries. Williamson admitted to sending the letter-bombs that killed Ruth First, Jeanette Schoon and her child Katryn. Williamson showed little remorse and believed that they were acceptable targets because they were supporting the ANC in an armed struggle.

Tutu had to preside over a very tricky TRC hearing concerning Winnie Madikizela -Mandela. After Winnie returned to Soweto in 1986, she collected a gang of vigilante youths that called themselves the peculiarly named Mandela United Football Club. These thugs liked to root out police informers. Various parents testified that their children had disappeared after being beaten up by members of the Mandela United Football Club. Winnie accused a fourteen-year-old boy, Stompie Seipei, of being a police informer and one of her acolytes, Jerry Richardson, beat Stompie to death. Richardson had already been sentenced to life in prison for the murder, but now Tutu wanted Winnie to ask for forgiveness. She reluctantly did so, although many doubted her sincerity. Nelson and Winnie soon divorced on account of her highly erratic behaviour.

On 21 July 1997 Ilse Fischer (Wilson) and Ruth Fischer (Rice) appeared before the TRC. Alex Boraine chaired the hearing and Hugh Lewin was one of the commissioners. The hearing was primarily concerned with the treatment of Bram Fischer in prison. Ilse detailed Bram's shameful lack of proper medical treatment and praised Denis Goldberg's efforts in caring for him. Ilse said that all she and Ruth really wanted was for something like this to never happen again. Boraine concluded the hearing with these remarks: "Bram Fischer was a son of Africa and knew no distinction in race or creed or language and thus stands as an enormous symbol of unity in a very divided society and you must be very thankful that even though he was in obscurity for so long, somehow that light went way beyond the prison cell and way beyond his death. There are many, many people who paid tribute to him today and you have done that and we hope that the hope you express, that because of this it is less likely to happen again, will come true. Thank you very much."[66]

Frank Chikane returned to South Africa in 1987 to take up the position of General Secretary of the South African Council of Churches (SACC). Frank's predecessors were Desmond Tutu and Beyers Naude. It was Beyers Naude that had strongly urged the appointment of Chikane as his successor. On 1 September 1988 the security police bombed Khotso House, the head offices of the SACC. At a hearing before the TRC Johan van der Merwe, the former National Commissioner of Police, sought amnesty and claimed that he had received his orders to bomb Khotso House from the Minister of Law and Order, Adian Vlok. On a trip to Namibia in 1989 Chikane fell dangerously ill. He recovered after four days but then on a trip to the United States in 1990 he was again struck down with a severe illness. Doctors determined that his underwear had been poisoned. In 2007 Adian Vlok and Johan and der Merwe pleaded guilty to ordering the poisoning and were given lengthy suspended jail sentences. In 1990 the Apostolic Faith Mission apologised and reinstated Frank as a pastor. Frank resigned as General Secretary of the SACC in 1994 and went to Harvard University to complete a degree in public administration. Mandela urged him to return to South Africa and serve as a special advisor to the government. Chikane rose to the position of director-general. He has never been seduced by the trappings of power, he has maintained his home in Soweto, and continues to pastor and worship with his mother, wife, and children at the Apostolic Faith Mission church in Naledi, Soweto.

There were many noble revolutionaries that sacrificed a great deal to make a difference in the struggle against apartheid. Some of them endured long years in prison. Some, like Nelson Mandela, emerged from prison and had a huge impact on the successful transition to a post-apartheid society. Bram Fischer was one the greatest of the noble revolutionaries. At another time and another place Bram would surely have been a great statesman. The ANC never co-opted Frederik Van Zyl Slabbert to serve in government. This was a great pity because Van Zyl Slabbert was another leader, who at another time and place would also have been a great statesman. On 14 May 2010 Van Zyl Slabbert died peacefully at his home. Nelson Mandela married Graca Machel, the widow of Samora Machel, on his eightieth birthday. Then on 14 June 1999 Mandela resigned as president, saying that at almost eighty-one he was too old to continue. Mandela retired gracefully and remained a global icon until his death on 5 December 2013.

The ANC government has not been a success and it has descended into inefficiency, greed, and corruption. There are many noble revolutionaries that must be so disappointed. Tim Jenkin, the Pretoria Central prison escapee, puts it like this: "The ANC of the liberation struggle was a different party that bears its name today. The good name of the ANC was hijacked by a gang of thieves, and the current entity that calls itself ANC has little to do with the ANC that I was once proud of serving."[67]

Many of the noble revolutionaries, none less than Bram Fischer, believed that communism was the antidote to apartheid. The dream of a communist utopia never became a reality and the ideology of communism has been thoroughly discredited. Stephanie Kemp accepted that the struggle to bring about a just world in the name of communism is in ruins and she writes: "In the 21st century there is a crater in understanding the world and how to change it for the better. For a century it has been so crystal clear – a binary world of good and evil, and we were on the side of a forward march of history. We marched with Marx, Engels and Lenin clutched firmly in our beliefs. But this is no longer true and there has been nothing to replace our clarity of understanding and how to go forward with Communism at the centre of our dreams for a better world."[68]

The noble revolutionaries that fought against apartheid should never be forgotten. Many noble revolutionaries are now commemorated through the renaming of public places, buildings, parks, and streets. In Johannesburg, D F Malan Drive is now called Beyers Naude Drive, Harrow Road is now called Joe Slovo Drive, and Hendrik Verwoerd Drive is now called Bram Fischer Drive. In Durban, the north freeway has been renamed Ruth First Drive. Bloemfontein airport is now called Bram Fischer International Airport. The names of apartheid's protagonists have been rapidly removed.

Bram Fischer would play down his contribution, but his name will live forever. This is how Nelson Mandela concluded the first Bram Fischer memorial lecture on 9 June 1995:

> "The policy of apartheid created a deep and lasting wound in my country and my people. All of us will spend many years if not generations recovering from that profound hurt but the dictates of oppression and brutality had another unintended effect, and that was it produced the Oliver Tambos, the Walter Sisulus, the chief Luthulis, the Yusuf Dadoos, the Bram Fischers, the Robert Sobukwes of our time – men of such extraordinary courage, wisdom, and generosity that their like may never be known again. Perhaps it requires such depths of oppression to create such heights of character. My country is rich in the minerals and gems that lie beneath its soil but I have always known that its greatest wealth is its people, finer and truer than minerals or diamonds. In any history of our country two Afrikaner names

will always be remembered. Happily, one is still with us, dear comrade Beyers Naude. The other is Bram Fischer. The people of South Africa will never forget him. He was among the first bright beacons that attracted millions of our young people to fervently believe in a non-racial democracy in our country. Bram Fischer was a son of the soil. His spirit lives on."[69]

Bibliography

Abrahams, Lionel, *Bosman at his Best: A Choice of Stories and Sketches by Herman Charles Bosman* (Human & Rousseau, pe Town, 1965).

Ancer, Jonathan, *Betrayal: The Secret Lives of Apartheid Spies* (Tafelberg, Cape Town, 2019).

Bizos, George, *Odyssey to Freedom* (Random House, Houghton, South Africa, 2007).

Clingman, Stephen, *Bram Fischer: Afrikaner Revolutionary* (Jacana, Johannesburg, 2013).

Davies, Norman, *Europe: A History* (Pimlico, London, 1996).

First, Ruth, *117 Days* (Hachette Digital, London, 2006).

Frankel, Glenn, *Rivonia's Children* (Weidenfeld & Nicolson, London, 1999).

Gilbert, Martin, *History of the Twentieth Century* (HarperCollins, New York, 2001).

Giliomee, Herman, *The Afrikaners: Biography of a People* (C. Hurst & Co., London, 2003).

Goodman, David, *Fault Lines* (University of California Press, London, 2001).

Grant-McKenzie, Ian, *Forward in Faith* (CTP Book Printers, Cape Town, 1998).

Jenkin, Tim, *Escape from Pretoria* (Jacana Media, Auckland Park, 2020).

Johnson, R.W., *How Long Will South Africa Survive: The crisis continues* (Jonathan Ball, Jeppestown, 2015).

Joseph, Helen, *If This Be Treason* (Kwela Books ebook, Cape Town, 2017).

Kemp, Stephanie, *Through an Unforgettable Storm* (Myebook. co.za, 2017).

Lapierre, Dominique, *A Rainbow in the Night* (De Capo Press, Philadelphia, 2009).

Lawson, Kenneth, *Venture of Faith* (Hortors Printers, Johannesburg, 1968).

Lewin, Hugh, *Bandiet Out of Jail* (Umuzi, Cape Town, 2012).

Lodge, Tom, *Sharpeville* (Oxford University Press, Oxford, 2011).

Malan, Rian, *My Traitor's Heart* (The Bodley Head, London, 1990).

Mandela, Nelson, *Long Walk to Freedom* (Little, Brown and Company, London, 1994).

Meredith, Martin, *Diamonds, Gold and War* (Simon & Schuster, London, 2007).

Meredith, Martin, *Fischer's Choice* (Jonathan Ball, Johannesburg, 2002).

Meredith Martin, *The State of Africa* (Simon & Schuster, London, 2005).

O'Malley, Padraig, *Shades of Difference* (Viking, New York, 2007).

Pakenham, Thomas, *The Boer War* (Jonathan Ball Publishers, Johannesburg, 1979).

Papenfus, Theresa, *Pik Botha and His Times* (Litera, Pretoria, 2010).

Sampson, Anthony, *Mandela* (HarperCollinsPublishers, London, 1999).

Slovo, Gillian, *Every Secret Thing* (Hachette Digital, London, 2009).

Sparks, Allister, *The Mind of South Africa* (Mandarin, London, 1991).

Sparks, Allister and Tutu, Mpho, *Tutu: the Authorised Portrait* (Pan Macmillan, Johannesburg, 2011).

Suttner, Raymond, *Inside Apartheid's Prison* (Ocean Press, Melbourne, 2001).

Suzman, Helen, *In No Uncertain Terms* (Sinclair-Stevenson, London, 1993).

Van Zyl Slabbert, Frederik, *The Last White Parliament* (Sidgwick & Jackson, London, 1985).

Van Zyl Slabbert, Frederik, *The Other Side of History* (Jonathan Ball, Jeppestown, 2006).

Welsh, Frank, *A History of South Africa* (Harper Collins, London, 1998).

Wilson, A.N., *After the Victorians* (Hutchinson, London, 2005).

William Wright, *A British Lion in Zululand* (Amberley, Gloucestershire, 2017).

Yeats, Charles, *Prisoner of Conscience* (Random House. London, 2005).

Endnotes

Most of the details concerning Bram Fisher's life are taken from Stephen Clingman's book *Bram Fischer: Afrikaner Revolutionary.*

Most of the details concerning South Africa's history from the establishment of the refreshment station at the Cape in 1652 until the formation of the Union in South Africa in 1910 is based on Martin Meredith's account in his book *Diamonds, Gold and War.*

Henry Allum's description of the Marshall Square police station is based on Ruth First's description in her book *117 Days.*

Henry Allum's account of meeting General Hendrik van den Berg is based on Stephanie Kemp's meeting with him in her book *Through an Unforgettable Storm.*

Desmond Tutu and Nelson Mandela were both awarded the Nobel Peace prize. Vilikazi Street in Soweto is the only street in the world that contains the homes of two Nobel prize winners.

The author was the school prefect that answered Beyers Naude's question during the tea at the home of the headmaster, Jan Breitenbach. The question and reply are in accordance with the author's memory.

Desmond Tutu's sermon and comments are based on quotes from Allister Sparks' and Mpho Tutu's biography *Tutu: the Authorised Portrait.*

Frank Chikane's encounters with the police are based on David Goodman's accounts in his book *Fault Lines.*

1.   A. N. Wilson, *After the Victorians*, p. 229.
2.   Stephen Clingman, *Bram Fischer*, pp. 91-92.

3. Martin Meredith, *Diamonds, Gold and War*, p.365.

4. Ibid., p. 411.

5. Ibid., p. 422.

6. Kenneth Lawson, *Venture of Faith*, p. 21.

7. Martin Meredith, *Diamonds, Gold and War*, p.514.

8. William Wright, *A Lion in Zululand*, p. 39.

9. Herman Giliomee, *The Afrikaners,* pp. 403-404.

10. Stephen Clingman, *Bram Fischer,* p. 148.

11. Nelson Mandela, *Long Walk to Freedom*, p. 81.

12. Stephen Clingman, *Bram Fischer,* p. 167.

13. Lionel Abrahams, *Bosman at his Best: A choice of stories and sketches by Herman Charles Bosman,* p. 10.

14. Ibid., p. 141.

15. Thomas Pakenham, *The Boer War,* p.304.

16. Alister Sparks, *The Mind of South Africa,* p. 144.

17. Stephen Clingman, *Bram Fischer,* p. 170.

18. Ibid., p. 178.

19. Ibid., p. 179.

20. Ibid., p. 190.

21. Glenn Frankel, *Rivonia's Children*, p. 59.

22. Gillian Slovo, *Every Secret Thing,* location 714.

23. George Bizos, *Odyssey to Freedom,* p. 177.

24. Helen Joseph, *If This Be Treason,* location 446.

25. Stephen Clingman, *Bram Fischer,* p. 229.

26. Helen Joseph, *If This Be Treason,* location 531.

27. Tom Lodge, *Sharpeville,* p. 105.

28. Nelson Mandela, *Long Walk to Freedom*, p. 264.

29. Ibid., pp. 312-313.

30. Glenn Frankel, *Rivonia's Children*, p. 99.

31. Nelson Mandela, *Long Walk to Freedom*, p. 354.

32. George Bizos, *Odyssey to Freedom,* p. 277.

33. Padraig O'Malley, *Shades of Difference,* p.146.

34. George Bizos, *Odyssey to Freedom*, p. 300.

35. Ibid., p. 307.

36. Stephen Clingman, *Bram Fischer,* pp. 372-373.

37. Ibid., p. 378.

38. Ibid., p. 384.

39. Helen Suzman, *In No Uncertain Terms*, p. 69.

40. National Security Memorandum 39 found at www.kora.matrix.msu.edu.

41. Stephen Clingman, *Bram Fischer,* p. 390.

42. Martin Meredith, *The State of Africa*, p. 418.

43. Helen Suzman, *In No Uncertain Terms,* pp. 149-150.

44. Hugh Lewin, *Bandiet Out of Jail*, pp. 302-304.

45. Stephen Clingman, *Bram Fischer,* pp. 403-404.

46. Martin Meredith, *The State of Africa*, p. 313.

47. Ibid., p. 421.

48. Donald Woods, *Asking for Trouble,* pp. 305-306.

49. Alister Sparks and Mpho Tutu, *Tutu*, p. 112.

50. Ibid., 112.

51. Dominique Lapierre, *A Rainbow in the Night,* p. 143.

52. Donald Woods, *Asking for Trouble*, p. 314.

53. Frederik van Zyl Slabbert, *The Last White Parliament.* p. 117.

54. Ibid., p. 117.

55. David Goodman, *Fault Lines,* p. 42.

56. Alister Sparks and Mpho Tutu, *Tutu*, p. 94.

57. Alister Sparks, *The Mind of South Africa*, p. 331.

58. Ibid., p. 347.

59. Ibid., p. 350.

60. P W Botha Rubicon speech found at www.omalley.nelsonmandela.org.

61. Anthony Sampson, *Mandela*, p. 349.

62. Frederik van Zyl Slabbert, *The Other Side of History*, p. 48.

63. Alister Sparks, *The Mind of South Africa*, pp. 358-359.

64. Martin Meredith, *The State of Africa*, p. 440.

65. Ibid., p. 440.

66. Alex Boraine concluding remarks at Bram Fischer TRC hearing found at www.justice.gov.za/trc.

67. Tim Jenkin, *Escape from Pretoria*, p. 385.

68. Stephanie Kemp, *Through an Unforgettable Storm,* location 4650.

69. Extract from 1995 Bram Fischer memorial lecture by Nelson Mandela found at www.mandela.gov.za.

Acknowledgements

I thank my wife Gillian, for her unfailing encouragement, for reading numerous drafts of the manuscript, and for suggesting improvements. All errors, faults, and inaccuracies in the text remain mine alone.

In November 2024 my much loved brother Timothy died. His wife, Maeve, died four months earlier. They both lost their fights against cancer. I now have no relatives in South Africa.

I thank my good friends Leon Jacobs in Johannesburg and Mike Simson in London for our frequent conversations over the past forty years about South African politics and every other issue. Thank you Sylvie Blair for your professional help in publishing this book.